Impressively Free

Impressively Free

*Henri Nouwen as a Model
for a Reformed Priesthood*

Michael W. Higgins and Kevin Burns

Paulist Press
New York / Mahwah, NJ

Cover image by Curly Pat / Shutterstock.com
Cover design by Lynn Else
Book design by Sharyn Banks

Library of Congress Cataloging-in-Publication Data

Names: Higgins, Michael W., 1948– author.
Title: Impressively free : Henri Nouwen as a model for a reformed priesthood / Michael W Higgins and Kevin Burns.
Description: New York : Paulist Press, 2019. | Includes bibliographical references.
Identifiers: LCCN 2018052188 (print) | LCCN 2019013668 (ebook) | ISBN 9781587687631 (ebook) | ISBN 9780809153923 (pbk. : alk. paper)
Subjects: LCSH: Nouwen, Henri J. M. | Priesthood—Catholic Church. | Pastoral theology—Catholic Church.
Classification: LCC BX4705.N87 (ebook) | LCC BX4705.N87 H5425 2019 (print) | DDC 282.092—dc23
LC record available at https://lccn.loc.gov/2018052188

ISBN 978-0-8091-5392-3 (paperback)
ISBN 978-1-58768-763-1 (e-book)

Published by Paulist Press
997 Macarthur Boulevard
Mahwah, New Jersey 07430

www.paulistpress.com

Printed and bound in the
United States of America

To the memory of John Baran,
Commonweal's *"Fr. Nonomen,"*
whose exemplary pastorship in writing
and personal witness continues
to inspire multitudes after his death
at fifty-nine in March 2018

My spiritual life was a bush hacked to the ground with blunt shears, but under the mashed branches, in the undergrowth, sap was flowing.

Stephen Hough

...the body of the faithful is one of the witnesses to the fact of the tradition of revealed doctrine, and because their consensus through Christendom is the voice of the Infallible Church.

Cardinal Newman

CONTENTS

INTRODUCTION

A Broken Vessel of Holiness

It is generally agreed upon, even by the most casually optimistic of church watchers, that Catholicism's hemorrhaging of its clerical personnel continues to have a substantive impact on its capacity to "deliver on its mission."

Whereas once the identity of the Catholic priest was reverenced even by the priesthood's critics, it now lies tarnished, irreparably damaged by a combination of redundancy of function brought on by secularism, pastoral irrelevancy occasioned by the emancipation of the Catholic laity, and considerable internal dysfunction generated by the extensive clerical sex abuse scandals.

This is not to say that the many priests who labor valiantly in the vineyard do so without recognition and support. There are countless priests who struggle to realize a postconciliar vision of pastoral collaboration, who carry the pain of isolation and opprobrium with dignity, and who remain faithful servants of the Lord throughout their lives in the knowledge that they retain the respect and love of those they serve. But that respect and love is no longer guaranteed by virtue of their office; it is only earned by virtue of their character.

Just a quick scan of movies and novels over the last century will show how the public's understanding of the role and personality of the Catholic priest has changed so seismically. That public is both Catholic and non-Catholic in its composition.

Priest protagonists played by Bing Crosby (*The Bells of St. Mary's*, *Going My Way*, *Say One for Me*), Karl Malden (*On the Waterfront*), Gregory Peck (*The Keys of the Kingdom*, *The Scarlet and the Black*), Spencer Tracy (*Boy's Town*, *The Devil at 4 O'clock*), and Tom Tryon (*The Cardinal*) were sympathetic figures, heroic and self-sacrificing in their ministry, exemplars of a rugged and practical holiness.

Contrast these sanitized models of spiritual perfection—even given their minor flaws—with the priest portrayals by Linus Roach (*Priest*), Brendan Gleeson (*Calvary*), Philip Seymour Hoffman (*Doubt*), Sean Bean (*Broken*), and the damaged priest-predators in the television series *Oz* and *Rescue Me*.

There has been such a radical collapse of prestige, social profile, and public respectability, such a breakdown so comprehensive and unforgiving.

The lovable priest-pastor cut in the image of a sweet and bungling Father Brown has been replaced by a manipulative and hypocritical cleric. One type replaces another type, and both are merely partial portraits of complex human beings.

Novelists have been more successful in capturing the personal conflicts and tensions that define the real blood-and-guts priest. Although Catholic piety has long been fed an unhealthy diet of hagiographic fiction, recent works have been more probing, transparent, and insightful in their treatment of Catholic priests. Novels like Linden MacIntyre's *The Bishop's Man*, John Boyne's *A History of Loneliness*, Andrew

O'Hagan's *Be Near Me*, and Jennifer Haigh's *Faith* all succeed in creating priest characters caught in a web of tortuous ambiguity, personal breakdown, vocational fidelity, and spiritual darkness that makes them convincing in their pain and admirable in their struggles.

Priests have been permanently toppled from their pedestals (at least in large sections of the Catholic world), and no group has benefitted more from this cosmic alteration of status than priests themselves. They have been liberated from a compromised credibility. But the costs have been great, and a strategy of restoration has long been afoot to recover the more devotional image of the priest that existed prior to the Second Vatican Council and was untouched by the sex scandals that began to unfold in the 1980s and that have yet to be staunched.

Although the flood of charges, allegations, rumors, and indictments that have cumulatively and aggressively undermined the church's credibility have been in part addressed through new protocols, judicial procedures, mandated pontifical commissions, and more accountable episcopal leadership, the deeper systemic causes have only been peripherally treated. More, much more, needs to be done at the structural and formational levels.

It is reasonable to conclude that the declining appeal of priestly ministry is the result of the scandals, but, in truth, there are several other factors involved, all culminating in a precipitated drop in clerical ranks. Although in some jurisdictions vocations to the priesthood are on the rise, there remains a wide gap between the new recruits and the aging clergy with a death rate that is higher, much higher, than the replacement rate.

One senior Irish cleric put it boldly:

> The difficult truth for the Irish Catholic Church is that Irish priests are disappearing. It is now mathematically certain that in less than two decades they will be significantly fewer, significantly older and that those still able to function will be the equivalent in practice of "sacrament machines" rushing from parish to parish—until the light is eventually extinguished.[1]

The poignant impact of such an observation is grounded in part in the knowledge that the writer continues to labor in the fields despite working in the shadow of extinction. Melodramatic? Most likely. Impossible to imagine Catholic Ireland, even post-Catholic Ireland, denuded of its iconic clergy? Perhaps, but only perhaps. It is that desperate.

In 2009, *America* magazine in the United States issued a "modest proposal" wherein the editors reminded their readers that "silence and fervent prayer for vocations are no longer adequate responses to [our] priest shortage."[2] The centrist Jesuit magazine underscored the discomforting truth that the strategies of coping—clustering parishes, reducing the parish priest to a circuit rider, heightened parish rationalizations—only contribute to an accelerated isolation and demoralization among a diminishing clergy and, in the process, impoverish the Christian communities these priests are ordained to serve.

The training of priests is fundamental to any rejuvenated effort to replenish the presbyterate. But even here there is an ever-widening discrepancy between those prelates keen on reinvigorating the ancien régime, as is the case with St. Augustine's Seminary in the Archdiocese of Toronto, and those prelates, as is the case with the Archdiocese in Paris, keen on having their students for the priesthood live in groups of five or six in a parish house outside the standard seminary environment. There are numerous iterations that exist outside these two models as well.

But the operating moral and pastoral imperative to get it right, to revitalize a priestly ministry shorn of the attributes and destructive legacy of clericalism, remains intact, and no one articulates the urgency of that imperative more starkly than the Oblate priest and spiritual writer Ronald Rolheiser:

> Some years ago, I heard an Evangelical minister state: as Christian churches, we have the living water, the water Christ promised would quench all fires and all thirsts. But this is the problem: we aren't getting the living water to where the fires are! Instead we are spraying water everywhere, except where it's burning. He's right. The answer to the mass exodus from our churches is not to blame the culture; it's to make better churches![3]

That won't happen until there are better priests, and to create an abundance of fine and mature priests for our time is no mean challenge. There are ecclesiological, theological, canonical, and anthropological issues that need to be creatively tackled before such priests can be "produced." Key to any success on this front are the spiritual models or exemplars that the institutional church puts forward for emulation. The time for the Curé d'Ars has passed. Recovering the mystique of the priesthood is a doomed effort. What is necessary is the crafting of an image of presbyteral ministry stamped with evangelical zeal, appealing pertinence, and heroic possibility. No better model can be found than Henri J. M. Nouwen.

On September 21, 1996, while on the way to St. Petersburg to shoot a documentary with a Dutch film company of his already storied *The Return of the Prodigal Son*, Nouwen, priest, spiritual writer, a professor at several universities, retreat giver, and decade-long L'Arche coworker and pastoral mentor, died of a heart attack in his homeland, the Netherlands.

His friends and countless admirers were simply stunned. The loss of such a charismatic and influential figure as Nouwen was felt not only in the immediate community but around the world.

A prolific writer—with over three dozen books—and a much called-upon speaker and preacher, Nouwen's presence in the Catholic world was secure and his popularity in the Protestant world, Evangelical specifically, was growing.

But who in fact was this Henri Nouwen? On what was his reputation based? It can't simply be that Hilary Clinton ranks him as her chief spiritual writer.

Nouwen had many vocations, including noninstitutional contemplative, pastoral psychologist, spiritual counselor, missionary, and scribbler of the heart. These vocations were his way of trying to channel his energy to maximize the good he could do, and they were also threshold moments when he tried to ascertain the direction he felt his ever-enticing God was calling him to take. They were a mark of his restlessness, his sometimes muddled and messy compulsion to serve the Word, and they were also a mark of his pioneering pastoral imagination.

Nouwen wrote in his posthumously published *Sabbatical Journey: A Diary of His Final Year*, "I am convinced that it is possible to live the wounds of the past not as gaping abysses that cannot be filled and therefore keep threatening us but as gateways to new life."[4]

Nouwen would be the wounded healer for others as well as himself.

Nouwen's writings—scores of books, thousands of letters, and a legion of translations—are a testament to his productivity and legacy, his fecundity as he would call it. Some of these books are journals, many others extended homilies, but they also include epistolary responses to acute human searching, sustained meditations on biblical themes, and well-crafted riffs on spiritual concepts that free us from cliché.

He could be variously sentimental, mushy, cloying, and crushingly needy. In his "letter" to journalist Fred Bratman, *Life of the Beloved*, Nouwen's penchant for overkill and his labored expressions of affection are in abundant evidence: "Deep friendship is a calling forth of each other's closeness.... Your life and my life are, each of them, one of a kind...our lives are unique stones in the mosaic of human existence."[5]

But mostly Nouwen was measured, penetratingly observant, immediately accessible, and occasionally luminous. In the epilogue to *The Road to Daybreak: A Spiritual Journey*, he reflected on the seeming capriciousness of God's grace:

> The last thing I ever expected from going to the Daybreak community was this truly abysmal experience of being ripped apart from the inside out. I expected to love with and care for mentally handicapped people, supported by a deep friendship and surrounded by a beautiful network of Christian love. I was not prepared to have to deal with a second loneliness....It is dark agony. It is following

Jesus to a completely unknown place. It is being emptied out on the cross and having to wait for new life in naked faith.[6]

Such exquisite honesty and transparency as this underscores the perduring appeal of Nouwen as a spiritual quester who self-discloses rather than disguises, probes rather than exhorts, and humbles himself in the presence of the awesome silence of the Holy One.

It is not easy to place Nouwen. His vocations were many. Theologians have difficulty situating him within one of their organic spiritual traditions; Catholic intellectuals see him as a cult figure, the darling of suburban matrons; psychologists have serious reservations around his methodology and his academic pedigree; pedagogues find his inspirational teaching style problematic.

But his readers love him—unconditionally. No matter what, he is their friend; he is a friend to thousands upon growing thousands. He cultivated close relationships, never abused hospitality, and reveled in the warm intimacy of their companionship.

That is why the substratum, the foundation upon which all his diverse vocations were explored, remained his priesthood.

Some twenty years now since his death it is instructive to see him in this *new* light: a postconciliar prophet of a reformed presbyteral model. Nouwen, in other words, as an exemplar of a priesthood that is contemporary, nonclerical, enabling, and effective. A ministerial priesthood in keeping with the ecclesial vision of Pope Francis.

In the chapters that follow, we explore the genesis and evolution of Nouwen's multilayered understanding of priestly ministry, and in the process, we have discovered how this most self-revealing of twentieth century spiritual writers created a redeeming notion of priesthood that could serve as a creative and hopeful trajectory for reform and revitalization in a time of identity turmoil.

Nouwen avoided ecclesiastical controversies like the proverbial plague. He saw himself simply as a pastor, called to witness to the saving power of God's unconditional love, centered on Jesus, the unique embodiment of that love. And he did this through his teaching, his preaching, his writing, his numberless friendships, and his living qua priest. At the heart of everything for Nouwen was his priesthood, and his priesthood was at the nexus of Divine and human interaction.

Denis Grecco, a professor and systematic theologian at St. Peter's Seminary in London, Ontario, once served as Nouwen's graduate assistant at Regis College, Toronto School of Theology. Nouwen asked him one day, "What is your starting point for priesthood?" and Grecco responded with "ministry."[7] Nouwen rejoined, "That's interesting. I don't know what to do with ministry." Intrigued, Grecco pressed Nouwen for an explanation because, he reasoned, everyone thought of Nouwen as being all about ministry. He asked Nouwen about his own starting point, and Nouwen's response was simple and direct: communion. Nouwen told him, "Everything that a priest does flows from his communion with God." Grecco says that in this brief exchange, he learned two things about the spiritual life of the priesthood as Nouwen understood and practiced it: "the centrality of the person and the significance of relationship and that both ways of thinking are key to his understanding of communion."[8]

Nouwen was every inch the priest—from the very beginning. From the playacting as priest of his preteen years—corralling his siblings to serve as his devout minicongregation as he presided in full liturgical vesture—to his early years in the seminary (his parents wisely discouraged minor seminary as an option) and through to his ordination and subsequent graduate studies in psychology and theology, Nouwen never doubted his vocation. He doubted his worth, the efficacy of how he lived his vocation, the very fecundity of his ministry, but not that he was called forth by God to serve as a presbyter.

Over time his sense of vocation would undergo some profound transformations. Teaching on both Catholic (University of Notre Dame, Boston College, Regis College) and on secular (Yale and Harvard) campuses, Nouwen weathered throughout the late 1960s, the 1970s, and the early 1980s the numerous challenges that beset both the church and the academy: the erosion of the old securities, the assaults on authority, the growing disinclination to affiliate with institutions, the rapid spread, and as some would have it, contagion of Gallic-inspired critical theory in the halls of the academy, and he did so with both anguish and genuine searching.

In the classic Nouwen modus operandi, he inserted himself into the joys and tumults of his time and place, embraced new situations as occasions of growth—working in a Latin American barrio, lecturing in a divinity school, testing the contemplative waters of a Trappist monastery, and living in a L'Arche home as an assistant and as a pastor—all with the understanding that he was called to be an instrument of God's grace.

In his 1985 reflection, *The Selfless Way of Christ: Downward Mobility and the Spiritual Life*, he made clear his conviction that irrespective of how we lived our particular vocation—cloistered, lay, sacerdotal—our common vocation was to define our spiritual life as "a life in which we keep making connections between God's story and our own."[9] We insert ourselves into the Christ narrative, a narrative of redemptive love.

But that narrative can be deeply disquieting, sundering the treasured "truths" we hold of ourselves and of the one to whom we are to conform our lives. In a searing self-disclosure in his diary, *¡Gracias! A Latin American Journal*, shortly after touring some Peruvian Catholic churches with their grisly combination of the gaudy and the macabre in their devotional art, he noted that "the nearly exclusive emphasis on the tortured body of Christ strikes me as a perversion of the Good News into a morbid story that intimidates…but does not liberate them….Maybe deep in my psyche I too know more about the deformed Jesus than about the risen Christ."[10]

To move from the debilitating images of the deformed to the risen Jesus required both a distancing from his Dutch preconciliar seminary formation and a sustained and honest confrontation with his own emotional and spiritual inadequacies. It is that relentless self-honesty, coupled with his promethean compassion, that fueled Nouwen's spiritual writings and made him the go-to person for millions of readers hungering for spiritual direction.

Uninterested in clerical gamesmanship, he preferred the fragile and hospitable Cardinal Joseph Bernardin of Chicago, who welcomed him warmly during his dying days with cancer, to the imperious and protocol-loving Cardinal Bernard Law of Boston, who reprimanded him for coming to the chancery without his clerical collar. Nouwen did not think of priesthood as a clerical redoubt, a bastion of privilege, or an entitlement.

His liturgies were canonically valid but informal; his spiritual counseling, exploratory but orthodox. Nouwen saw himself as the wounded healer and not as an ecclesiastical judge or gatekeeper.

Nouwen's frankness around issues of sexuality and his willingness to self-disclose on matters of emotional fragility make him a model at a time when many bishops are keen on retaining traditional seminaries and priesthood-formation strategies that highlight the recovery of a now discredited neo-Tridentine template promoting "John Paul II and Benedict XVI priests."

It is a long way from his early years as a preseminarian romanticizing a life of priestly service to a young cleric satisfied that he is the possessor of the truth to a 1995 diary entry when he observed,

> My conviction as a young man was that there was no salvation outside the church and that it was my task to bring all "nonbelievers" into the one true church. But much has happened to me over the years. My own psychological training, my exposure to people from the most different religious backgrounds, the Second Vatican Council, the new theology of mission, and my life in L'Arche have all deepened and broadened my views on Jesus's saving work. Today I personally believe that while Jesus came to open the door to God's house, all human beings can walk through that door, whether they know about Jesus or not. Today I see it as my call to help every person claim his or her own way

to God. I feel deeply called to witness for Jesus as the one who is the source of my own spiritual journey and thus create the possibility for other people to know Jesus and commit themselves to him.[11]

Deeply christocentric, the universal pastor has become an *alter Christus* in a different and less conventional sense, no longer restricted to cultic functions, free of a caste system that engenders a sense of separateness, in love with a flawed and scrambling humanity, a broken vessel of holiness.

What better model of the Catholic priest can we find than this?

For decades, the identity of the Roman Catholic priest has been in uneasy flux as many have struggled to secure a definition, a purpose that would be in creative continuity with the past and yet attuned to the shifting sociocultural paradigms of our time. At the Second Vatican Council, various decrees were promulgated that spoke to the status, vocation, or office of baptized believers: *Apostolicam actuositatem* (on the Apostolate of the Laity), *Perfectae caritatis* (on the Adaptation and Renewal of Religious Life), *Christus dominus* (on the Pastoral Office of Bishops), and *Presbyterorum ordinis* (on the Ministry and Life of Priests). It is generally agreed among *periti* or the theological experts at the Council, the Council fathers, and historians and theologians of the Council itself that the decree on the priesthood was weak, the poorest of the four.

Throughout this extended period of postconciliar turbulence, Nouwen wrestled with the meaning of priesthood and how it could be exercised in different contexts, responded with great empathy to those who anguished over the relevance of their vocation, and offered hope to those who despaired of their ministry.

It is instructive to consider Nouwen's evolving and maturing understanding of priesthood by finding an analogue in the fiction of that master novelist of Catholic angst and heroic struggle: Graham Greene.

Over the course of several decades, Greene explored three key iterations of sacerdotal crisis in his novels *The Power and the Glory* (1940), *The Honorary Consul* (1973), and *Monsignor Quixote* (1982).

His ideal priest must speak for the alienated, the abandoned, and those without hope; he won't comfort the settled, nor console the governing elite. If the priest is the *alter Christus*, the other Christ, he must also be a credible Christ, not a sacramental functionary but a "suffering servant." An exacting standard, perhaps, but Greene had a great tolerance for failure—grand or partial.

The whisky priest of *The Power and the Glory*, the guerrilla priest of *The Honorary Consul*, and the priest-quester of *Monsignor Quixote* are all criminals in the eyes of the law, canonical and civil.

Weak vessels all! The whisky priest has no illusions about his character: he tells his hunter, the contemptuous lieutenant, that he is not a saint; he is not even a brave man. He accepts the judgment of a fellow priest, one who has fled to safety, that he lacks firmness of character, and he freely allows that he has broken his vows. Father Rivas, the guerrilla priest, is no speculative theologian, and he struggles to understand the reality he calls God and that his reluctant companion in arms, Dr. Eduardo Plarr, calls the "horror." Monsignor Quixote is considered suspect by his new assistant, Father Herrera, because he prefers God's love to God's justice and prefers pastoral compassion to the norms of moral theology. His bishop sees him as a source of great scandal, a dangerous simpleton.

But at no time does their humanity more recommend itself than in periods of acute questioning, searching doubt, and anguished unbelief. In such moments, their priesthood is not eclipsed but ennobled. Greene's priests are most like Jesus not in the degradation of the cross nor in the triumph of the empty tomb but in the exquisite torment of Gethsemane:

> The whisky priest, the guerrilla priest and the priest-errant are not conventional clerics. The *alter Christus* as rebel is engaged, ultimately, in nothing short of the most perfect priestly act: *kenosis*. The priest-rebel of Greene's fiction is a persistent reminder of the author's predilection for the fallen and disobedient as the prism through which can shine the disturbing light of faith.[12]

Nouwen's life as a priest was far less dramatic than Greene's fallen clerics. The heroism, folly, and arresting theatre of Greene's priest-rebels was not Nouwen's personal narrative. But a close reading of the novels and their priest protagonists reminds us of the unique qualities of compassion, creative empathy, struggling self-awareness, and wrenchingly beautiful self-scrutiny and pure intentionality that define Nouwen at his best.

In his letter of March 29, 1994, to a Dutch friend who was shortly to be ordained, Nouwen encapsulates the essence of his own self-understanding as a priest:

What I most want to say to you is that living a deep and intimate relationship with your Lord Jesus will allow you to be a source of healing for many people as you walk through life full of contradictions, conflicts and violence. I also want to say to you how important it is to be surrounded by good, caring friends who will hold you close to Christ by their affection, their care and their encouragement. Finally, I want you to fully trust that when you stay close to Jesus and to those who in the name of Jesus will embrace you with their love, you cannot be other than a source of life to others.[13]

The crisis of definition around priesthood is with the church still. Pope Francis has made clear his growing alarm over the deficiencies of seminary training, the antiquated process of vocation discernment, the myopic curriculum, and most especially the corrosive effects of clericalism.

Dramatic change is called for—bold, prophetic, and visionary. The style and substance of Nouwen's priestly vocation—his premier vocation—provides precisely the kind of Christian depth and human maturity the church needs. His personal ministry as a priest serves as a marker for a rejuvenated and meaningful ministry for our tremulous, fragmented, yet hope-filled church.

In 1971, after fourteen years of ordained ministry, Nouwen published *Creative Ministry*, a book that attracted attention on both sides of the Atlantic. In this early work, he presented the case for ministry as a self-defining mission. It is a definition that, decades later, we believe, points toward a progressive reinvention of the role of the priest. Nouwen wrote that those whose vocation is that of priest or minister

elect to follow an uncertain path where success may not be
experienced in their lifetime:

> They know they will not see their purpose realized,
> and they consider themselves only a guide to it.
> *They are impressively free toward their own lives.*
> From their actions it becomes clear that they con-
> sider their own existence of secondary importance.
> They do not live to keep themselves alive but to
> build a new world of which they have already seen
> the first images and which so appeals to them that
> the borderline between their life and their death
> loses its definitiveness.[14]

What will emerge over the course of his maturing ministry is
the realization that being "impressively free" allows for the
priest as conduit of grace rather than sacramental dispenser,
vulnerable among the vulnerable, compassionate attendant in
the field hospital that is the church.

A PRIEST IN THE MAKING

A Time in which All Boundaries Were Clear

Henri Nouwen declared his intention to become a priest in 1938 when he was six years old. His delighted grandmother, Sarah de Monk Ramselaar, arranged for a seamstress to make child-sized vestments for him and for a carpenter to construct a miniature altar with a tabernacle that was eventually set up in the attic of the family home. Playing a priest became a serious business for the young Nouwen. He reveled in the opportunity to organize friends and family members to act as servers, deacons, and bishops, even delivering sermons to them as they compliantly played along.

The Nouwen and Ramselaar families had deep Catholic roots. Henri's mother was one of eight Ramselaars, his father one of eleven Nouwens. The Dutch biographer Jurjen Beumer characterized the Nouwen family as "incorruptible, pious and very Catholic," and Ramselaars as "gentle people with an artistic bent...also traditional Catholic, but without the pious traits of the Nouwens."[1]

The Ramselaar and Nouwen family lines joined in 1931 when Maria Ramselaar and Laurent Nouwen married. Henri, or Harrie as he was known within the family, was born the following year in Nijkerk, followed by Paul in 1934, and a decade later, Laurent (Junior) in 1944, and then Laurien in

1945. Laurent Junior described Catholic Holland of the 1930s as a time when religion was the dominant and defining identity. "In society you belonged either to Protestants or you belonged to the Catholics. And [our parents] were from this Catholic background," he explained.[2]

The Nouwens and Ramselaars were Catholics in clear conformity with their pope, Pius XI, who, in 1937, wrote, "We can command: it is not enough to be a member of the Church of Christ, one needs to be a living member, in spirit and in truth, i.e., living in the state of grace and in the presence of God, either in innocence or in sincere repentance" (*Mit Brennender Sorge* 19). They took their faith seriously and with great loyalty. Nouwen biographer Michael O'Laughlin describes the dominant Catholic attitudes in the Netherlands at that time: "Catholicism of Nouwen's youth in the Netherlands was in almost obsessive conformity with the official policies of the Vatican."[3] The Nouwens and Ramselaars were Catholics in the manner that pope Pius XI had in mind when, in 1935, he wrote, "Blessed are those Christian parents who are able to accept without fear the vocations of their sons, and see in them a signal honor for their family and a mark of the special love and providence of Our Lord. Still more blessed, if, as was often the case in ages of greater faith, they make such divine visitations the object of their earnest prayer" (*Ad catholici sacerdotii* 82).

In responding to their six-year-old son's declaration that he wanted to be a priest, the Nouwens and the Ramselaars would have paid serious attention to the warning contained in the next paragraph of the same encyclical: "A long sad experience has shown that a vocation betrayed—the word is not to be thought too strong—is a source of tears not only for sons but also for ill-advised parents; and God grant that such tears be not so long delayed as to become eternal tears" (*Ad catholici sacerdotii* 83).

There would be no such tears for them. Nouwen's parents had no intention of getting in the way of their young son's chosen career. His mother encouraged it and his father made sure that his son would be ready for it when the time was right. The early intimations in childhood of a proposed way of life as an adult are what the psychologist Carl Jung called "islands of consciousness which are like single lamps or lighted objects in the far-flung darkness," when we look back on them later in life.[4] Such flickers of interest "contain a new, very important series of contents belonging to the perceiving subject himself, the so-called ego."[5] In the decades that followed, Henri Nouwen's books and journals charted his unwavering commitment to gathering up the fragments of his emerging vocation, and they mapped out the growth and maturity of his self-perceptions, as a child, as a man, and finally as a priest.

Life in Holland turned upside down for all its citizens, religion notwithstanding, when in May 1940, the German occupation began, forcing the Dutch royal family to go into exile. Cultural historian Jeroen Dewulf says that the occupation has become critical to understanding subsequent events—cultural, political, and religious—in the Netherlands. The Dutch "continue to relate contemporary debates to the Second World War," he writes. "Modern Dutch identity can indeed not be understood without reference to the occupation."[6]

The occupation changed the way of life for the entire population. Up until that event, Catholics in the Netherlands had their own distinct culture, as did Protestant denominations, and indeed various politically affiliated groups. The groups lived very different, in fact separate, lives. Their businesses and their cultural and social relations were generally kept within denominational or political confines. Historians describe this as *verzuiling*, or pillarization, the way the Dutch country has historically reinforced strong attachment to and membership within certain divisions or pillars (*zuilen*).[7] Historically, there were four dominant pillars: Catholic, Protestant, Social Democrat, and Liberal silos. Each was so well established that large sectors of Dutch society were, for decades, able to experience life within a specific silo, within a distinct cultural/religious/political community that was decidedly separate from the other three. Each had its own school system, publishing, and media, as well as commercial and social networks.

Long before German troops entered the Netherlands, the "gentle" and "artistic" Ramselaar family had settled in Amersfoort, a small town equidistant from Utrecht and Nijkerk. There, the family business, a Catholic enterprise, was a department store. Maria's mother had to take over this business when her husband died unexpectedly. Her daughter Maria looked after the bookkeeping. Two other Ramselaar children, Anton, known to the family as "Toon" (1899–1981), and Gertrude (1902–59) entered religious life. Uncle Toon, as Henri knew him, was a priest and later monsignor in the Archdiocese of Utrecht. He would go on to an illustrious career in the Dutch Roman Catholic Church that included the presidency of Apeldoorn's minor seminary, serving as a *peritus* during the Second Vatican Council, and becoming a major voice in Catholic-Jewish relations. Henri Nouwen's Aunt Gertrude was Sister Marie Augustine, a member of the Zusters de Goede Herder (Sacred Heart Sisters). Uncle and aunt exerted a close and lasting influence

on the Catholic formation of their beloved nephew, especially after he declared his calling to the priesthood.

Despite their relative comfort, the Nouwens and
Ramselaars, like every Dutch family in the 1930s, were forced
to adapt to severe economic disruptions and political insta-
bility. Events in the United States (the Wall Street Crash of
1929) and across the border in Germany (the rise of National
Socialism and the chancellorship of Adolf Hitler) made for
frightening and uncertain times. Henri Nouwen was eight
years old when the occupation began and the traditional pillars of Dutch society began to crumble. His father, then a tax
lawyer, sought to keep the family safe while trying to avoid
the possibility of getting caught up in the forced labor policies of the occupiers. He built a hiding place in one home
and kept the family on the move, from Nijkerk, to Venlo,
then the small village of Bossum to the north of Hilversum
(where Maria Nouwen convinced a group of priests to set
up a Catholic school for her son and six other classmates[8]),
The Hague, then Scheveningen, and finally to Nijmegen by
the time the war was over. As Pope Pius XI had warned the
Catholics of Europe as early as 1937, "The more the ene-
mies attempt to disguise their designs, the more *distrustful
vigilance* will be needed, in light of bitter experience" (*Mit
Brennender Sorge* 39 [emphasis added]).

The Catholic bishops of the Netherlands filled in the
details of what such distrustful vigilance could involve.
Following the occupation, they released a pastoral letter
forbidding Catholic cooperation with the Germans. Early
in 1941, they asked parishes and all other Catholic institutions across the country to withhold any information from
the German High Command that related to finances and
personnel. This was followed by a directive that all Catholic

publishers should refuse the German order that their materials had to be cleared through Nazi headquarters prior to their publication. In 1943, they encouraged Dutch Catholics to practice civil disobedience rather than help their occupiers hunt out Jews for transportation to extermination camps.[9]

Distrustful vigilance certainly characterizes Laurent Nouwen's wartime activities when his family's personal security was at risk and food shortages were increasingly common. *Der hongerwinter* is the name Dutch citizens gave to the extreme food shortages of 1944. Despite their relative affluence, Maria and Laurent Nouwen were challenged to keep their children fed. "The last years of the war were very difficult for the family," recalled Laurent Junior. "Henri and our brother Paul had to go to the farms to find food and they went on those expeditions, which for them were adventures."[10] In addition to such dubious adventures, there was regular church attendance and formal education in the various Catholic schools the Nouwen children attended.

Historically, Catholic education has operated under special arrangements with the state, often making it vulnerable. Dutch Catholics felt relatively protected because, since 1815, there had been constitutional, if not financial, support for denominational education. Despite this constitutional protection, there was a divisive campaign in 1917 called "the school struggle" for state funding for Catholic and Protestant schools. Political pressure from and between Catholic and Protestant "pillars" resulted in state funding for schools of both denominations, as well as other nonstate-established schools operating within the other two pillars: Social Democrat and Liberal. These nonstate schools operated alongside what are known today in the Netherlands as "public-authority" controlled schools. The Pacification Law of 1917 was a response to

Dutch Catholics who acted as brokers, as the Jesuit sociologist John A. Coleman explains, among Catholic appeals for school funding, "Protestant demands for schools with the bible and socialist pleas for school reform." A compromise was found that "joined together the questions of electoral reform and subsidies for schools."[11] Under the 1917 law, Catholic men, and then two years later, women, were granted full voting rights.

The private Catholic schools, such as the one at Bossum that Henri Nouwen and his brother attended were not "private" independent schools as we might think of today. The Catholic school in the village of Bossum, although initiated locally by the Nouwen family, would have been considered by Dutch authorities as private, and under Nazi occupation, they would become suspect.

The Catholics of the Netherlands were not a defensive minority. When Uncle Toon entered the Archdiocese of Utrecht in 1922, the Catholic population in the country was 35.6 percent. By the time Henri Nouwen was born, it had increased slightly to 36.4 percent, and by the time he was fifteen, it was 38.5 percent. The later "collapse" of Catholic organizations in the Netherlands, as some observers call it, would not begin until the 1960s, when Henri Nouwen had already begun his first sojourn in the United States. This rapid secularization happened at a time of depillarization, changing Dutch society fundamentally.[12]

As a Catholic schoolboy of the 1930s and 1940s, Henri Nouwen would be less involved in these raw statistics and complex politics than in the biblical characters and parables that were part of the curriculum intended to help children like him to become informed Catholics and literate, numerate, well-rounded citizens, despite the Nazi presence within their midst. The typical curriculum included stories from Scripture, as well as the lives of the saints, common practice in Catholic primary education around the world. All Dutch Catholics were taught about their country's patron saint, interestingly from the north of England, Willibrord, the first bishop of Utrecht who, in the words of Pope Benedict XV, "brought the radiance of the gospel to Holland" (*Maximum illud* 2).

Willibrord is "the man who first turned the thoughts of the English people to foreign mission" and "the first English missionary who laboured with success on the continent."[13] Born in Yorkshire around 658, he entered a monastery at Ripon, before relocating to a monastery in Ireland, where he was ordained. He was still busily engaged in missionary work when the Venerable Bede wrote about him in his *History of the English Church and People*.

Over time, Henri Nouwen would come to share at least two characteristics with this octogenarian Anglo-Saxon priest and patron saint: live most of his life in a foreign country and preach and teach in a foreign language. But before that could happen, he had to successfully complete his primary and secondary education, in the hopes that the German presence in his homeland would come to an end and that its Catholic schools might survive. In 1944, an impatient twelve-year-old Henri Nouwen told his father he wanted to enter the minor seminary at Apeldoorn, the traditional feeder system into the major seminary. His father informed him he would have to wait. "'You are not ready to make a decision about the priesthood,' my father told me. 'You better wait until you are eighteen.'"[14] Rather than evidence of doubting his son's maturity, this decision speaks to concerns about the occupation. This was a time when Canadian and other allied troops had begun their defense of the Netherlands and the Nouwens did not want their son living elsewhere at a time of great uncertainty. It would be safer to keep him closer to home, and they kept him at the local Catholic gymnasium or high school. They enriched his education by arranging poetry readings and discussions about art and artists, hosted in the different homes they frequently moved to. The life and work of Rembrandt and Vincent van Gogh were included in this mix of in-school and in-home education.

In his later books, Henri Nouwen tends to portray his father as inflexible and critical. "Many of our meals were interrupted with my father's commands: 'Elbows off the table,' 'Wait until everyone is served,' and 'Don't talk as you eat.'"[15] His brother Laurent counters this interpretation: "Unfortunately, I find that the image of my father has been too harsh. Henri was, in some ways, an impossible person, as well. He was not an easy person....He absorbed a lot of tension from people around him. That was maybe because he was uncertain, maybe it was because of the doubts he had himself."[16]

Those doubts had to do with emotional security. Laurent explains that throughout his childhood and beyond, his gangly and physically uncoordinated brother spent a lot of time worrying about whether he was loved or not. "He had a great doubt. He felt he wasn't accepted as a person or he didn't fit in. I think he asked our mother from an early age for confirmation that he was loved. He would ask her, 'Do you love me?' And our mother would say yes, not only in her words but by her relationship with him."[17] But it was never enough. Writing about his parents toward the end of his life, Nouwen concedes, "Even though they assured me hundreds of times

27

that they loved me I never seemed fully satisfied with their answers and kept on asking the same questions."[18]

Nouwen's secondary education concluded as the occupation ended and the war was over. Their devastating impact on the country would be felt for decades. No longer seeking to avoid forced labor, Nouwen's father moved the family once more, no longer clandestinely, this time to The Hague, where Henri Nouwen enrolled in the Jesuit-run Aloysius College to complete a preparatory year before moving back to Apeldoorn.

Aloysius College, named after the patron saint of male purity, was established during the First World War in 1917. Laity replaced the Jesuits in 1971, and the college closed in 2016. Nonetheless, the college had a distinguished tenure with some notable alumni, including many politicians, jurists, and a few Jesuits, among whose number is the former Superior General, Peter-Hans Kolvenbach. Both Henri and his brother Paul were graduates and their time under the Jesuits was formative, though not so formative as to turn them into Jesuits. The Ignatian influence on Nouwen's early education and formation is further discussed in the next chapter.

This final preparatory year gave Henri Nouwen the opportunity to reflect on the nature of the priesthood. In 1935, Pope Pius XI had presented a blueprint for the priesthood at a time in history that he characterized as "unparalleled in its need for the mercy and pardon of God" (*Ad catholici sacerdotii* 7). The encyclical *Ad catholici sacerdotii* offers what some would call today a strategic plan for priestly formation and the seminaries around the world charged with the implementation of its contents. In this encyclical, Henri Nouwen, a candidate for priestly formation, would discover a challenging and complex job description that he would need to prepare for. Priests, asserted the pope, are "mediators between God and humanity" (no. 8), who have "power over the very body of Christ" (no. 16), and also "the power to remit sins" (no. 20). The priest is the "appointed 'dispenser of the mysteries of God'" (no. 17) who occupies "a place midway between God and human nature...bringing to us absolving beneficence, offering our prayers to Him and appeasing the wrathful Lord" (no. 29). The priest "accompanies the Christian throughout the pilgrimage of his life to the gates of Heaven" (no. 19). "The minister of God is a father of souls" and "a veritable father of the poor" (no. 49) and also "stable and perpetual...with the indelible character imprinted on his soul whereby he becomes 'a priest forever'" (no. 22). Priests "of the Latin Church in higher Orders are bound by a grave obligation of chastity; so grave is the obligation in them of its perfect and total observance that a transgression involves the added guilt of sacrilege" (no. 40).

Toward the end of the encyclical, Pius XI turns his attention to those who run the seminaries: "What a terrifying account, Venerable Brethren, We shall have to give to the Prince of Shepherds, to the Supreme Bishop of souls, if we have handed over these souls to incompetent guides and incapable leaders" (no. 76).

There was another model of the priesthood that was being widely circulated and discussed in the Netherlands at that time. In 1937, *Dagboek van een dorpspastoor* appeared in bookstores across the country and received a lot of attention in the Catholic and secular press. It was the Dutch translation of the 1936 novel by Georges Bernanos, *Journal d'un curé de campagne* (*The Diary of a Country Priest*). The book takes the form of a diary written by a nervous young priest, insecure over his humble origins, during his first posting to a small parish in rural France. He is an awkward outsider whose increasing ill-health is seen as weakness by his parishioners. The children he teaches taunt him. Rumors begin to spread that he may be an alcoholic. Older priests offer him advice, sometimes pragmatic, often cynical. He begins to sense that his ministry is a failure. Then cancer overcomes him before he can discover how the example of his quiet, grace-filled suffering has become a parable for the people he seeks to serve.

The reviews in both the Dutch Catholic and secular press were very positive. In October, the national daily, *De Telegraaf*, described the novel as a simple book that presents the intimate (and sometimes desperate) thoughts of an unassuming village parish priest concerning his relationship to his parish, its people, and his faith. It commented on how the priest's thoughts are presented in ways that reveal his commitment and his deeply intuitive knowledge about life and its many problems. It concluded that the novel was a work of uncommon purity, simplicity, and passionate truthfulness, and a truly convincing and tragic book of great merit.[19] A month later, a provincial paper picked up on the word *intuitive* in its description of the young priest. The review praised the novel as an important work about a physically broken human being who possessed a wondrous intuitive gift: his ability to bring grace, blessing, and peace to even the most confused souls.[20] The anonymous reviewer used the word *gebroken*, meaning "broken," to describe this ailing priest. Another Dutch word, not used in the review, will become a central image for Henri Nouwen in all the books he will eventually write. That word is *verwond*, meaning "wounded."

Celebrating the Bernanos novel fifty years after its publication, the Harvard psychologist Robert Coles offers insights into the book's lasting contribution and uses language that, like the abiding image of woundedness, has striking applicability to the postordination life of Henri Nouwen. First, the novel takes the form of a diary, a literary convention that Nouwen will use for some of his best-selling books. Coles says that the diary convention permits

> a candor, a lack of self-consciousness and self-importance, so that gradually this ailing, seemingly confused, melancholic young priest becomes to the reader a virtual incarnation of divine grace. His unpretentious, stumbling, honestly earnest manner, his mixture of knowing sadness and naiveté, his moments (and longer) of self-doubt, followed by quiet spells of prayerful trust in the Lord's intentions for him and for everyone, all are evidence for the reader of what a true *homo religiosus* is like inwardly.[21]

These will become key words for understanding Nouwen's career: unpretentious, lacking self-consciousness and self-importance, aware of his stumbles, honest and earnest, underlying sadness, naiveté, self-doubt, and prayerful trust. At this stage in his life, the preseminary Henri Nouwen is youthfully innocent, a *puer religiosus*. Michael O'Laughlin presents the image of Nouwen as a "wise child" or the *puer aeternus* of Jungian theory: "Throughout his life, Nouwen displayed a childlike quality that managed to be both naïvely idealistic and yet wise at the same time."[22] His preseminary life, despite the tribulations of war, was relatively comfortable. Looking back on them years later, he describes this period as "life in the garden of youth," a time in which he reveled in the experience of devotions and prayer, his love of theology and spirituality, and most of all his "strong sense of vocation."[23] His family had been nothing but supportive, nurturing and protecting him throughout a turbulent period in the history of the Netherlands. Precarious as the 1940s had been for his parents, they managed to maintain something of a normality for their growing family. Their two oldest sons received a solid Catholic education, the Ramselaar family business in Amersfoort continued, and their participation in Catholic liturgical and sacramental life was relatively uninterrupted.

The way Henri Nouwen describes his preseminary youth certainly reflects a pre–Second Vatican Council worldview of Catholicism that could also describe the experiences of other European or North American Catholics of the period. At the same time, it reveals the impact of his childhood within the profoundly pillarized Dutch society of the 1930s and 1940s. Looking back on that era, two years before his death, Nouwen wrote,

> I was born and raised in a Roman Catholic family, went to Roman Catholic schools, and lived a life in which I related exclusively to Roman Catholics. It was a time in which all boundaries were clear.... These very clear boundaries gave me a sense of being in the right place, being wholly protected, and being very safe. I never met anyone who was divorced, who had left the priesthood, or who was gay. It was clear what I was going to do as a priest.[24]

But what kind of priest might that be? The young curé in the Bernanos novel is reminded by a more experienced priest of the dangerous space between the hermetically sealed life inside a religious institution and the experience of the unexpected messiness of life as it is lived beyond its walls. He cautions the young priest that the seminary "is not the world you know—real life is not like that."[25] The eighteen-year-old Henri Nouwen would certainly discover this in time. He did not need to rely on the example of fictional priests. In sharp contrast to the vulnerability of the example of the Bernanos *dorpspastor* were two influential priests he knew intimately. Two of them would exert a powerful influence on his preparation for the priesthood and how he lived out that vocation in the decades following his ordination. Uncle Toon was ordained in 1922 and Bernard Alfrink in 1924. These priests helped Nouwen to give form and meaning to his understanding of the concept of priesthood. Both had managed to create their own, somewhat atypical "model" of priesthood as they rose through the ranks of the strict hierarchical institution that was the Archdiocese of Utrecht.

Anton Ramselaar was thirty-two years old when his nephew was born and had been a priest in the Archdiocese of Utrecht for ten years. Following his ordination in 1922, he began typical parish work in Haaksbergen, in eastern Holland, close to the German border. After two years of parish life, Anton undertook further studies, this time in Rome, where he became an expert in Gregorian chant. He returned to the Netherlands in 1927 and served, initially, as chaplain in Nijkerk and then in Soest, close to the Ramselaar family home in Amersfoort. Anton's ministry took a very different turn in 1929 with his appointment as chaplain at the archdiocesan cathedral, St. Catherine's, in Utrecht. Now in a major urban setting, he turned his focus to youth work and the

Catholic Scouts movement, becoming its spiritual director in 1936.

In addition to organizing educational programs for Catholic youth, from 1936 to 1941, Anton worked with the creative community behind *De Gemeenschap* (The Community), a cultural magazine for Catholic Youth founded in 1925. All the major Catholic literary voices of the Netherlands in the interwar period wrote for or illustrated this magazine, including the poets and novelists Jef Last, Bertus Aafjes, and Gerrit Achterberg. The magazine also published translations of articles by Jean Cocteau and Jacques Maritain.[26] Because of its antifascist focus, the magazine was shut down under the occupation. The art and literary historian Anton van Duinkerken was editorial director for several years. Van Duinkerken (the nom de plume of Willem Jan Marie Anton Asselbergs) eventually became a much-loved member of faculty, teaching art history at the Catholic University of Nijmegen from 1952 until his death in 1968. Nouwen's graduate work there in 1966 is discussed in the next chapter.

Archbishop Johannes de Jong appointed Anton Ramselaar president of the minor seminary in Apeldoorn in 1945. In time, the minor seminary expanded its focus to become, in 1953, a high school *(gymnasium)* open to the broader Catholic community, not only for teenaged boys pursuing priestly apprenticeship. Ramselaar maintained links with his cathedral, St. Catherine's, and was made a canon in 1946. Two important developments, the first in 1951 and the second in 1952, set him on radically different paths when he became involved in two major international initiatives. Each will frame the rest of his highly independent career as a priest.

First, with the support of the Dutch Catholic politician Anna de Waal (who was about to become the first female cabinet minister in the Netherlands, serving as Secretary of State for Education in 1953), he established the *Katholieke Raad voor Israël* (Catholic Council for Israel).[27] The goal was to increase Catholic awareness of the cultural and theological meaning of Israel, starting in the Netherlands, where memories of Dutch collaboration with the Nazis with Jewish deportations were especially bitter and unresolved. As Marnix Croes of the Research Centre of the Dutch Ministry of Justice writes, "For scholars of the Holocaust, the low survival rate of the Jews from the Netherlands remains a mystery. Of the 140,000 people (native and immigrant) whom the Nazis considered 'full' Jews in 1941, only 27 percent survived the occupation." Croes contrasts these statistics with the survival rate for Belgium's 66,000 Jews: 60 percent, and France's 320,000 Jews at 75 percent.[28]

Amid all the grim statistics were remarkable and terrifying testimonies that were just beginning to be circulated in the Netherlands and around the world. In 1947, *Het Achterhuis*, the Dutch edition of Anne Frank's diary, was published. It contained a story that was news to some people and a provocative reminder to others. The previous year, the psychotherapist and extermination camp survivor Viktor Frankl spent nine days dictating a short book that went on to sell more than nine million copies: *Ein Psycholog erlebt das Konzentrationslager* or *Man's Search for Meaning*.[29] Frankl's influence in North American psychology circles was greatly assisted by the Harvard-based psychologist Gordon Allport. He wrote a preface to the English language edition, comparing Frankl's importance to that of Freud, describing the book as "a compelling introduction to [logotherapy] the most significant psychological movement of our day."[30] Allport also invited Frankl to Harvard as a guest lecturer. Chapter 5 details how Allport offered advice to Henri Nouwen concerning the direction and focus of his work in psychology.

Ramselaar's second major initiative began in 1952, when he took over the leadership of the *Fédération Mondiale de la Jeunesse Féminine Catholique*, an international organization for young Catholic women. These two issues: Jewish-Christian relations and the role of women in social action, were of vital importance to the Dutch Catholic community and in the remaining decades of Ramselaar's career, they also became defining concerns that would bring him into the orbit of the Vatican. As he researched and wrote about these major initiatives, they also became the subject of highly animated conversations over dinner in the Nouwen household, where he was a frequent guest.

Nouwen's year at the minor seminary Apeldoorn was spent under the watchful eye of his uncle. Uncle Toon's constantly evolving and unconventional job description with its international travel, conferences, and publishing was a close and constant example that stood in stark contrast with the limpid self-reflections of the fictional *dorpspastor*.

Then there was the example of Father Bernard Alfrink, who was one year older than Uncle Toon and, like him, also attended the major seminary at Rijsenberg. Alfrink was ordained in 1924. His priestly vocation was singularly academic, with graduate studies in Old Testament Scripture at the Pontifical Biblical Institute in Rome, culminating in a doctorate in 1930. This enabled him to teach at the major seminary he had attended in Rijsenberg, where he contributed to the Canisius translation into Dutch of the Old Testament published in 1939. During the occupation, the Rijsenberg seminarians were moved into smaller premises, and Alfrink continued working on a book on the Synoptic Gospels. After the liberation, he was appointed to teach Old Testament Studies at the Catholic University in Nijmegen, and the book he had been working on all through the war years, *Het Passieverhaal der Vier Evangelisten*, a synoptic analysis of the gospel texts on the passion of Christ, was published in 1946. Alfrink remained at the university until 1951. His "work" as a priest was primarily academic, focused on research, teaching, writing, attending conferences, and consulting with his bishop. On weekends he ministered at local parishes, where some complained that his sermons were too long, too academic, and too difficult to follow.[31] Alfrink's rise within the Catholic Church and his unwavering support of Nouwen are detailed in the next chapter.

In his final year as a teenager, Nouwen, who had been fixated on the idea of becoming a priest since the age of six, carried his suitcase up the steps of Utrecht's major seminary in Rijensberg to begin the required studies for the priesthood. As he looked back on this time, many years later, he characterized himself as an individual who was "restless, nervous, intense, distracted and impulse driven."[32] In addition to the socks, shirts, and breviary inside that suitcase, he also carried, deep inside, unresolved emotional and psychological issues that would take many years for him to articulate, let alone address, beginning with that nagging uncertainty about being loved.

Viktor Frankl captures the ambiguity of this young seminarian's difficulties whose future ministry to others, no matter what form that would take, would only become effective when this inexperienced minister had addressed some maturity issues, especially those related to the experience of loving and being loved. "No-one can become fully aware of the essence of another human being unless he loves him," writes

Frankel. "By the spiritual act of love he is enabled to see the essential traits and features in the beloved person; and even more, he sees that which is potential in him, that which is not yet actualized but yet ought to be actualized."[33]

Nouwen did not enter the seminary with the intent of becoming a priest psychologist. His intent was to become an ordained minister who would, eventually, serve the Archdiocese of Utrecht. The rigorous all-male process he experienced there is described in the next chapter. Some issues he managed to deal with right away, others were ignored or patched over, left for him to address later in life.

In 1931, the year that Maria Ramselaar and Laurent Nouwen were married, Carl Jung captured the essence of the biographical arc that this young idealistic seminarian would follow. Each of us, Jung proposes, must work with the "illusions and assumptions" formed in childhood. Dealing with them as we age and mature is a "fight waged within oneself as well as outside," especially if we persist in believing that earlier dreams and convictions are "eternally valid, and make a virtue of unchangeably clinging to them."[34] This is another way of expressing the words of St. Paul: "When I was a child, I spoke like a child, I thought like a child, I reasoned like a child; when I became an adult, I put an end to childish ways" (1 Cor 13:11). The remaining chapters in this book will illustrate how the "inner fight" that Carl Jung describes captures the experience of Henri Nouwen as he prepared for and developed his role as an ordained priest. Nouwen managed to push some issues aside, but as Jung cautions, "Many—far too many—aspects of life which should also have been experienced lie in the lumber-room among dusty memories; but sometimes, too, they are glowing coals under grey ashes."[35]

THE SEMINARY YEARS

In the "Between" of the I-Thou

Henri Nouwen was ordained to the Roman Catholic priesthood in 1957, a time of postwar reconstruction in the Netherlands, a time of restoration—political and social—of the order of things that preceded the Nazi occupation, a time of reclamation, of robust Catholic confidence.

It was not uncommon for young boys, whether from an avowedly devout family or from one with a minimalist approach to practice, to think of a priestly calling. It was, after all, a vocation, a profession if you like, swathed in prestige, with a high level of social respectability. It was a career choice that ensured a materially comfortable life, and minus the foreswearing of an active sex life, provided consolations as much as it demanded sacrifices. Henri Nouwen was not an outsider, an eccentric dreamer, a romantic exotic, when he entertained thoughts of becoming a priest. It was as natural for most Catholic males and as predictable as puberty, which was about the time that alternate options began to surface in the male mind. Though not in Nouwen's case, evidently.

Both before and after pubescence, young Nouwen, dressed up as a presiding celebrant provided with vestments courtesy of his dotting maternal grandmother, took to his makeshift altar with an abundant piety, an exuberant love of drama, and a preternatural seriousness:

By the time I was eight years old, I had converted the attic of our home to a children's chapel, where I played Mass, gave sermons to my parents and relatives, and set up a whole hierarchy with bishops, priests, deacons, and altar servers among my friends.[1]

It is not often, perhaps not even natural, that a preadolescent youth homilize, and to an artificial congregation made up of admiring if not mystified adults and long-suffering siblings and companions.

It seems that Nouwen was made for the sacerdotium.

Former graduate teaching assistant for Nouwen at Harvard and one of his biographers, Michael O'Laughlin, draws on the work of American psychologist James Hillman to demonstrate that a charismatically gifted person, someone who will make a significant impact on his generation in his chosen field, will exhibit early signs of his maturing vocation. O'Laughlin concludes that "Henri Nouwen certainly fits Hillman's model: at a very early stage in his life he gravitated almost magnetically towards his calling or mission."[2]

That sense of mission evolved when Holland was still a Nazi-occupied territory—although the tide of the war was already changing—and the need for some stability was paramount. He would later observe that the larger context of his vocation to the priesthood, the backdrop as it were to his embryonic gift for priesthood, was the war with all its hideous aftershocks, saturation bombing of Rotterdam, local bomb shelters, invading troops, and the prevailing fear of imminent death.

Instead of the minor seminary—now generally recognized as a formation tool of limited value—Nouwen attended the local gymnasium and then, immediately following the end of the war, the family relocated to The Hague, and he was sent to complete his secondary schooling to the Jesuit high school, Aloysius College, whose Ignatian training certainly helped to shape Nouwen's sensibility. Such schools were made to do so. John Padberg, Jesuit historian and authority on the educational philosophy that informs the pedagogical work of the Society of Jesus, argues that the schools of today continue to realize the four essential reasons for Jesuit education as outlined by Diego Ledesma, a sixteenth-century member of the then-new order in the church:

> Ledesma said, first of all, that Jesuit schools provide a way in which people can effectively, practically earn a living: that is, there is a practical reason for education. Secondly, they provide for the right governing of society and the proper making of law and public affairs. In other words, there is a social reason for education. Thirdly, he said that Jesuits have schools because they provide (I'm using his baroque term, now) for the ornaments, splendor, and perfection of the rational nature of man. In other words, there is the liberalizing effective end of education. Finally, he said, and this is almost a quotation although I don't have it in front of me, 'What is most important, is that education helps lead humankind, men and women, most securely to their last end, God our Lord.' In other words, there is a religious motive for the Jesuit educational enterprise. So you've got a practical, a social or civic, a cultural or liberal, and a religious motive for Jesuit education.[3]

Although Nouwen's time with his Jesuit educators was of a limited duration, their mode of instruction, emphasis on *eloquentia perfecta*, discipline, and commitment to doing all things *ad majorem Dei gloriam* would not have been lost on the impressionable lad from Nijkerk. His incorporation of aspects of Ignatian spirituality—the foundational work of which is the *Spiritual Exercises* of St. Ignatius of Loyola—into his own pastoral ministry, prayer life, and religious epistemology and aesthetics would be later, more mature developments. This early taste of the Jesuit ethos at Aloysius College would prove to be foundational.

Preaching, teaching, and catechizing all involved the Jesuits in the cultivated arts of articulation and persuasion. The centrality of the Word—in preaching and teaching—would influence everything from their missionary activity throughout the globe to their theatre, architecture, and fostering of the classical arts.

Nouwen's gift for preaching—although innate and grounded in his love of the Scriptures and in his predilection for dramatic expression—received embryonic nurturing in the Jesuit college in The Hague.

At the age of eighteen, Nouwen entered the preparatory seminary in Apeldoorn for one year prior to beginning his six years of study in Rijsenburg, the major seminary, confirming for himself a path that would lead to ordination as a priest of the Archdiocese of Utrecht. During these years of methodical study, years spent under a scholastic regimen that demanded little in the way of creative thinking—in fact, it discouraged all forms of intellectual curiosity and intellectual resilience—Nouwen gave every evidence of enjoying the camaraderie and collegiality that defined seminary living, the kind of bonding that ensured a measure of emotional balance in a structure that feared emotion.

The curriculum had remained largely unchanged for generations—a heavy dose of neo-Scholastic Thomism (not the more profound and generative variation known as Transcendental Thomism sweeping the theological faculties at the universities at the time but operational *outside* the seminary world) coupled with a magisterial teaching style that placed a premium on docility, deference, and manic note-taking. The scholastic formation he received was normative, logical, firmly entrenched, and, at heart, anti-intellectual.

He studied natural philosophy, cosmology, epistemology, philosophical psychology, logic, metaphysics, dogmatics, homiletics, canon law, apologetics, ascetical theology, and other subjects peculiar to the narrowly defined theological disciplines deemed suitable for those destined for parochial ministry. The social, natural, and liberal sciences were foreign to that insular world and seen either as a threat or as an indulgence.

Nouwen made what he could of that world which was regimented, tradition-bound, and a priori in its methodology because, after all, the seminary was a timeless structure, hallowed, isolated from the secular sphere. This was the only place where you went to become a priest. The rarified atmosphere of priestly formation guaranteed that the ethos of the priest as *other*, the sense of holy exceptionalism, was preserved and fostered.

Not all was bleak and doom. Friendships were made, intelligent members of the priestly professoriate encouraged more than conformity in their classes. A mature prayer life could develop under the direction of enlightened clerics, but the structure was unbending, the course of studies fixed, and the rigorous scrutiny of all candidates by seminary staff to ensure that an orthodox mind and appropriate presbyteral decorum was firmly in place. It was a "disciplined life of supplication and sublimation," as Nouwen biographer Michael Ford notes, a life in which

> their own bodies had to be kept rigorously in check. They were to shower in light robes so they never saw each other fully naked, and they had to sleep with their arms crossed at the top of their chests, above their bed covers. The body was not to be trusted. Prone to sinful and destructive meanderings, it was the mule to be whipped on the way to the kingdom. Years later, when some friends were laughing at a 1940s manual they had found about teaching sex to children, Nouwen refused to find it funny: "That's what it was like for us in the seminary," he protested. "You don't understand what it was like."[4]

Although life at Apeldoorn was regulated and conventional in its daily *horarium* with few surprises, the real boon for Nouwen was to be found in his relationship with the rector of the seminary, Monsignor Anton C. Ramselaar, his Uncle Toon. Dutch Nouwen biographer, minister, and theologian Jurjen Beumer, identifies the special attraction Nouwen had for his uncle and the unique role Ramselaar played in the post-1945 "religious" world of the Netherlands:

> Because of the important role of Ramselaar [in building mutual understanding and respect between Catholics and Jews, T. H. M. van Schaik's book

Familiar Strangers: The Relationship between Catholics and Jews in the Netherlands, 1930–1980 profiles Toon and] marks him "as a man of the world: an amiable presence with a broad interest in culture, artistically gifted, blessed with a fine perception of what was brewing, courteous and considerate in his relationship with women and a man of means to boot." Henri was very fond of his uncle.[5]

Life at Apeldoorn was merely a prelude for the serious training that would begin at the Philosophicum Dijinselburg with its requisite two years of philosophy followed by the four years of theological training at Rijsenburg. These years of formation with their prescribed texts, magisterial teaching style, isolated environment, cultic focus, and defensive posture toward the outside world, reflected centuries of inculcation.

It was not until the Council of Trent in the sixteenth century that we get the blueprint for seminary education, a form of training that has lasted largely unaltered for five centuries. Dealing with the poor education of many of the parochial clergy, with the persisting problems of clerical laxity and the abuse of clerical concubinage known as Nicholaism, and with the formidable threat posed by the reforming churches, the Council Fathers at Trent were desperate to establish colleges for the moral and intellectual shaping of priestly candidates. They needed to impose some clear shape on the hitherto sketchy and inadequate preparation for orders of the regular clergy, and to that end the Council, with its Decree on Seminaries, sought to implement an organized program of studies and a monastic-style spirituality. And this was to be achieved in an isolated environment cut off from the temptations of a tumultuous world of conflicting theologies and of temptations of the flesh.

As Maryanne Confoy remarks on this decree in her work *Religious Life and Priesthood: Perfectae Caritatis, Optatam Totius, Presbyterorum Ordinis*,

> These schools sought to isolate and protect priestly candidates from the dangers of the world, to educate and form priests who would serve the church and keep their parishioners away from the aberrations of the era. The intention of the entire Tridentine Decree on Seminaries was to protect endangered youth by removing them from the world and to fortify them in their priestly vocation.[6]

By the time Nouwen had reached the major seminary, Rijsenburg, and commenced his six years of philosophical and theological schooling for ordination as a diocesan priest, he was poised for a new and encompassing program that was distinguished less by its intellectual rigor (seminaries are not hothouses of vibrant debate, unchecked curiosity, and robust independent thinking) than by its clerical camaraderie, its sense of common molding for a sacred destiny, its exalted notion of separateness. It was, in his own words, a "safe, secure, and happy environment,"[7] a place marked by "masculine piety, solidarity and a good sense of humour."[8] He liked the feeling of togetherness and common purpose, and although in later years would come to see the inherent deficiencies of an "enormously clerical life which could appear rather sectarian and ghettoish,"[9] he was content, indeed happy, progressing through the years in an institution that shaped generations of priests.

But even in this seemingly utopian setting, Nouwen had difficulties: he deplored the hazing of first-year students, found the jokes and exaggerated masculine ribaldry and jocularity offensive, and longed to be in "a real university" at times. In his mature years as a priest, he came to deeply regret the lack of intimacy among his classmates, the underlying fear of sexuality that permeated the environment, and the paucity of insight around spirituality itself. Everything was ritual, rubric, and regimentation.

He recalls that the official seminary attitude toward the spiritual or ascetical life was summed up by the rector of the seminary with his already legendary distillation of the trifold stages of the mystical unfolding:

> I remember the famous story when the rector, who was responsible for our spiritual formation, reputedly said: "Yes, as far as the spiritual life is concerned, you have the *via purgativa*, meaning that you have to pull the oars yourself, followed by the *via illuminativa*, meaning that you have to sail with the wind blowing into your sails, and then there is the *via unitiva*, but I don't need to talk about that because you will never reach that stage anyway. Don't think too much of yourself, don't act *too* spiritually, because we are just boys, ordinary boys, with our feet planted firmly on the ground."[10]

Such an attitude, neither rare nor eccentric at the time, embodied the deep suspicion of anything that smacks of pietism, unmanly devotionalism, religious impracticality, and "feminine fussiness" around the interior life. The institution's rugged masculine spirituality was further secured by its anxiety around "particular friendships," friendships that were exclusive and had a tinge of the homoerotic about them, friendships that crossed the line on forbidden physical tactility.

Nouwen, ruminating years later on the emotional reserve of his seminary peers, observed,

> I felt closely connected with my classmates, but they were not the kinds of connections that led to individually deeper relationships. I think that perhaps the whole philosophy around "particular friendships" prevented somewhat the development of enduring deep connections and especially for the strong affective bonds for which I have always felt a strong need. There was solidarity, but not a whole lot of intimacy, and that I have always regretted.[11]

Although Nouwen maintained throughout his life in priestly ministry an authentic fondness for his contemporaries in the seminary at Rijsenburg, he lamented the absence of anything approaching intimacy as this absence diminished the emotional life of all of them. But he was not without bonds of esteem and affirmation as well as a record of achievement: he was elected the "president" of his senior class; his first article appeared in *Streven*[12]; and it was on the Mariology of John Henry Newman, a thinker for whom he developed a profound and long-lasting admiration. He became actively involved in a project that provided religious objects to the persecuted church in the former Yugoslavia, and he cultivated contacts with Protestant theologues in an effort to begin an ecumenical dialogue long before they became popular. Most importantly, he saw the stark limits of seminary training with its heavy emphasis on obedience.

These limits were never in more clear evidence for him than when following a natural flood disaster in Zeeland some sixty miles from the seminary, he sought to go and help out only to face stiff opposition from the seminary authorities. His frustration was palpable:

> It's crazy, but we seminarians were forbidden to participate in the disaster relief and supposed to be proper and attend to our obligations at home. I am still so mad with myself for my failure to rise above the system, to have the courage to say, whatever the authorities think, I will just go to Zeeland, if need be run away, and then it will be up to them to decide if they want to take me back. I am amazed at how little independent I was, at least emotionally, that I did not even have the freedom to simply say that I am a grown man and I will do what I consider it important to do. I may have been twenty-years old but I was still a little boy.[13]

The experience of having his desire to help his fellow citizens in a time of crisis stamped down left a permanent scar. But it also proved to be a transformative moment:

> Later, when I ended up in the United States during the Vietnam War and the Civil Rights protests, I became actively involved, with the memory of the incident at Rijsenburg always fresh. I would not allow what happened to me then to be repeated ever again. It is interesting that I still think back on the Zeeland incident with a feeling of self-reproach.[14]

Many years after his ordination, and very shortly after he arrived in the United States to begin his fellowship in psychiatry and religion at the Menninger Foundation in Topeka, Kansas, Nouwen proved to the dismay of his clerical colleagues at the Menninger that the obedience to authority that defined his reaction to Zeeland would not be replicated. The then-Benedictine monk Richard Sipe recalls Nouwen's social activism, in sharp contrast with his priestly confreres who were not inclined to leave the corridors of the clinic for the corridors of conflict:

> Henri was especially notable in that his social activism translated into taking part in the historic civil rights march from Selma to Montgomery, Alabama. The first one, on March 7, 1965, was blocked at the Edmund Pettus Bridge and there was a brutal repression of the marchers, with many injured. Two weeks later Martin Luther King Jr. called on church leaders and people of faith to gather in Selma for a second march on the capitol. Henri was there. He wrote that 'I felt my skin turn black and I slowly began to realize what it means to be black.' In this he was different from the rest of us. Our social activism was easily tempered—mute, even. We were interested, of course, but Henri plunged right in and taught his American colleagues something about ourselves.[15]

The lesson of Zeeland and Rijsenburg, the guilt of inaction, the lockstep acquiescence to authority, and the dimming of the little voice, his conscience as he called it, was never to be repeated. Selma would ensure that.

Rijsenburg's intellectual and spiritual ethos was not Ignatian. In fact, as Nouwen lamented, nothing by way of an organic spirituality was taught, spiritual formation was cultic and rubrical, operational if you like, and not centered on the cultivation of a prayer life. This would come postordination for Nouwen—the prayer life, that is—and the "professional" field of spirituality, much in its infancy, would become his lifelong project.

But if Rijsenburg was not Jesuit in any way, it did embody much of the theological timbre associated with Jansenism. In that, the seminary was largely indistinguishable from Catholic Dutch society at large. Jansenism, a tendency or development in the Catholic Church toward ascetical and ethical rigorism, was a reaction to Reformation humanism and Jesuit moral laxity. Its founder, the Flemish theologian Cornelius Jansen, deplored the emphasis on voluntarism and moral libertinism that he saw gnawing away at the church's spiritual vitals. His approach to theological and moral matters was sifted through a narrow Augustinian perspective and his work *Augustinus* was highly influential in some circles including the Port Royal convent that housed Jacqueline, the mystical sister of the mystic-mathematician Blaise Pascal. Nevertheless, the core of his teaching was condemned by Pope Innocent X and the Jansenist approach to the reception of communion was repudiated by Pope Pius X. Still, the Jansenist-tinged sensibility, if not doctrinal inclination, lingered in the Low Countries, Quebec, and Ireland well into the twentieth century.

Although Jansenist spirituality, in the words of systematic theologian William Thompson-Uberuaga, can be defined as "the special bowstring-tight tension between attunement to divine transcendence and moral earnestness,"[16] the psychological dimension of such a tension has had at a popular level a more negative than sublime impact. Often equated with the puritanical wing of Calvinism, Jansenism on the devotional and moral planes—much removed from the abstract debates around St. Augustine's conception of grace—has resulted in severe anxiety around, if not repression of, matters sexual.

> The Jansenist legacy, although an admirable corrective to the laxity that diluted Catholicism's attachment to the heroism of the Gospel, was mostly deleterious in its effects: a flesh-despising asceticism that bordered on a Manichean hatred of the body, an over-reliance on self-abnegation as the primary route to holiness, and a theological conceptualization of God greatly dependent on the Calvinist notion of predestination.[17]

While the abstruse disputes around Jansen's theology would continue for centuries, the tone, emphasis, and body-fearing dimensions of his teaching in the world of pastoral praxis would have some scarring consequences. Nouwen was not untouched by Jansenist ideas and religious sensitivities. The impact was not good.

Although the doctrinal debates central to Jansenism were not marginal to orthodox Christianity—questions around the reconciliation of the absolute gratuitousness of divine grace with personal responsibility and free will—the movement became increasingly identified not with dogmatic propositions but with a *mentality*, a spiritual and moral disposition that was astringent and even legalistic. The Roman magisterium eventually killed the movement per se with the papal bull *Unigenitus* in the early eighteenth century, but it persisted in other ways. Theologian Konrad Hecker correctly notes that "organized Jansenism survived only in the Netherlands, where it still exists as the 'Church of Utrecht,' now united with the Old Catholics."[18] Doctrinally and ecclesiologically schismatic, Jansenism qua movement is largely a spent force; as a moral and spiritual perspective it infiltrated mainstream Catholic life and its institutions. Nouwen encountered Jansenist inclinations in religious practice, ascetical formation, and in the general puritanical sternness more widely associated with Calvinism.

Many years after his seminary training and ordination, Nouwen was directly confronted with his inner Jansenism by his spiritual guide and psychological counselor, the psychiatrist-abbot John Eudes Bamberger. Distraught over his vocational direction and spiritual tumult, Nouwen sought on two occasions in the 1970s at the Trappist Abbey of the Genesee in upper New York State to find inner focus. Bamberger was perplexed by the then Yale University professor's "seeming incapacity to rise above his 'psychological self-hate,'" and in a letter to Nouwen, he observed that "St. Francis de Sales, in his earlier years, had a trial very similar to yours...a great spiritual trial of faith and of relation to God, but it too had its psychological side and was reinforced—and even precipitated—by the Jansenist idea of God."[19] In a later letter, he underscores that delimiting conception of God and its debilitating consequences for Nouwen: "I am sorry that you continue to be afflicted...at bottom it continues to result from your over-stern image of Christ, through your experiencing Him rather by means of your own self-condemning superego than by discovering what His mercy really is."[20]

Rijsenburg did not create that "over-stern image" but it did consolidate it. And it would take decades to dislodge it.

His major seminary experience was formative in more ways than one: he relished the camaraderie, the clerical club atmosphere, the sense of common purpose. Although he had reservations about bouts of boorish behavior, concerns about the curriculum and the magisterial approach that discouraged intellectual curiosity, as much as anxiety around the high priority accorded obedience and conformity, these were late life reflections and not "in the moment" impressions.

His ordination to the priesthood in St. Catherine's Cathedral in Utrecht was a joyous moment—receiving the oils from his Ordinary and his first chalice from his revered Uncle Toon—with the members of his family in attendance, the culminating act of a multiyear training regimen realized in the grand and solemn choreography of the ordination liturgy. It was high drama enacted on the altar and in the emotional life of the *ordinandus*, and he captured something of its intensity in *Can You Drink the Cup?*:

> It was Sunday, July 12, 1957. Bernard Alfrink, the Cardinal Archbishop of the Netherlands, laid his hands on my head, dressed me with a white chasuble, and offered me his golden chalice to touch with my hands bound together with a linen cloth. Thus, along with twenty-seven other candidates, I was ordained to the priesthood in St. Catherine's Cathedral in Utrecht. I will never forget the deep emotions that stirred my heart at that moment.[21]

The cultic role of the priest, molded *in persona Christi*, was manifestly the primary definition of priesthood at the time. It was a definition that Nouwen wholly accepted. There would be no reason to think otherwise given his conventional formation.

Even so, the spiritual stirrings, the inchoate spiritual dissatisfaction, were there in embryo. He couldn't identify or formulate the nature of his deeper yearnings for intimacy, nor elaborate a notion of priestly ministry grounded on a personal relationship with Jesus. These would come in time, through a maturing ministry, profound insights sifted through emotional anguish, and a questing sensibility that was uncomfortable with religious complacency and conformity. Robert Jonas, a doctoral student at Harvard University who befriended Nouwen, sagely observes of Nouwen's understanding of his own priesthood,

> He was a maverick priest, under the hierarchy's radar. For him, a personal relationship with Jesus was paramount. In his early years as a priest the relationship was with Christ—remote and revered. But in his mature years he came to see that a personal relationship with a doctrine, an abstraction, was not life sustaining. After all, Jesus would often ask 'Do you love me?' His deepening spiritual relationship to Jesus became, in my view, a relationship with the *eternal presencing of Someone for all of us*. Jesus is found in the 'between' of the I-Thou, revealed in the personal disclosure.[22]

In 1957, and not only in Holland, priesthood was a sacral institution with rigidly articulated expectations, codes, and accountabilities. The anguished self-questioning, plummeting numbers, identity turmoil, and indifferent, if not overtly hostile, societal attitudes characteristic of our present era were simply unthinkable in the 1950s.

What Dr. Michael M. Winter writes in a letter to the editor of *The Tablet* lamenting the current drop in quality of priestly candidates would have been deemed unjustified, beyond the pale, sixty years earlier:

> Young men of intelligence and with well-integrated personalities...rarely offer their services. Yet the compulsory element in the celibate life provides secure haven for other individuals who have not yet achieved mature integration of all the elements in their emotional life. Although they are comfortable in the clerical caste, with its distinctive clothing and titles, it is not always clear that they have the talent for spiritual leadership.[23]

When American liturgist Rita Ferrone observes of the contemporary seminary training ethos in the United States that "our bishops fear the corrupting influence of 'non-priests' so much that their tender recruits are sequestered, not even allowed to share a classroom with lay catechists, much less learn from them or strive to integrate themselves with the people they will serve,"[24] such a sentiment would be seen as incomprehensible at the time of Nouwen's priestly formation.

When Canadian ecclesiologist Cathy Clifford writes of the clerical resistance to Pope Francis's efforts at both reform and renewal of the priesthood that we should not underestimate "the level of resentment against Francis's critiques of the culture of clericalism so deeply ingrained and grounded in a passionate adherence and defense of a perception of the sacred *over and against* a hostile world because it is a challenge to the very identity of men schooled in a very particular notion of priestly identity—one from which both the ordained and the laity must be liberated,"[25] the church of the pre–Vatican II world would have judged such a conviction heretical, Protestant to the core.

The great chasm that now exists between the time of Nouwen's sacerdotal formation and our own is wide and getting even wider. Much has unfolded in the intervening years between 1957 and our time, some of which has been revolutionary in its impact and, consequently, has generated its own reactionary or restorationist impulses. Nouwen bridged this tumultuous time, and his own spiritual and theological maturation provide us with a cipher into a different epoch, a model of creative change, and an icon of priestly wholeness that is grounded in the real and not the fictive.

Nevertheless, as Nouwen's priestly career began, change was in the air. Theologians were thinking new ideas, postwar Europe was restive, the Pacelli papacy was in its death throes, and a new era was about to begin.

EARLY MINISTRY

A Church in the Process of Freeing Itself

The morning after his ordination, Nouwen celebrated his first Mass in a convent chapel, but that experience is as nothing compared to the sheer delight and pride that a family takes on the occasion of the first *public* Mass celebrated by the new priest. Such delight and pride were palpable among the extended Nouwen family as they gathered in the parish church of Our Lady of Lourdes in Scheveningen, not far from The Hague. Nouwen was flush with the new energy and abundant good feeling that accompanies the successful completion of years of study, the culmination of a dream that has long sustained one's progress through life, the realization that what was an ending is also a beginning.

Nouwen's time in parochial ministry was very limited. He was not destined for a chancery position, a rectorship, an administrative position in the local curia, and he was not being slotted into the regular parish structure. Although Cardinal Alfrink did ask Nouwen if he would pursue further studies at one of the Roman pontifical universities—the Gregorian, in fact, the best of the lot—with the likelihood of a seminary teaching appointment as part of the bigger plan. Nouwen countered with a proposal to enroll in doctoral studies at Nijmegen University in its graduate psychology program. Not for the last time, Alfrink gave authorization to do so.

It was 1957, and although there were remarkable centers of new theological and philosophical thinking springing up in the church—for instance, the *Nouvelle Théologie* with loci in France and Germany and numbering among its adherents or expostulators such luminaries as the Jesuits Pierre Teilhard de Chardin, Henri de Lubac, Karl Rahner, and Jean Daniélou, Dominicans Yves Congar, Edward Schillebeeckx, Marie-Dominique Chenu, as well as Hans Küng, Joseph Ratzinger, and Hans Urs von Balthasar—and although liturgical reforms, chiefly carried by Benedictines, and ecumenical ventures, modest but encouraging, were also bearing fruit in the church, its European expression particularly—life in the institutional church was still insular, it was fearful of the forces of secularism, its face set against the world, its ecclesial perspective greatly circumscribed.

Despite its "natural" conservatism, the Dutch church was restive, and under the leadership of Alfrink, is was poised for change. As one Council authority says, "When we turn to the Church in the Netherlands we are in contact with a Church that was in the process of freeing itself from its minority and ultramontane complex."[1] Freeing itself, but far from freed, and with a distance to go.

All the more surprising then that Alfrink would willingly approve Nouwen's request for advanced studies in the social sciences. This was not the norm, specifically in the case of diocesan priests. But as Alfrink seems to have already intuited, Nouwen would rarely conform to the norm. The paucity of advice and direction he received in his own seminary formation in the area of spirituality no doubt contributed to his determination to find ways of interconnection between the study of human behavior and motivation with the study of the divine subjects. He would perforce marry these interests. Or he would try. Nijmegen would be his port of departure.

It would be at this Catholic university where Nouwen would be first exposed to phenomenological psychology, a school of thinking that his classmate, close friend, and fellow psychologist Peter Naus would describe as a methodology grounded in the Husserlian approach. That is, in epistemology, and by extension psychology, one had to "go back to the thing in itself." Nouwen understood this as a summons to retrieve, or relive, the original experience. His writing, says Naus, betrays his

> phenomenological bias as he tries to get into the experience of anxiety, the experience of being in a competitive relationship, etc. He thinks and feels as a phenomenologist and not as a behaviourist; as a clinical psychologist he was trained to get into the experience of the patient. To the degree that he was successful in mapping out that experience from the inside, he was able to allow his readers to discover, to recognize, themselves.[2]

As Nouwen was working his way through his studies, a series of quite dramatic episodes in the Catholic Church was unfolding. In 1958, the long-reigning papacy of Pius XII (Eugenio Pacelli) came to an end, and the election of a pope, John XXIII (Giuseppe Roncalli), markedly different from his predecessor in style, appearance, world experience, and spiritual outlook, implied a paradigm shift. Then, the convocation of an ecumenical council, or world gathering of bishops, was both unanticipated and hope-generating. Things in the *ecclesia* were shifting, and there was some trepidation in the air. But more important still: there was great excitement.

When the episcopacy convened in Rome for the first of four sessions of what was to be known as the Second Vatican Council (SVC), an assembly of bishops, *periti* (theological experts), and invited guests, who would meet once a year in autumn from 1962–65, they had little idea that they were embarked on an undertaking that would revitalize, destabilize, and massively reshape the direction of the Catholic Church for generations to come. At the heart of it was one Bernard J. Alfrink from Utrecht, and with him was Monsignor Anton Ramselaar, Nouwen's Uncle Toon, who as discussed earlier, was an expert on Jewish-Catholic relations.

Also present, periodically and not in an official capacity, was Henri himself. He could not have been immune to the vitality, visioning, politicking, and spiritual vibrancy that defined the SVC itself.

But of special importance in all this was the critical role played by Alfrink. The Dutch church, a minority church, marginal to the seat of power, found in its Primate a thinker and leader of impressive resilience and forward thinking. Alfrink's active presence in the Council is indisputable. He was a key player among the progressive bishops, a number that also included amongst its leadership Josef Frings, cardinal archbishop of Cologne, Franz König, cardinal archbishop of Vienna, Giacomo Lercaro, cardinal archbishop of Bologna, Giovanni Battista Montini, cardinal archbishop of Milan (the future Pope Paul VI), Achille Liénart, cardinal archbishop of Lille, Julius Döpfner, cardinal archbishop of Munich, Léon-Joseph Suenens, cardinal archbishop of Malines-Brussels, and Paul-Émile Léger, cardinal archbishop of Montreal. These hierarchs were essential agents of change and renewal, completely committed not only to the documents of the Council but also to the process that produced them. This was a process as fully democratic, collegial, and transparent as could be achieved in a structure accustomed to stability, continuity, and holy obedience or compliance, *obsequium religiosum.*

The Council itself was the work of two popes—John XXIII, the pope who called the Council and survived to see only the first session concluded, and Paul VI, the pope of the Council, who brought it to fruition over the next three years. The Council—papa Giovanni's "insight tested in prayer"— accomplished many things that have virtually reshaped the structure of the church beyond the point of mild adaptation but falling short of a radical facelift. The list includes decentralization of some decision-making, strong support for the principle of collegiality, deep recognition of the importance of meaningful dialogue both within the church and between the church and other religions, and internationalization of the Roman Curia. By the time the Council concluded on the Feast of the Immaculate Conception, December 8, 1965, it had produced sixteen documents of varying weight, quality, and authority: *Lumen gentium* (Dogmatic Constitution on the Church), *Dei verbum* (Dogmatic Constitution on Divine Revelation), *Sacrosanctum concilium* (Constitution on the Sacred Liturgy), *Gaudium et spes* (Pastoral Constitution on the Church in the Modern World), *Inter mirifica* (Decree on the Instruments of Social Communication), *Unitatis redintegratio* (Decree on Ecumenism), *Orientarum ecclesiarum* (Decree on the Eastern Catholic Churches), *Christus dominus* (Decree on the Bishops' Pastoral Office in the Church), *Optatam totius* (Decree on Priestly Formation), *Perfectae curitatis* (Decree on the Appropriate Renewal of Religious

Life), *Apostolicam actuositatem* (Decree on the Apostolate of the Laity), *Presbyterorum ordinis* (Decree on the Ministry and Life of Priests), *Ad gentes divinitus* (Decree on the Church's Missionary Activity), *Gravissimum educationis* (Declaration on Christian Education), *Nostra aetate* (Declaration on the Relationship of the Church to Non-Christian Religions), and *Dignitatis humanae* (Declaration on Religious Freedom).

These documents—constitutions, decrees, and declarations—have been received and implemented with varying degrees of success since the Council. Some served as springboards for serious change, others provided foundational shifts in ecclesiological thinking that have had an impact on Catholic self-understanding that will endure for generations, and still others proved insufficiently relevant in content and focus.

The composition of these documents, the politics of lobbying for their promulgation, the curial maneuverings to either stymie or significantly retard those documents that the conservative faction perceived as limiting curial power and that of the supreme pontiff, the endless jostling behind the scene as reformers and traditionalists struggled to prioritize and direct the workings of the Council—all these factors contributed in the end to the very design and structure of the documents themselves.

The eminent Vaticanologist and papal biographer Peter Hebblethwaite astutely observed that the Council documents have a certain structure and

> basically answer three questions. The *first* question is: What is the Church? It is a curious thing in a way that the church had not reflected on what it

was. You don't find a theory about what the church is until the nineteenth century with people like Johann Adam Mohler and then later in the twentieth century with Karl Adam and Yves Congar. It was necessary, then, for the Council Fathers to arrive at a self-understanding which was faithful to tradition, of course, but which unveiled aspects of tradition that had been forgotten. The main thing was to see the church as the people of God on a march through history, a history in which everybody is endowed with charismatic graces. From there is a radical equality among the people of God, a point that is underscored in the opening paragraphs of *Lumen gentium* and then and only then do you move on to talk about the priesthood, the episcopate, the papacy. The ordering is right and revolutionary in its way. The *second* question flows from the first: What are the different roles in the church and how are they to be understood? On this point you will note that the Council documents go through the role of the bishop, the role of the religious, and the role of the laity quite systematically, and then they move on to the various, if you like, activities of the church. For instance, the liturgy. The life of prayer in the church undergoes some serious re-evaluation: we now have the introduction of the vernacular and the slow elimination of Latin. You can't have, argue the Council Fathers, a strange barrier coming between the people and the expression of prayer. And, finally, the third question: With this new understanding of church and the altered roles exercised by its members, how are the church's complex and multi-variegated relationships with society and other faith groups defined? On this point, what you see evolving is a discovery or rediscovery of the church's fundamental Christian humanism and a recognition of the supreme importance of relating to other Christians through a shared baptism, of acknowledging the special question of the Jews, the value of religious liberty, and the pastoral demands to respond to the joys and hope, anxieties and pain, of the modern world.[3]

There were many who opposed the unfolding intentions of the progressive wing of the Council, however, and the traditionalist wing found itself pitted against the reformers or liberals, although these labels proved inadequate in defining the genuine shades of difference that often existed among the bishops as well as among the bishops and some of their theological experts.

There was no quibbling about Alfrink's label or position. He was a far-seeing progressive, comfortable with engaging the world on equal terms rather than through the lens of anathema and judgment, committed to the papal Johannine vision of renewal, and energized by the power of the Spirit he saw working—sometimes overtly and sometimes subtly—in the cut and thrust of argument and conviction that shaped the direction of the Council. He was a shaper of the Council's politics. He was not on the sidelines. He was at the heart of things.

From the outset of the Council there were challenges around preparatory drafts, working documents and strategies concerning control and direction. Who would manage the Council? The central administration, the Roman Curia, saw itself as the driving power behind an ecumenical council that they neither anticipated nor wanted. The worldwide episcopate, similarly surprised by the convening of a council, were of diverse mind around the intention behind and the process invoked around the Council's deliberations. A power struggle was in the offing from the beginning.

Resistance to the original design of the Council's modus operandi set in early. Efforts to frame discussions, prioritize items, and manage procedures were stunningly defied by several senior prelates who decided to flex their collegial muscle and remind the apparatchiks on the Tiber that a council is a collegial exercise of the magisterium, not an exercise of the more uniquely constrained papal magisterium. It is an illustration of the church's bishops working *cum* (with) rather than *sub* (under) Peter with the authority of such an assembly taking precedence—or at least enjoying equivalence—with the pontiff who convened it. That was not the thinking at head office.

Elected to the Council of Presidents and a central figure throughout all the sessions, Alfrink championed a culture of ecclesial openness, of *parrhesia* (candid speaking), and the use of a rhetoric of persuasion over a rhetoric of condemnation. Jesuit historian John W. O'Malley has succinctly encapsulated the change in tone, timbre, and style characteristic of the conciliar experience:

> I will summarize in a simple litany some of the elements in the change in style of the Church indicated by the council's vocabulary: from commands to invitations, from laws to ideals, from threats to persuasion, from coercion to conscience, from monologue to conversation, from ruling to serving,

from withdrawn to integrated, from vertical and top-down to horizontal, from exclusion to inclusion, from hostility to friendship, from static to changing, from passive acceptance to active engagement, from prescriptive to principled, from defined to open-ended, from behavior modification to conversion of heart, from the dictates of law to the dictates of conscience, from external conformity to the joyful pursuit of holiness.[4]

Such a qualitative shift from one paradigm of ecclesial governance and behavior to its opposite cannot be anything other than as wrenching as it is invigorating, divisive as it is unifying, hope-inspiring as it is fear-generating. Bishops needed to wend their way through this minefield of competing expectations and resistances to find a common ground that allowed for the constraints of tradition to find dialogue with the yearnings for change. No easy task.

From the outset, Alfrink was seen as a staunch ally of Pope John XXIII and his intention was to establish two fundamental principles that would determine, direct, and define the purpose and outcomes of the Council: *aggiornamento* (updating) and *ressourcement* (historical recovery).

Of *aggiornamento*, O'Malley writes,

Three aspects were special about the *aggiornamento* of Vatican II. First, the changes done in the name of *aggiornamento* were sometimes obvious reversals of what had broadly been considered normative. Second, no previous council ever took the equivalent of *aggiornamento* as a leitmotif, as a broad principle rather than as a rare exception, with its implication that the Church should change in certain regards to meet the times rather than the times change to meet the Church....Third, the council took as axiomatic that Catholicism was adaptive even to the "modern world."[5]

Of *ressourcement*, O'Malley writes that it "entails a return to the sources with a view not to confirming the present but making changes to conform it to a more authentic or more appropriate past, to...a more profound tradition."[6]

With both terms, explicit and implicit, one can detect a sympathy, however cautious, for change, for a more comprehensive understanding of the need for change, the capacity for change. Alfrink was onside. He feared neither the prospect of change nor its reality. For him, change was a bulwark against the ossification of truth, the deadening of the Spirit, the debilitating fear that accompanies both intellectual and institutional hostility to malleability, to adaptation. He was a firm champion of John XXIII's pastoral strategy of dialogue and accommodation over the more normative approach of judgment and anathema.

Yves Congar, in his diaries of the Council, noted that in a very early intervention Alfrink affirmed his credentials as a Roncallist who was opposed to the political and ecclesial manipulations of the Curialists who were eager to limit the scope of the Council and were governed by protectionism and fear rather than by openness and resilience. He stood in public opposition to a schema, or template, of operating that ran counter to the intentions of the pope as enunciated in his address at the opening of the Council:

Cardinal Alfrink: The text [*schema*] is not in accordance with the spirit of the Pope's opening speech. That is, not to repeat what has already been defined....But the *schema* repeats what is contained in all the manuals. The Pope declared that the purpose of the Council was to formulate doctrine in a way suited to our time. Moreover, the *schema* sheds no light on the matters discussed in recent theology.[7]

Congar's meticulous private diary is an insightful chronicle of the politicking, lobbying, struggles, and visions of the various key Council fathers, the adroit and maladroit maneuverings of scheming prelates, the frustrations and outrages articulated by both those with something to lose and those facing unanticipated stumbling blocks, and the joys and anxieties in grappling with a process fraught with risk yet replete with promise.

Alfrink figured prominently among the list of bishops quoted by Congar, often with nuanced admiration, and he remained throughout all the sessions a player of consequence. He held the trust of both Council popes, was respected by the majority of *periti*, viewed as a progressive by both religious and secular journalists, and served as a lightning rod for the organic conservatives and the obscurantists.

In his diary entry for October 15, 1964, Congar notes that for "Alfrink: the image of the priest and of the priesthood in the world of today is inadequate. The questions that engage priests today are not dealt with or are dealt with superficially. It needs to be looked at again. Applause."[8]

In addition to calling for a renewed and relevant look at the presbyterate, Alfrink championed many other "liberal" positions, earning for the entire Dutch episcopate the soubriquet of schismatics. In time, the Roman Curia's apprehensions around perceived Dutch waywardness, mounting concerns around the hyper-Protestantizing tendencies of Dutch Catholicism, and the secular drift of Holland's Catholic leaders, resulted in a Dutch Synod convoked to deal with the excesses of the regional church. But that would be some time down the road, following the Council's conclusion in 1965.

During the time of the Council itself, Alfrink was the Dutch star.

Nouwen, like Alfrink, was in many ways constitutionally a conservative priest. Neither was a reckless renegade hell-bent on dismantling tradition, and neither was inclined to polemics or fashionable causes. They were both men of discernment, intellectual resilience, pastoral attentiveness, and openness to the Spirit. They could change; indeed, they did change, and they understood that change, in all its myriad manifestations, was a sign of an organism's health and adaptability. Not just change for its own sake, unthinking change, but change as a result of insight, a shift in horizon, a receptivity to grace.

Nouwen, although ordained before the Council, became a son of the Council, its teachings, spirit of renewal, and its intellectual fecundity. He discovered, as did the Catholic world at large, the richness of the Scriptures. He was reanimated in his desire to know not just the Jesus of history and the Christ of faith but also the centrality of a personal relationship with the Lord. He saw a restored vitality to the liturgy as a means for building up a eucharistic people, and he appreciated for the first time the special vocation of the priesthood of all believers, the common baptism of the people of God, the charism of the laity. In many ways, a faithful priest to the end of his life, loyal to his bishop in Utrecht, and sensitive to the needs of priests in a time of definitional tumult, Nouwen's vocational understanding began in the 1960s, greatly driven by the new thinking of the Council, along a trajectory of friendships with the laity that was by 1996, the year of his death, astounding in its number and influence.

Nouwen's relationship with Alfrink, who was both a biblical scholar of merit and a Council father of distinction, was not a conventional one. He learned from his Ordinary refreshing insights into contemporary ecclesiological life, the foundational role of pastoral discernment in the exercise of priestly ministry, and the essential wisdom that effective service to the church and the world is determined best by prioritizing the person over the rubric and the law of mercy over the law of ecclesiastical compliance. Nouwen would live his life as a priest greatly informed by the sagacity and witness of his religious overseer, the Primate of the Netherlands.

Although Alfrink was swept up in the whirligig of Council life, he continued to maintain contact with the young cleric who was studying psychology at Nijmegen. Nouwen's seven years at the Catholic university were years of growth and discovery, but they were also years that underscored the limitations of the pure academic life for meaningful pastoral ministry—at least for him. He benefitted clearly from his exposure to phenomenological psychology, the competing and often combative Freudian and Jungian systems, and the cut and thrust of university life. But the kind of work he was keen on—the integrated blend of psychology with spirituality—was not a specialty at Nijmegen. His prospectus for a dissertation examining the case-method approach of the pioneering pastoral visionary Anton Boisen was not approved.

The approach of his committee was more quantitative in its emphasis and he needed to introduce many revisions to his thesis plan. He declined to do so. He needed to go elsewhere. He wrapped up his work—obtaining the *doctorandus*, a professional qualification below the research doctorate—and would once again seek the permission of Alfrink to embark on a new but convergent path: a fellowship at the Menninger Foundation for Psychiatric Research in Topeka, Kansas. Not surprisingly, Alfrink approved.

An appreciative Nouwen wrote to his bishop:

The MF [Menninger Foundation] is regarded by many as the Rome of the psychiatry world and it is undoubtedly the centre where the most positive attention is given to the relationship of psychiatry with religion. Ministers and priests from all corners of the United States, and various other countries, come here for a full year of training and intense collaboration of psychologists, psychiatrists, social workers, etc. and all in an ecumenical framework, which opens up many new perspectives in new areas of the apostolate. I know that the topic of theological formation holds a special interest for you and it is right here that the problems surrounding this framework are at the very centre of attention.[9]

Alfrink's anxiety around theological formation was two-pronged: the program of training for future priests and their ongoing theological education, and the emergence of a new catechetical direction for mature adult lay instruction. The former remained a priority for him, and after the Council, the urgency around theological formation for priesthood became an ecclesial imperative.

The work that Nouwen would do in Topeka would be exploratory, pioneering, and critical, and is detailed in the next chapter. At one point, Alfrink actually traveled to visit Nouwen at the Menninger, and his support for his young cleric's intellectual and spiritual forays into postconciliar uncharted waters was a natural extension of his unfinished work as a Council father.

The Council documents dealing with priesthood were a source of contention in the *aula* of St. Peter's Basilica—the large venue where the bishops gathered for deliberation and voting. Much of what was debated, mulled over, crafted with skillful consensus, and eventually approved and promulgated, remained more tentative probes than radical rethinking.

But there were changes afoot.

The Second Vatican Council's major ecclesial accomplishment—structurally speaking—was the rediscovery of collegiality. In part, this was to offset the imbalance created by the First Vatican Council's exclusive emphasis on the petrine primacy and papal authority. The role of the presbyter, the simple parish priest, was broached, but in no significant way addressed. Some wags quipped that if the First Vatican Council was the pope's council and the Second Vatican Council was the bishop's, the priest is doomed to wait for the Third Vatican Council. The laity will have to satisfy themselves with a few synods, pontifical documents, and periodic gestures of recognition. It is Blessed Cardinal Newman, often spoken of as the hovering spirit of the Council and an invisible *peritus*, who is reported to have responded to Bishop Ullathorne's troubling question, "Who are the laity?" His witty riposte was that "the Church would look foolish without them." If a

Council father was asking the question: "What is the priest-hood in our time?"—and it is clear that many of the bishops were indeed asking that question, if predominantly off-record and in coffee conversations, but occasionally on the floor—the answer in the end was incomplete.

The schema, or working document, *De sacerdotibus* (On the Life and Ministry of Priests) was introduced by the archbishop of Rheims, François Marty, in early October 1964, during the third session of the Council. In his introduction, Marty outlined the thrust of the document, its tone, and its strategic omissions, emphasizing a traditional model of priest underscored by the overarching conciliar theme of the "call to holiness." The vexatious issues—the problems and serious challenges facing modern priests in anticlerical cultures, perennial questions around the witness value of celibacy, and the possibility of reintroducing into the practice of the church the charism of a married diaconate—were left off the table. Minor matters, such as the elimination of the medieval practice of priestly compensation via benefice, were competently addressed. But the resulting schema hardly satisfied the majority of bishops and the liberal cardinal archbishop of Chicago, Albert Meyer, who was the first to speak. He succinctly articulated the view of most of those in session when he called for major revisions, a recognition that the priests were as deserving of the substantial and serious attention accorded the bishops and the laity. The result was that the document was sent back for reworking and expansion. More, much more, was required.

A month later, another schema—*De institutione sacerdotali*—a much shorter document dealing with the priesthood, was introduced and it received enthusiastic and nearly unanimous approval. This document called for the

decentralizing of priestly training by having local episcopal conferences design the seminary curriculum. It
established the primacy of the spiritual over academic formation, although the latter was not to be neglected. It also
ensured that biblical studies would now receive priority of
place.

Eventually, at the end of the third session, this schema
would emerge—adjusted, amended, and expanded—as the
official Vatican Council document *Optatam totius* (On the
Training of Priests). The other document, which would eventually become *Presbyterorum ordinis* (On the Ministry and
Life of Priests), would be approved at the end of the fourth
session. Its passage would be both more complicated and
fraught. In the end, despite an overwhelming vote for its
acceptance because of its more substantive content and potential import, it was a disappointment withal, an anemic document. Meyer's apprehension that it would not be for priests
what the other documents were for bishops and laity would
be vindicated.

Though not entirely. If celibacy was taken off the agenda
for discussion—Pope Paul VI saw a discussion of the law/
requirement/gift of celibacy as potentially very divisive for
both the Council and for the Western church. He decided,
accordingly, to reserve the matter to himself. Then, in 1967,
two years after the Council ended, he issued his least persua-
sive and prophetic encyclical, *Sacerdotalis celibatus*. The
heated debates around *Presbyterorum ordinis* had not been
without effect, even if the result was a poor comparator to
the companion documents on the bishops and the laity. There
was still much to celebrate, as outlined by Council historian
John O'Malley:

In choosing *presbyter* over priest (*sacerdos*) to designate the reality, the Council engaged in... *ressourcement*. "*Presbyter*" was the older of the two terms. Retrieved from the New Testament and early Christian sources, it suggested a broadening of definition beyond administering the sacraments and offering sacrifice, which is what priest as *sacerdos* implied and which since the Middle Ages had been the standard understanding of it. The presbyter's role was three-fold, expressed in a conventional triad: "prophet," that is, proclaimer of the Word of God; "priest," intercessor for and with the community and minister of the sacraments; and "king," leader of the community. In the text, as in others in the council, these three terms underwent important redefinitions, as when "king" was equated with servant."[10]

Although the cultic functions of the priest would remain intact, the pastoral, socially engaged, and outward-looking functions of service to the faith community and beyond would emerge to counterbalance the ritualistic and rubrical obligations of the priest. That would in turn introduce an aperture into the carapace of priestly identity that would have reverberating consequences throughout the Council initially, and then throughout the universal church.

From the outset, Alfrink remained firmly committed to the dual functions or orientations of the modern priest. Without jettisoning the *sacerdotal*, he embraced the *presbyteral*, not as dualities but as complementary dimensions of effective ministry.

Nouwen would be onside.

The Vatican Decree on the Ministry and Life of Priests (*Presbyterorum ordinis*) may have been flawed with its undeveloped theological rethinking—the *what* of ministerial priesthood—but it did grasp the need for the *how*, for the essential changes in pastoral approach necessitated by diverse historical, cultural, and social tensions in a rapidly altering post–World War II theater:

> The world which is entrusted today to the loving ministry of the pastors of the Church is that world which God so loved that He gave His only Son for it. The truth is that though entangled indeed in many sins this world is also endowed with great talents and provides the Church with the living stones to be built up into the dwelling place of God in the Spirit. Impelling the Church to open new avenues of approach to the world of today, this same Holy Spirit is suggesting and fostering fitting adaptations in the ministry of priests.[11]

Alfrink was a major advocate for enlightened and innovative adaptations, and he knew from his experience of the cut-and-thrust of conciliar debates that progress—rightly discerned and intelligently promoted—requires constant nurturing. A renewed presbyterate for the universal church was a necessity; a renewed presbyterate for the Dutch church an urgency. One of the reasons why he actively encouraged wide coverage of Council events in all the Catholic media, made himself available for interviews, mandated information sessions for the laity and priests at large, and preached regularly and passionately on the Council, was his abiding belief that renewal of church life required the highest level of commitment to its implementation. And that originated at the top of the hierarchical ladder: the primatial see itself, Utrecht.

Throughout the tumult and excitement generated by the Council, Nouwen, like his bishop, embraced the now much maligned "spirit of the Council," that is, the rush of energy, new expectations, unleashed frustrations, and multitudes of experimentations and probings, that in time threatened to sunder the unity of the Dutch church and cripple communion with Rome, its very institutional continuity with the past. But that would come in the full decade following the Council's conclusion.

At the time of the Council's conclusion in 1965, Alfrink's hopes for ecclesial renewal were unchecked and the openness of his flock undimmed. Nouwen meanwhile was busily pursuing his research fellowship duties in the United States, exploring the connections between phenomenological psychology and the insights of the pioneer thinker Anton Boisen, acclimating to American life, corresponding with his clerical peers back on the Dutch front, and adjusting to the interactions between secular society and Catholicism in a tempestuous decade.

After any seismic event, there are aftershocks. Following the conclusion of the Council, the bishops returned to their respective dioceses, the theologians returned to their respective academies, and the journalists returned to their respective media outlets, but no one returned to the status quo. Things were changed and utterly so, and that augured well for some and ominously for others.

The minority that either opposed the Council outright— the renegade French archbishop Marcel Lefebvre, for instance, and his Society of St. Pius X with its quaint and subversive nineteenth-century ultramontanist sensibility—and the larger minority that remained within the Roman communion but quietly resisted the conciliar reforms, would not be appeased by the aftermath of the Council, as if the restoration of the *ante status quo* was ever on the horizon. Pope Paul VI was no less a pope of the Council than John XXIII.

But the incorporation of the Council's decrees into the life of the universal church, however, would be regional and driven by the commitment of the individual bishops as well as the recently recharged national conferences. That meant, of course, that the *aggiornamento* and *ressourcement* so beloved of the Council fathers and their *periti* would vary markedly from diocese to diocese, country to country.

Some countries, like Ireland, Poland, and Portugal—homogenously Catholic if not Erastian in their history—remained largely untouched by the Council. Other countries, like Canada, Belgium, and Germany were moderate or centrist in their application of the Council's calls for renewal and reform. And still others, Holland most notably, minority Catholic jurisdictions primed to break free of their ghetto Catholicism, were hyper keen on change, the breaking down of encrusted barriers, and the full rejection of the *ancien regime*. With a progressive hierarchy, a much-loved primate in Alfrink—scholar and pastor extraordinaire—change was the new lifeblood of the national church, and it couldn't come fast enough. Therein lay an unexpected and potentially lethal tension that even Alfrink and his enlightened local curia couldn't fully manage.

The various successes of the Dutch church, the brilliant, prophetic, and indeed first post–Vatican Council compendium of Catholic Teaching known in English as *A New Catechism: Catholic Faith for Adults* raised Roman hackles. Various pastoral councils flexed their new muscle with little heed to head office on the Tiber, and numerous ecumenical initiatives, liturgical experiments, and doctrinal forays of dubious orthodoxy flourished. So many high expectations were doomed to some disappointment, and they set in quickly.

Nouwen was largely insulated from the immediate post-SVC tremors, after all, the U.S. Catholic Church was similar to the Dutch church in its minority status and therefore constitutively conservative and parochial, albeit with some strong radical wings of inquiry and experimentation. His experience of the Council's renewal efforts, now that he was living in the United States, was more gradualist and less accelerated. And that fit nicely with his temperament, his dislike for partisan advocacy, his very spiritual disposition.

In a letter written to his friends Holy Cross priests Claude Pomerleau and Don McNeill while visiting his home in Holland on December 29, 1973, Nouwen acknowledges his own growing ambivalence over the cult of change, his anxiety around the wholesale rejection of tradition, and the tendency to constrict the divine:

> In general, the Church [in Holland] is still in the "critical mood" and therefore does not seem to realize the great need for home, for candles, for statues, for incense and for all the things which helped us in the past to feel close to God and to each other. I do not say that we should go back to the early days but we definitively should respond to this enormous need and show God again as a loving, caring, gentle God under whose wings we can find refuge. I am less and less clear what is good or bad religion, what is regressive or progressive, but I am more and more convinced how important it is to respond to

real needs and to prevent ourselves from narrowing
God to one or two images.[12]

Although Nouwen's ambivalence regarding the church
of his birth might suggest that he was unhappy with its quick
discarding of its hallowed traditions, rites, and devotional
practices, and that would be in fact correct, it is as true that a
nostalgic Catholicism, a religion enmired in an ersatz emo-
tionality, is undesirable, a caricature of Christianity, a perversion. For Nouwen, in these still early years after the Council
(1965–73), his pastoral ministry is largely restricted to university communities, research centers, theological schools,
and the intentional eucharistic celebrations he presides at
with his ever-growing number of friends. Questions around
the nature of priesthood and questions of ontological and
dogmatic orientation do not occupy his attention or define
his own understanding of the priest as *in persona Christi*, an
understanding that is not theological but pastoral, an understanding that is at war with our efforts to narrow "God to
one or two images."

How one marries tradition and custom with innovation
and experimentation was quickly developing into a lifelong
project for Nouwen. His exploratory work on Anton Boisen,
his cultivation of phenomenological psychology and its
refined tools of methodology and insight, and his deep devotion to the reforms of the Second Vatican Council provided
him with a template for contemplating the challenges facing
a Catholicism in flux. It also provided him with the template
for his spiritual self-understanding: the creative blending of
psychology with spirituality, the adept use of Scripture to
reveal both universal and personal truths, the vocational cer-
titude around pastoral priority in his priestly life.

One of the key developments of the Council that would have a lasting impact on Nouwen's ministry and spirituality, and that would speak to his "creative blending," was the document *Nostra aetate*, on the relation of the Catholic Church to non-Christian religions, a conciliar declaration that paid particular attention to those of the Jewish faith. Nouwen's Uncle Toon had a warm relationship with the Jewish community and shared Alfrink's conviction that Catholic-Jewish rapprochement post-Nazified Europe and postoccupation Holland was an implicit key to the Roncalli vision.

The struggles to agree on the final text of this document were fierce, although not as contentious as with other conciliar documents. Key figures who served as *periti* for *Nostra aetate* included Austrian clerics John Osterreicher and Joseph Neuner and American Paulist Thomas Stransky, as well as the Augustinian Canadian Gregory Baum, a special protégé of the Jesuit Cardinal Augustin Bea, the presiding, if overly cautious, driver of the document. Baum was an especially central figure in the drafting of the document in its initial phase.

Baum has been clear that "John XXIII wanted a document on the Jews because he was profoundly scandalized by the anti-Jewish rhetoric in the Christian tradition."[13] When Cardinal Bea asked for a volunteer to write the first draft, Baum came forward because he had experience in the area, having already published a book in the year prior to the opening of the Council that directly addressed the history of Christian anti-Judaism and anti-Semitism. The book was published under the title *The Jews and the Gospel: A Re-Examination of the New Testament* and was subsequently reissued with a more germane title. *Is the New Testament Anti-Semitic?*

Although the final document would have a specific reference to the Jews, three-fifths of the approved text deals with issues around all non-Christian religions, the role of salvation, and the bold affirmation that the Catholic Church "rejects nothing that is true and holy in these religions."[14]

Concerns around the use of *deicide* or God-killing, and the pressure to formally repudiate this spurious charge against the Jews—an insidious justification for the numerous judicial sanctions, pogroms, and persecutions suffered by the Jews over two millennia—proved to be a greater obstacle than initially realized. Theological anxieties, regional political considerations, Orthodox-Catholic relations, the perspective of Eastern Rite Catholics, the fraught circumstances of Arab Christians, and the ingrained conservatism of several curial prelates all guaranteed a rougher ride than originally thought. There was also heated debate around the very document itself: Should it be revised, dropped, or all references to anti-Semitism eliminated in order not to enflame the warring parties in the Middle East?

In the end, the document was promulgated, *deicide* was included, and the political pushback was less intense than anticipated. As Congar noted, "Twenty years after Auschwitz, it is impossible that the Council should say nothing."[15] He was right, and he was vindicated.

Alfrink, Ramselaar, and the young Nouwen would have been pleased.

The significance of Jewish life and spirituality for Nouwen—his numerous Jewish friends, his many rabbi colleagues, and his respect for Jewish scholarship—is evidenced by his emotionally moving *Life of the Beloved*, in part a response to the searching heart of journalist Fred Bratman, and by the following testimonial from one of Nouwen's Jewish students at Yale, Dean Hammer:

> I was raised in the synagogue and in the Jewish tradition—but it was through Henri and participating in his Eucharists that I came to believe that even as a Jew I belonged round the table. I also think Henri's theology of compassion was a linchpin of the ministry of peace and justice activism. In this ministry of compassion there was a radical intersection of the lowest of the low meeting the outcasts, as well as the highest of high meeting presidents of state and highest leaders of all denominations. I was always impressed with how he spanned the spectrum.[16]

Nouwen's priestly self-understanding was expansive, not restrictive—that he would invite nonbelievers around the table was not an indication of theological syncretism, indifferentism, or spiritual flabbiness. It was a mark of his deep love for the Eucharist, his abiding compassion, his distaste for exclusivism, and his visceral commitment to community-building, but it would not be at the cost of the sacrament's integrity, his canonical obligations, or his priestly formation.

He stretched the limits; he didn't discard them.

THE AMERICAN CRUCIBLE

A Deep Incision in the Surface of Our Existence

In Leonard Bernstein's 1957 musical, *West Side Story*, the star-crossed lovers of William Shakespeare's feuding Italian families are reimagined along race and language divides and transported to New York, the land where everything is imagined to be free. The Jets claim Manhattan and are in a turf war with the mostly Puerto Rican Sharks. The Jets joke about their interactions with psychiatrists, social workers, judges, and the police. They try to convince the suspicious cop, Officer Krupke, "Like, inside, the worst of us is good."[1]

Bernstein will eventually come to represent for Nouwen a rare creative artist who offered him insight into the complex relationship between a minister and those being ministered. Part of Bernstein's appeal was his very Americanness. Along with many thousands of Europeans in the years following the Second World War, Nouwen looked to the other side of the Atlantic with a mixture of awe and fascination. The free and open creative adaptation of traditions and the willingness to innovate held his interest. Beyond the venerated clinics of Vienna were innovative adaptations of psychological principles and a growing library of influential American resources from such figures as Anton Boisen, Karl Menninger, Carl Rogers, A. H. Maslow, Erik Erikson, Jerome

Bruner, and Harvard's Gordon Allport. In addition to reading their books, Henri Nouwen had already visited their homeland several times. America was not a theoretical abstraction. He traveled in the United States during his seminary and graduate formation, serving as a volunteer chaplain on the Holland-America shipping line in what were the twilight years of mass Atlantic crossings by sea.

What was a work-experience interlude in chaplaincy for him was a life-changing moment for others. From 1945 to the 1970s, half a million people left the Netherlands to live elsewhere. About one-third chose Canada as their destination,[2] and most of those arrived in the immediate postwar period and ended up working on farms in Ontario and Alberta.[3] The settlement pattern in the United States was different. "Only about a fifth went to the United States," writes historian Roger Daniels. "Later Dutch immigrants…tended to settle in metropolitan New York and in California. Very few were farmers."[4]

It was after one of Nouwen's Atlantic crossings as chaplain that he arranged through the office of Boston's Richard Cardinal Cushing to meet with the Harvard-based psychologist Gordon Allport to discuss pastoral psychology and the possibility of pursuing further studies with him at Harvard. In his 1937 book on personality, Gordon Allport had thrown a challenge to traditional psychology, calling on it to "expand its boundaries, revise its methods, and extend its concepts to accommodate more hospitably than in the past, the study of the single concrete life."[5] Such a tradition of openness to innovation and confidence in the "corrective patience"[6] of psychology attracted Nouwen. Allport cautioned his professional colleagues and readers about the oversimplification that can enter the psychologist's understanding of "the client." He used the example of biographers who seek to impose a coherency that might not otherwise be present. "The writer wishes to extract 'the essence' or meaning of the life. In so doing remarkable unity emerges, more than was ever present in the animate person."[7] The same problem can hinder the case study method where a psychologist seeks clues within the incidents of a person's life in the hope that "one true pattern of unity will emerge by sheer virtue of the 'systematic relevance' of one incident to another. Thus, the case study is tested only by its internal intelligibility, by its self-consistency."[8]

Allport advised Nouwen to explore the innovative program that combined theoretical work with practical clinical, psychological counseling and pastoral care at the Menninger Clinic in Topeka, Kansas. The program was introduced in 1954 specifically for members of the clergy. Two experts in the work of Anton Boisen happened to be on the Menninger staff: the clinical psychologist Seward Hiltner, who was one of Anton Boisen's first students, and the Dutch-born clinician Paul Pruyser, who had moved to the United States in 1943 to pursue his doctorate at Boston University, which he completed in 1953.[9] The Menninger Foundation was established in 1925 by Dr. Charles Frederick Menninger and his two sons, Karl and Will, as a treatment-focused alternative to the incarceration of people with mental illness.[10] Karl Menninger's book *The Human Mind* was published in 1930, and the Foundation launched the peer-reviewed *Bulletin of the Menninger Clinic* in 1936. A decade later saw the creation of the Menninger School of Psychiatry, which for years was one of the largest schools of psychiatry in the United States.[11]

Nouwen found a creative way to combine Allport's advice with Alfrink's continuing support. He would bring his studies of Anton Boisen, the American founder of the clinical pastoral education movement, to a conclusion by applying for the two-year Menninger program. He sought and received the blessing and financial support of his archbishop. In August 1964, he traveled to Topeka, Kansas, to enroll as a fellow in the religion and psychiatry program at the Menninger Clinic, joining eleven other trainees. He remained there until December 1966.

Pastoral counseling was his focus and the founder of that pioneering movement was Anton Boisen. It was in Boisen's work that Nouwen discovered the key phrase that will weave itself through most of his subsequent work: "the wounded healer."

Key to understanding Anton Boisen's influence on Henri Nouwen is Christopher De Bono, whose 2012 doctoral dissertation reveals both the depth and the significance of the Boisen-Nouwen connection.[12] "What we have with Anton Boisen is this startling insight that maybe a psychotic experience is of religious significance. His fundamental idea is that our spirituality is relational, that we need to work it through our crisis experiences, and that perhaps in this crisis we discover something about the ultimate," explains De Bono.[13]

What Nouwen and Boisen had in common was "a shared insight that some suffering remains. Some of these wounds we can have for our whole life and yet they can be a source for understanding, and certainly for Anton Boisen and Henri Nouwen, a place where God gets in, where God is present."[14]

Boisen studied and interpreted his own difficulties, making himself his own case study. Nouwen was not yet a published author, but the work he would eventually publish, much of it based on his journals, would use autobiographical components as a basis for analysis and reflection. The

Presbyterian Anton Boisen was forty-four when he experienced one of the five psychotic breaks he describes in his autobiography. This one resulted in a year-and-a-half spent as a patient in a mental hospital. It was the crisis that gave him his true vocation: to serve as a chaplain in a mental health center and to transform it into a center for training and research into religion and psychiatry.

Boisen was born in Indiana in 1876, studied languages, and after his first breakdown, switched to the study of forestry. He then suffered another mental collapse, and after recovering from that, he enrolled in New York's Union Theological Seminary. He successfully completed that training in 1911 and began ministry as a Presbyterian minister. During the First World War, he worked for two years with the YMCA in Europe, returning to the United States in 1917. He suffered another psychotic break in 1920, and it was during this hospitalization that his final sense of calling became clear. By 1924, he had recovered enough to serve as the chaplain at the Worcester State Hospital in Massachusetts, where he set up the program in clinical pastoral education. In 1932, he moved to the Elgin State Hospital in Illinois, where, three years later, he suffered another break when the subject of his unrequited love, Alice Batchelder, died and he was incapable of attending her funeral. As Boisen explains in his memoir, "I look upon this episode as another problem-solving experience. Its meaning I find in the clarification of my relationship with Alice."[15] That same year, he returned to the Elgin State Hospital and completed *Exploration of the Inner World*, published in 1936, followed by *Religion in Crisis and Custom* in 1955, and *Out of the Depths* in 1960. He retired from the Elgin State Hospital in 1954 and died there in 1965.

De Bono meticulously charts Nouwen's responses to the work of Anton Boisen and the development of the "wounded healer" image. He begins with Nouwen's assertion that it is impossible to understand Anton Boisen's "innovation of the clinical case method in theological education and practice" without taking into account Boisen's "'own case,' specifically his 'intensely autobiographical' uses of it."[16] In Nouwen's analysis, Boisen's experience of the "unreachable love" of Alice Batchelder "was not only the main motive of his suffering, but also the main motive of his creative work."[17]

Boisen was interested in psychological practices built on the life experiences of a "living human document," as he called his patients. "I have sought to begin not with the ready-made formulations contained in books but with the living human documents and with actual social conditions in all their complexity."[18]

One of the first things Nouwen sought to do when he arrived in Kansas was to seek out the actual living human document of Anton Boisen. He was then a patient in the Elgin State Mental Hospital in Illinois, where he had spent many years as its director. He was now in failing mental and physical health. In his thesis, De Bono includes a copy of the three typed pages in which Nouwen described his encounter with the person he had greatly admired and who was now sitting in a wheelchair in a not-very-clean room.[19] They discussed the person whom Boisen said was his strongest influence (Freud), and he asked Nouwen about his experience of celibacy ("The fact that I was a priest intrigued him."). Then things started to fragment for Boisen, leaving Nouwen with an observation that anticipates both the direction and the language of so much of his ministry once his studies are formally and finally over: "Seeing a man so closely and being able to experience how a deep wound can become a source of beauty in which even the weaknesses seem to give light is a reason for thankfulness."[20]

The wound as a source of beauty, illumination, and, potentially, healing—Nouwen was still working through these ideas when he returned to Topeka. There he consulted with Seward Hiltner and Paul Pruyser for their insights into the application of Boisen's theories. Seward Hiltner believed that Boisen was trying to create a new theology for pastoral work and that his ideas were gaining traction in counseling circles. Hiltner writes, "Behind the particular form of [Boisen's] thesis, we should note, is the assertion that the study of actual and concrete forms of human experience, especially where ultimate issues are at stake, is theological if we bring theological questions to it. It is not merely psychology or psychiatry incorporated by theologians. It is a point in theological method."[21]

In the work of Pruyser, Nouwen was challenged to recognize the complex interplay of the perspectives of the clinician and the pastor that Boisen brought to this work. Like Nouwen, Boisen was an ordained minister, one whom Pruyser described as someone "not content with merely describing what he saw in the members of his odd flock." As a pastor, Boisen "tried to understand the process of this patient's cataclysmic episodes with a view to helping them come to a good ending. Recording and reporting is not the same thing as aiding and helping them come to a good ending."[22]

For the next two years, in the company of eleven fellow students, Nouwen immersed himself in the Menninger Clinic's laboratory of American ideas about religion, psychology, pastoral care, clinical practice, and theology. He was not the only Catholic in the clinic's decidedly Protestant environment. Richard Sipe, then a Benedictine from Minnesota, was also in the program. After eighteen years in religious life, Sipe would withdraw from the order to continue his studies and practice of psychology, with a research focus on celibacy, including a longitudinal study of people in religious life, their sexuality and experience of celibacy.[23] Sipe and Nouwen would stay in communication into the 1990s.

"Henri Nouwen was one of four priests in that program. I was a Benedictine. There was a Jesuit from Australia and a Dominican from Chicago," explains Sipe. "The four of us were part of the group of twelve that went through a one-year program of training in counselling and psychiatry in pastoral care. Its founders were very devout Presbyterians, from several generations of devout Presbyterians. They were very open to religion. The integration of religion and science was very respectful and there was a free exchange between religion and psychiatry and also ideas between religion and psychiatry."[24]

Nouwen's openness challenged the other members of the program, but they were certainly impressed when he managed to get his bishop (now cardinal) to come from Utrecht and see for himself the kind of work that the clinic and program were pursuing. Jurjen Beumer says that although Nouwen immersed himself in American political and religious culture and felt at home, "the idea that he would stay had not entered the picture yet. It was his intention to introduce what he had discovered and learned in Topeka into the program of religious education in the Netherlands."[25]

One of the staff psychologists at the Menninger was John F. Dos Santos, also Catholic, who connected right away with the fresh-from-Europe Nouwen. Dos Santos explained in an interview how he saw great potential in his European colleague because of his different educational and cultural background "and his promise as a mentor, counselor, and teacher."[26] When Dos Santos was invited by Father Theodore Hesburgh, president of Notre Dame University, to launch a full program in psychology at the university, he encouraged Nouwen to join him.

Nouwen wrote Alfrink with yet another request:

This morning, Eminence, I received a letter from Dos Santos. Maybe you remember him. When you were in Topeka he was still connected with the research institute at the Menninger Foundation. His letter includes an invitation to lecture at Notre Dame for the coming semester and for a variety of reasons this is attractive for me. I really like to teach, especially in those areas outlined in his letter of offer. After a long student life, it is very appealing to lecture on the basic subjects. Besides, I have been assured there will be ample opportunity to work on my thesis. I have gathered most of my materials but am not as far along as I had hoped to be. This offer from John will give me the opportunity to work in the USA, making use of the facilities in both South Bend and Chicago. Also I will be in the position to connect with people who have helped me with my work up to now. And last, but not least, the attractive salary will allow me to pay off several debts and allow me to feel less dependent upon others. At the beginning of December, my Foundation scholarship will end and this salary would give me the chance to stay here at my own cost.[27]

Alfrink was persuaded and added a request that Nouwen bring his experience and knowledge for a semester or two to the Netherlands. Nouwen's transatlantic connection would remain, and largely on Nouwen's terms.

Dos Santos believed that the example of the Menninger dialogue between religion and psychology had served to break long-standing resistance within the American Catholic Church to psychology, fearing it as a potentially faith-disrupting influence. He believed having an ordained priest who also happened to be a trained psychologist would certainly help in this early development of the department. In 1966, he offered Nouwen a position of visiting professor with responsibility for teaching courses in clinical psychology, developmental psychology, personality theory, psychology of religion, and pastoral psychology.[28] This was a short-term offer, and although the initial agreement was for him to teach at Notre Dame for two semesters, with the encouragement of Notre Dame's president Hesburgh, Nouwen remained on staff in Indiana until 1968.[29]

In 1990, Lawrence Freedman's book about the Menninger Clinic was published. Nouwen read it and reflected on this two-year interlude before he moved on to Notre Dame. He described his time in Kansas as "the most formative years of my life as a student. The Saturday Colloquia with Dr. Karl [Menninger] will always remain one of my most precious memories. During that time I so enjoyed the support and friendship...Paul Pruyser, Dr. Seward Hiltner...and John and May Alice Dos Santos. It was John Dos Santos who brought me to N.D."[30]

One of the reasons for withdrawing from Notre Dame was that university-based, research-driven psychology was not the kind of work that interested Nouwen. He was far more interested in pastoral and counseling interventions. The tensions between a more clinical/technical approach to psychology and the more pastoral approach are undercurrents in Nouwen's early published works. It was writing about his two-year teaching experience at Notre Dame that marks the launch of Nouwen's publishing career. His first books were based mostly on lecture notes for his counseling and psychology courses: *Intimacy: Essays in Pastoral Psychology*, published in 1969, and *Creative Ministry* in 1971.

De Bono has researched the references to the work of Anton Boisen in Nouwen's published work and archival holdings. Despite Nouwen's substantial research into the life and work of Boisen, the direct references to him are relatively few, although their focus is revelatory, especially two scholarly articles. Nouwen wrote the first in 1968, when he was still at Notre Dame, and the second in 1977, when he was on faculty at Yale Divinity School.[31] These articles, De Bono explains, bookend Nouwen's first and last direct focus on Anton Boisen, "the person he had spent so much time studying."[32] In the first article, Nouwen explains the importance of understanding Boisen's use of autobiography. Boisen's inspiration is his own mental health circumstances. "This was the motive for the exploration of his inner world, this brought him through the wilderness of the lost, which he calls 'a little known country.'"[33]

In the second, Nouwen looks at how Boisen convinced his medical peers that ministers should rightfully be thought of as full members of therapeutic teams of helping professionals. "If today in hospitals and institutions where clinical training programs are established the chaplain-supervisor and his students...can participate in the staff discussions and are free to consult the files, they are indebted to the strong conviction of Boisen that the chaplain is also a scientist, specialized in the religious aspect of the case under consideration."[34]

These references by Nouwen are essentially academic because while he was preparing courses at Notre Dame, he was also trying to complete a doctoral dissertation on Boisen. His progress was interrupted and delayed by a contract for a book based on those very lectures. Nouwen dedicated his first book, *Intimacy*, to John Eudes Bamberger, "monk and psychiatrist, eminent guide through the complexities of the inner life." He quotes Boisen twice, beginning with his conviction that the function of prayer is to "find out what is wanted of us" and that which will provide "sources of strength which will make it possible for us to accomplish our task whatever it may be."[35] Nouwen adds a line of his own that prayer is what "opens our eyes for ourselves and through clarification enables us to step forward in the direction of hope."[36]

The second reference to Boisen in *Intimacy* relates to the concept of "living human documents." Nouwen likens the experience of ministering in a parish with clinical work in a hospital; both require professionals who know their field and who are willing to make creative contributions to it. "The parish is just as much a field of research for the priest as the hospital is for the doctor," he writes and then introduces Boisen's concept of living human documents.[37]

In addition to Boisen, Nouwen had long identified Thomas Merton as an important prophetic voice. One afternoon in May 1967, he further interrupted his work and traveled to Kentucky to meet with Thomas Merton in his hermitage on the grounds of the Abbey of Gethsemani. It was the only time the two met.

The meeting inspired him to write one of the first biographical and bibliographical explorations of Merton's spirituality. This was one of Nouwen's rare works as it was written first in Dutch and only later translated into English. Nouwen's career as an author began in English, not in translations from the Dutch. From the start, he was an author in a second language.[38]

At Notre Dame, Nouwen experienced a complex series of challenges to the direction his career was taking. The clinical research orientation of some colleagues was in sharp contrast with his more pastoral perspective. This was a familiar professional tension concerning the reputations of formal psychology and pastoral counseling that he understood very clearly, given his experiences at the Menninger. Paul Pruyser characterized this as a challenge of loyalties within a team that needs to show loyalty to its own particular discipline (nurse, psychiatrist, social worker, occupational therapist, and chaplain, for example). Despite their training within that discipline, each member should "proceed with fidelity to the team whose main task is to bring about transformation in the patients' presenting conditions, in the direction of betterment."[39]

A second challenge was the emerging gulf between the church into which he had been ordained in 1957 and the convulsive state of Catholicism in the Netherlands. Peter Naus, his fellow student in the psychology department at the University of Nijmegen, was appointed a visiting assistant professor at Notre Dame in 1996–97 and recalls a conversation: "We had lunch together almost every day. I had discussions with him about what concerned me at the university and also what was going on in the Church in Holland. I picked up at that time his reluctance to become active somehow, his reluctance to engage himself in the turmoil that was in the Dutch church at the time."[40] Despite this hesitation, after two years in Indiana, Nouwen returned to the archdiocese of Utrecht, where he would have to address once and for all the question of his academic focus. His preference, says Jurjen Beumer, was pastoral psychology, but that would require additional studies in theology. Back in the Netherlands he studied theology, passed his doctoral exams, and set about completing a doctoral degree in the Social Sciences Faculty of Nijmegen University: *De betkenis van Anton T. Boisen's acute psychose in verband met jijn vraag naar verhouding tussen geestesziekte en religieuze bekering* ("The Meaning of Anton T. Boisen's Acute Psychosis in Connection to His Search of the Relationship between Mental Illness and Conversion"). De Bono confirms that Nouwen "never actually defended this thesis either, settling once again for a (non-thesis) *doctorandus* degree and accepting to start teaching at Yale Divinity School in the fall of 1971."[41]

The invitation to teach at Yale was based, in part, on the success of Nouwen's books *Intimacy* and *Creative Ministry*. Once more, his cardinal archbishop supported his decision to return to the United States where Nouwen was not shy about setting out the conditions of his employment. With a clear sense of the credentialism in universities on both sides of the Atlantic, Nouwen set out to avoid any ambiguity about his now two *doctorandus* degrees. He set four conditions to joining the Yale faculty: that (1) he not be required to produce a dissertation; (2) he be made a permanent member of faculty within three years; (3) he be granted tenure after five years; and (4) he would establish his own criteria for any peer review of his work. The contract was signed. "Apparently Nouwen had become a very desirable commodity," muses Beumer.[42]

The Yale decade, 1971–81, sees the emergence of Henri Nouwen as an internationally acclaimed writer whose popular and much-translated books address, initially, questions of ministry and formation, and by the end of the decade, they take on new exploratory forms, blending autobiographical reflection, prayer, social commentary, personal tribulation, and spirituality. There were no doubts that conventional parish work was not going to be his priestly job description. For the time being he was a Dutch citizen residing in the United States.

Publishing is typically a year behind writing, and Nouwen's first published books address his insights during the two-year stay at Notre Dame. Within a year of arriving at Yale, no fewer than three Nouwen works appeared in bookstores, *With Open Hands*, *Pray to Live: Thomas Merton—Contemplative Critic*, and *The Wounded Healer*. Robert Derback visited Nouwen at Yale and describes the creative process he observed.[43] Nouwen would typically begin with informal conversations with large gatherings of students and friends. Next, these conversations would become more formal and focused, out of which would emerge a single or a series of crafted lectures. Then Nouwen would rework these lecture notes into a book. If you listen to the audio recordings of Nouwen's Yale lectures in the archive in Toronto, you can certainly hear phrases and anecdotes in their raw form that are carefully crafted and reworked into these Yale-era titles.

Interestingly, these first books contain no direct mention of Boisen, not even *The Wounded Healer*. This title quickly became the tag by which Nouwen came to be remembered. "Nothing can be written about ministry without a deeper understanding of the ways in which ministers can make their own wounds available as a source of healing."[44] Nouwen likens the wound of loneliness to the Grand Canyon, "a deep incision in the surface of our existence which has become an inexhaustible source of beauty and self-understanding."[45] The paradox of the Christian leader, Nouwen observes, "is that the way out is also the way in, that only by entering into communion with human suffering can relief be found."[46] Similarly, visitors to the Canyon discover that the only way in to it, the Bright Angel Trail, is also the only way out. The lines read like a paraphrase from his notes after visiting Boisen just a few years earlier.

The image of a healer who is wounded has its origins in Greek mythology. In 1961, Carl Jung used the myth of the centaur Chiron, the creature who is half horse and half human, to remind readers that the wounded healer was not a twentieth-century concept. "In the end," said Jung, "only the wounded physician heals and even he, in the last analysis, cannot heal beyond the extent to which he has healed himself."[47]

Nouwen's oversubscribed courses at Yale and the books that he wrote during that period (typically one a year) placed him firmly in the spotlight, with endless requests to attend conferences, give public lectures, and lead retreats. In 1974, as his contract with Yale stipulated, Nouwen was given tenure. He was also granted permanent residence status in the United States.

After three busy years of teaching, he arranged for a seven-month sabbatical. He hoped to spend it at the Abbey of the Genesee, where he had proposed he might live for the duration of his sabbatical, not as a guest, but as a monk following all the practices of monastic life as a Trappist. This idea surfaced after his first visit to Genesee some years earlier. Nouwen's decades-long exploration of Trappist practice and especially the life and work of Thomas Merton is detailed in the next chapter.

Nouwen saw this opportunity to spend time in the company of Trappists as a "break away" from his university work and to explore his "compulsions and illusions" and to live as "a temporary monk."[48] John Eudes Bamberger, his spiritual director at the Abbey of Gethsemani in Kentucky, was now the abbot at the Abbey of the Genesee in New York State, and Nouwen wanted to continue the experience of his wise spiritual guidance. After discussing the proposal with the members of the community, Bamberger wrote to Nouwen that he had been "voted in" by them and that his temporary monastic membership, although unorthodox, could begin.

Typically for Nouwen, every major life experience resulted in a book. At Genesee he worked on two very different books: a journal of his time there, *The Genesee Diary: Report from a Trappist Monastery*, and an exploration of his ministry entitled *Reaching Out: Three Movements of the Spiritual Life*. In this second work, Nouwen articulates his uncertainty about the kind of priest he has become and his mixed roles of minister, teacher, and writer. He has not "settled in" to his career and has some unfinished personal business to address: "I am still searching for inner peace, for creative relationships with others and for the experience of God, and neither I nor anyone else has any way of knowing if the small psychological changes during the past years have made me a more or a less spiritual man."[49] The three "movements" of the book concern the deepening of an experience in order to transform it from something negative into something that can become a positive influence. In this way, loneliness has the potential to be transformed into the experience of solitude, hostility can become hospitality, and illusion can be transformed into prayer.

Nouwen's biographer, Jurjen Beumer, identifies *Reaching Out* as the turning point in Nouwen's development as a writer, and by extension a critical moment in how he understands his identity as a priest. Nouwen is no longer writing "about" personal experiences but is, for the first time in Beumer's opinion, speaking "out of" them. This is the moment in Nouwen's career when, like Boisen, he has found a way to see himself as a living human document and can begin to use his own case study as he continues to try and understand his emerging vocation.

The books that followed reveal the extent to which Nouwen wrote not "about" but from *within* his insecurity, uncertainty, his affirmation-seeking neediness as he turned his attention to the elements of his ministry: praying, lecturing, preaching, writing, studying, and counseling.[50] "When God has become our shepherd, our refuge, our fortress," he writes in *Reaching Out*, "we can reach out to him in the midst of a broken world and feel at home while still on the way."[51] As the next chapter illustrates, Genesee offered a temporary glimpse of a certain kind of "home." But even fragments count. In 1990, at a similar turning-point moment midway through his time at L'Arche Daybreak, he used slightly different words to explain how he connected such fragmentary experiences. He said his compulsion to write from within his own living human document was the result of his awareness that his deepest vocation was "to be witness to the glimpses of God I have been allowed to catch."[52]

After seven months in the Trappist world, Nouwen returned to New Haven, Connecticut, to resume teaching and writing in the highly competitive culture of Yale. His colleague, now professor emerita and member of the Sisters of Mercy, Margaret Farley, characterized academic life at Yale as "the most pressured existence you could imagine in terms of the demands."[53] It was not long before some familiar but "troublesome visitors" returned in the form of "demons" that entered his soul once again to remind him that his sabbatical, although helpful, was not a permanent fix to his concerns. He certainly did not leave any of his "compulsions, illusions, and unrealities" back at the abbey. Nouwen was convinced, though, that his Trappist experience had provided him with one more glimpse of God's graciousness, a ray of light that broke through his darkness.[54]

In addition to teaching, Nouwen preached retreats and gave workshops. His notes for these became the contents of new books. His 1974 book, *Out of Solitude: Three Meditations of the Christian Life* (dedicated to his former Nijmegen and Notre Dame colleague, Peter Naus, and his wife, Anke), is an adaptation of homilies he gave at Battell, the United Church on Christ at Yale. It contains a glimpse of a different kind, a glimpse into Nouwen's understanding of the utility of certain kinds of books. In a section on the importance of consolation, he reflects on the paradox that consolation and hope are often found in the work of authors who, surprisingly, offer no answers to any of life's tough questions in their work. It is their courage in articulating the difficult circumstances of their own lives, honestly and directly, that offers readers "new strength to pursue our own search. Their courage to enter so deeply into human suffering and to become present to their own pain gave them the power to speak healing words."[55] His list of such writers includes Søren Kierkegaard, Jean-Paul Sartre, Albert Camus, Dag Hammarskjöld, and Thomas Merton. They are, in effect, living human documents writing from within the circumstances of their own case histories. Increasingly, this is the kind of work that Nouwen attempted to produce, often in the form of "pocket-sized" shorter works and works that combined words and visual images.

In the 1970s, it became common to produce books almost as if they were print versions of a documentary film, with (mostly) black-and-white photographs, usually lots of them, set against blocks of text. Nouwen's 1972 collaboration, *With Open Hands*, is one example with its striking photographs of actors and dancers in intense dramatic poses and with sparse texts in between. The work grew out of a series of discussions with students, and many of the photographs appear to be of university group projects in improvisational dance and drama. Nouwen continued to experiment with both the form and content of his books with *Aging: The Fulfillment of Life*, published in 1974. This is another example of early self-help, magazine-like publishing, setting words and images alongside each other. It contains eighty-five art photographs of people and nature by Ron Van Den Bosch, interspersed with inspiration texts about getting older from Yale graduate Walter Gaffney, former chief of staff at Connecticut's Department of Social Services, and Nouwen himself.

Nouwen's teaching methods were highly theatrical, and his classes often began with Taizé chants or current "pop" songs that were analyzed for their meaning. Gay rights activist and minister Chris Glazer took several of Nouwen's courses at Yale and remembers his "trademark flailing hands flapping like birds about to fly up to God."[56] Historian Robert Massie remembers seeing one of Nouwen's presentations and describes his fingers as "a ten-member liturgical dance corps that performed in front of him whenever he opened his

mouth."[57] Such high-performance theatricality engaged his
students deeply, as did the often surprising connections he
continued to make beyond liturgy and Scripture. In addition
to writers, Nouwen also paid a great deal of serious attention to the work of his favored visual artists and fellow coun-
trymen, Rembrandt and Vincent van Gogh. His Yale course
exploring the spirituality of the artist and his work ("The
Compassion of Vincent van Gogh") quickly developed a student waiting list. The deeply wounded van Gogh was "his
saint."

"Look at Rembrandt and van Gogh," he wrote, "With
true Dutch stubbornness, they trusted their vocations and did
not allow anyone to lead them astray."[58] Van Gogh's art
"heals and consoles me more than anything else,"[59] and
brought him in touch with his own "brokenness and talents
in ways nobody else could."[60]

In the difficult and truncated life of van Gogh, Nouwen
found a powerful wounded healer and spiritual fellow trav-
eler. "I cannot help thinking that the best way of knowing
God is to love many things. Love this friend, this person, this
thing, whatever you like, and you will be on the right road to
understanding Him better" sounds like a Nouwen quotation
from one of the books from his Yale decade. It isn't. It's from
a letter written in July of 1888 by van Gogh to his brother,
Theo.[61] He writes, "Try to grasp the essence of what the great
master artists, the serious masters, say in the masterpieces,
and you will again find God in them. One man has written or
said it in a book, another in a painting."[62] John Franklin of
the Toronto School of Theology, characterizes van Gogh's
paintings as a glimpse of the transcendent.[63] It is Vincent van
Gogh who offers Nouwen such glimpses in the 1970s. Before

long, his attention will turn to Rembrandt in an especially profound way.

Although Nouwen was mostly silent about Boisen, he mentioned him briefly in a 1977 work based on presentations at conferences for clinical pastoral education professionals. In *The Living Reminder: Service and Prayer in Memory of Jesus Christ*, Nouwen referenced Boisen for the last time in his published work. He introduced Boisen in the context of ministers and their role in assisting people to address memories that retain the power to wound. Boisen, explains Nouwen, understood the "psychic forces by which painful memories are rejected" and proposed "theology through living human documents."[64] But how this has been interpreted in pastoral counseling ever since, argues Nouwen, has tipped the balance toward behavioral sciences at the expense of the Bible. "Are we not talking more about people than about God, in whose name we come to people?" he asks. The primary vocation of the minister, he writes, is to "continuously make connections between the human story and the divine story."[65] Nouwen organized the book in three sections (healing, sustaining, and guiding) based on Seward Hiltner's guiding principles for ministry that seeks to balance concern for the spiritual life with input from the social sciences. Ministry and memory are intertwined. Here, Nouwen anticipated the words of Nobel Prize winning neuroscientist Eric Kandel, who in his 2006 memoir wrote, "Without the mental time travels provided by memory, we would have no awareness of our personal history, no way of remembering the joys that serve as the luminous milestones of our life. We are who we are because of what we learn and remember."[66] In 1977, writing in *The Living Reminder*, Nouwen says that our memories of "trust, love, acceptance, forgiveness, confidence, and hope enter so deeply into our being that indeed we *become* our memories."[67]

After three more years of teaching, Nouwen was planning his next sabbatical, which would take him to Rome for five months in 1978. He served as a scholar in residence at "the NAC," the Pontifical North American College, established in 1855 for the formation of diocesan seminarians from the United States. Nouwen's students were mostly seminarians and he gave them presentations on solitude, community, celibacy, prayer, contemplation, and ministry, which form the basis of *Clowning in Rome: Reflection of Solitude, Celibacy, Prayer, and Contemplation*, published in 1979. It was a dark time in many parts of the world, as Nouwen summarizes in his introduction, a time "clouded with an all-pervading fear, a growing sense of despair, and the paralyzing awareness that indeed humanity has come to the verge of suicide."[68] In the midst of such darkness stands the clown. It's an ambivalent image. In the traditional circus it is the role of the clown, in a larger-than-life costume and with exaggerated face makeup, to divert the audience's attention while the next act is being set up. In Nouwen's explanation, the clowns are in sharp contrast to the elegant tightrope walkers, muscular trapeze artists, or brave lion-tamers. They are more like "us" who watch such skill and bravery and are reminded "with a tear and a smile that we share the same human weaknesses."[69]

De Bono identifies Nouwen's discovery, in 1971, of the clown as metaphor for ministry in the work of Heije Faber in the Netherlands: "The clown is an accomplished artist whose work is the result of years of training and performance experience," but that work often appears improvised and spontaneous.[70] Paul Pruyser in the United States took up the clown metaphor, suggesting that those watching the clown (those being ministered to) get a "a new sense of humanity" because they are not overwhelmed by the appearance of clinical virtuosity.[71] Nouwen shifted the focus from those doing the ministry to those being ministered. The values he presents in the book, when lived out "authentically and generously" should not be seen as demonstrations of "spiritual virtuosity good for a select few, but a way of life which speaks to many."[72] Metaphors for ministry have the power to break through to something creative, and also the power to harm, just like that other frequently used image of the minister, the shepherd.

Where there are clowns there's always laughter and as the adage goes: where there's laughter there's often tears. In the summer of 1978, the then forty-six-year-old Nouwen arranged for his parents to visit him at Yale. Their time together was curtailed by his mother's sudden illness. Maria Ramselaar had to fly back to the Netherlands where she learned that she had a cancer that required immediate surgery. In the six days between her surgery and her death in the hospital at Nijmegen, Nouwen flew to the Netherlands to be with her. In his book *In Memoriam*, he writes with deep regret that he was making a telephone call outside her hospital room when she died. She was, he says, the lens through which he had viewed the world. They had exchanged letters regularly in which he outlined his plans, his ideas for books, and his uncertainties. She "followed every decision I made, had discussed every trip I took, had read every article and book I wrote, and had considered my life as important as hers....I had viewed the world through the eyes of her to whom I could tell my story."[73]

Four months after her death, Nouwen was back at the Abbey of the Genesee, deep in prayer, and writing once more. This time his work took the form of a prayer "journal" published as *A Cry for Mercy: Prayers from the Genesee*. He followed this with a book about the desert mothers and fathers, based on a course he gave at Yale. In *The Way of the Heart: The Spirituality of the Desert Fathers and Mothers*, Nouwen bridges their words and life experiences with his contemporary reflections on prayer, silence, and commitment.

When Nouwen first arrived at Yale in 1971, the United States was still convulsed by a war that seemed to have no end in sight. That year, the death toll of U.S. military in combat in Vietnam exceeded the 33,629 killed in the Korean War. President Nixon began the withdrawal of American troops from Vietnam, even as hostilities continued. Peace talks began in 1972, and a cease-fire agreement was signed by all parties the following year, though the war continued until April 1975. International news coverage focused on the image of overloaded U.S. helicopters swooping away hundreds of desperate refugees from Saigon rooftops.[74] Although undeniably a pacifist and horrified by war, Nouwen was uncomfortably ambivalent about the peace movement itself. Two years of national service were a requirement in the Netherlands, and after leaving the seminary, Nouwen had served with a mental health team, opting not to exempt himself, although as a priest he could have. In his writing about this, he justified his decision, explaining that he enjoyed the team spirit of the recruits and met people he never would have encountered. In their company, he said he "learned a lot about psychology, felt very useful, and made closer friends than during my six years in the seminary."[75] He said that divisions within and the tactics of the peace movements that he saw in the Netherlands and in the United States made him skeptical about antiwar demonstrations. He described them as distasteful and said that they renewed his "respect for the cleanliness, orderliness, discipline, and single-mindedness of those who served their country in the military."[76] He then placed peacemaking at the heart of the Christian vocation, using a decidedly Ignatian qualification that all such activities should be guided by St. Paul's words: "Whatever you do at all, do it for the glory of God" (see 1 Cor 10:31).[77]

By the end of the 1970s, warfare was taking a different form. Guatemala had entered its second decade of a violent civil war, the Sandinistas had removed the Nicaraguan dictator Anastasio Somoza though the war with the U.S.-backed Contras was far from over, and civil war was about to break out in El Salvador. The world's attention shifted from the legacy of the Vietnam War to events in Central and South America.

Nouwen looked back on this convulsive decade and his experiences at Yale as "tumultuous and full of anxious searching."[78] Yet the books he published in his final year at Yale, *Making All Things New: An Invitation to the Spiritual Life* and *Compassion: A Reflection on the Spiritual Life*, exude something approaching serenity. Nouwen said that he had had enough of the lonely and competitive life in academia and the tensions he continued to experience between his career and his vocation. He had reached the conclusion that it was a time to return, not to the Netherlands, but to a more basic form of ministry.

There's an entry in the diary of Georges Bernanos that captures the intriguing gaps between a writer's life experience and their creative output. In 1940, four years after the highly successful release of *The Diary of a Country Priest*, Bernanos wrote that the "artist's work is never the sum of his doubts and disappointments and sufferings, of what is good and bad in his life, but his life itself, transfigured, illuminated and reconciled."[79]

Nouwen looked once again to the example of Father Louis, the recently deceased Thomas Merton.

6

THE TRAPPIST TWIST

Stumbling over Compulsions and Illusions

In *Raids on the Unspeakable*, the American Trappist monk, poet, essayist, and literary polymath Thomas Merton observed of the contemplative life that it

> must not be construed as an escape from time and matter, from social responsibility and from the life of sense, but rather, as an advance into solitude and the desert, a confrontation with poverty and the void, a renunciation of the empirical self, in the presence of death and nothingness, in order to overcome the ignorance and error that spring from the fear of "being nothing." The man who dares to be alone can come to see that the "emptiness" and "uselessness" which the collective mind fears and condemns are necessary conditions for the encounter with truth.[1]

Nouwen's own experience of the contemplative life was more provisional than permanent, more tentative than existential, but it was transformative for him spiritually, helped to refine his notions of human fecundity over human productivity, and aided in the differentiation between the deep human need for solitude as opposed to the sterile offerings of a constrictive loneliness. Most importantly, it provided the

6

template that he needed to confront the big questions of nothingness and death.

If Nouwen was originally a romantic about monasticism—what it had to offer, the security provided by an unvarying *horarium*, the consolations inherent in a real as opposed to artificial community—his eyes were opened to the true dynamic of contemplative living by his spiritual director, the psychiatrist monk, John Eudes Bamberger:

> In the contemplative life every conflict, inner or outer, small or large, can be seen as the tip of an iceberg, the expressive part of something deeper and larger. It is worthwhile, even necessary, to explore that which is underneath the surface of our daily actions, thoughts, and feelings.
>
> The most persistent advice of John Eudes in his spiritual direction is to explore the wounds, to pay attention to the feelings, which are often embarrassing and shameful, and follow them to their roots. He keeps telling me not to push away disturbing daydreams or hostile meanderings of the mind but to allow them to exist and explore them with care.[2]

There are, then, dimensions of life highlighted by the structured or regulated contemplative vocation that can speak to the rest of humanity; there are charisms peculiar to the contemplative vocation for sure, but the "constituitive monkhood" common to all human questing, as world religions scholar Raimundo Panikaar rightly notes, is not confined to institutional expression alone.

Nouwen was drawn to contemplation because he recognized it as the lifeblood of effective Christian ministry; without it, social activism is without foundation and an active worship and sacramental life barren.

To bear fruit both spiritually and psychologically, one needs to be grounded in a contemplative disposition, one needs to attend to the interior life, one needs to nurture the longing for a generative solitude.

In short, one must be a contemplative *in* the world.

The discovery of that seminal truth was for Nouwen a journey that began with an encounter—partial, seemingly inconsequential, a moment with a living icon of holiness, under a tree, paying attention and enrapt with the awe that comes when in the presence of a great exemplar. Nouwen was starstruck.

And it happened at Gethsemani. The meeting was not particularly auspicious, rated a minimal acknowledgment in the Merton journals (Nouwen's name was misspelled) and the conversation was not epoch-making. Nouwen himself said that it was not "a very life-giving meeting."[3] Yet John Eudes Bamberger thinks that the encounter validated Nouwen's grasp of Merton's "essence" because, although this was there only meeting,

> yet by a sympathy of feeling and perception he has understood the central motivation force of Merton's life: meditation and prayer. He has seen this more truly and profoundly than some who, while claiming to be intimate friends of Merton, have altogether missed the point of his work and life through lack of feeling for his vision of God, humanity and the cosmos. There is nothing surprising in this fact. True understanding depends

not only on intelligence and proximity but above all on the heart.[4]

Merton introduced to Nouwen key concepts that would serve as the substratum of his own spiritual explorations and writings: detachment in poverty as a form of freedom; compassion as the new desert where one's self-constructed illusions are shattered; the role one is called to play as a reporter of one's own inner life; the critical differentiation between productivity and fertility in a meaningfully free life.

Merton entered Nouwen's bloodstream through his diaries, his various manuals on the spiritual life, his wirings on peace and nonviolence, his interfaith investigations, and his genre-bending fiction: works like *Thoughts in Solitude*, *No Man Is an Island*, *Seeds of Destruction*, *New Seeds of Contemplation*, *Gandhi on Non-Violence*, and *Zen and the Birds of Appetite*. It is especially interesting that he also read Merton's only published novel, the macaronic, Kafkaesque, and surreal hodgepodge, *My Argument with the Gestapo*. Nouwen did his homework, and it took him places where he would naturally not venture.

Merton became his abiding companion, a spiritual father, a mentor in the ways of the heart, and he did this by means of his considerable output as a diarist. After all, they met only once and Merton, at the time, was not much for this world. His ill-fated trip to the East was on the horizon. In a letter to his friend Fred Bratman, a Jewish journalist who inspired his 1992 book *Life of the Beloved: Spiritual Living in a Secular World*, Nouwen wrote that Merton's ability "to bring concrete burning issues of the day in connection with the spiritual search affected me very much....More than any of his books, it is his spirit and his way of approaching life that has influenced me deeply."[5]

In other words, Nouwen's "encounter" with Merton was not defined or limited by their cursory meeting on the abbey grounds. It was rather an ongoing and life-sustaining encounter predicated on his sympathetic and creative reading of the Merton to be found in his books, the Merton who inspired millions, the Merton who bore witness to his own personal struggles and ambivalences of heart and mind with a noble honesty.

That is the man whom Nouwen would emulate.

Nouwen's interest in the monastic life—the regulated structure that provides meaning in the course of a daily *horarium* built around the rhythms of prayer, labor, silence, and *lectio divina*—had huge appeal for the Dutch priest on the fast track of professorial success and on the cusp of national celebrity with his writings. In search of both a serious life of prayer and a life of community, Nouwen found in the Trappist Abbey of the Genesee in Piffard in upstate New York the oasis of his dreams, a sanctuary where he could do the heavy thinking around spiritual matters that a bustling faculty of divinity with its curious and intense students made close to impossible.

While at Yale University—and on one of his many sabbaticals—Nouwen arranged to spend seven months with the Trappist community at Genesee not

> as a guest but as a monk [and it] did not develop overnight. It was the outcome of many years of restless searching. While teaching, lecturing, and writing about the importance of solitude, inner freedom, and peace of mind, I kept stumbling over

my own compulsions and illusions. What was driving me from one book to another, one place to another, one project to another?[6]

By going to live as a monk-manqué—although Nouwen would see it in more devotional terms—he was hoping to find some solution, possibly temporary but ideally permanent, that would still his restless soul. That was not likely to happen then or later, but what the abbey gave him, besides the opportunity to write his first published diary, was the sustained exposure to Bamberger, the abbot-psychiatrist and spiritual director, who would guide a frequently distraught and guilt-ridden Dutch cleric through the minefield of his spiritual and emotional turmoil.

Nouwen was already familiar with Bamberger, and Bamberger, in return, had already developed an insightful perspective on the high drama that was Henri Nouwen-in-action. Bamberger writes on November 28, 1965, that

> beyond the obviously very healthy and wholesome aspects of your warm relations with people and your popularity, there is a measure of self-doubt that leads you to preserve a tension within yourself, and which probably accounts for the extent to which you feel more or less bound to go to social contacts, so as to maintain what you feel is the required effort. Perhaps more than anything else an understanding of this mechanism would make a more ordered, disciplined life possible for you....I think that before any kind of serious ascetic discipline can take the place in your life that it probably ought to have you'll need to get a good look

at this *need for reassurance from others that you are loveable.*[7]

That "reassurance" would never come in a way that could still his restlessness. It would elude him all his life. His "primary wound," his gut feeling that he was unlovable and the concomitant self-rejection that came with it, remained the driving pathology of his life and ministry.

But what his time at Genesee did give him—from that June to December of 1974—was an opportunity to replicate Merton as diarist, taste firsthand the alternating cadences of silence and chant, probe deeply the inner forces at work in his psyche, and feel, yes *feel*, the tangibility, the tactility even, of community.

Like Merton, Nouwen addressed a myriad of topics in his diary entries: nature, the change of the seasons, the beauty of the mundane, the work habits of the monks, his own manual labor, the books he read, his observations of the characters about him, his personal struggles, and his spiritual turmoil.

Throughout the diary the reader can see that Nouwen's sessions with his spiritual director, Bamberger, provide the *cantus firmus*, focusing his thoughts, steadying his emotions, generating new ideas. He wrestles with his compulsions, tries to balance the contradictions of his personality, and looks for guidance on the matter of his twin vocations. In a specially moving entry he observes that the way to the heart "always seems to be a quiet, gentle way. After Thanksgiving, I received a note from someone I do not know telling me how much she felt part of my life because of my writings. It seems that these are the most precious moments of life."[8]

Merton understood that precisely because of his writings he would have an ongoing impact on readers, that they would seek him out, that he had an obligation attached to his fame that amounted to an extension of his priestly ministry. His disciple, Henri Nouwen, came to understand that as well. In Nouwen's case, the contacts were driven less by cerebral concern than by pastoral necessity. His diaries created a new apostolate for him, his readers were his parishioners, and his vocation now included bringing hope to the disconsolate and the despairing.

Merton may have been his model, but his clientele would be different in kind. Their requests more urgent, their needs more pressing; it is the making of his universal pastorship.

Merton's diary writing was the principal genre that Nouwen could emulate, and he got better at it as the years unfolded—more disciplined, more self-disclosing, more honest. The diaries were not only confessional in that he could be self-revelatory in ways other forms of public discourse wouldn't allow or at least encourage, but a *confessional* for readers to vicariously connect with a spiritual father.

He also learned from Merton the indispensability of prayer: the cornerstone of the spiritual life. This is true not only of those professionally dedicated to praying, as it were, but for all those in search of a more integrated human life: a life open to the other and the Other, a life grounded in the immanent thirsting for the Transcendent.

It was during his second Genesee retreat, February to August 1979, that he crafted a volume of prayers titled *A Cry for Mercy*. The prayers are devoid of the sentimentality Nouwen was occasionally prone to, and they are often cast in the form of a colloquy with the Infinite Lover. They draw on both the general and the particular of human experience and as a consequence don't absolutize or render eccentric. Throughout the entire collection, which he dedicated to his Uncle Toon with the recognition that it was he who showed him the way to the priesthood, Nouwen talked about the commonplace, laced his reflections with biblical allusions, and spoke about various figures who had moved him, none more substantially than his nineteenth-century countryman, Vincent van Gogh.

In many critical ways, Nouwen identified with van Gogh: he was an isolated artist who regularly drank the bitter gall of rejection; his art and his spirituality were fused in the cauldron of his conflicting emotions; he yearned for human love but was frequently disappointed; he was incapable of finding a satisfying and mature outlet for his roiling sexuality; he encountered incomprehension and derision in the exercise of his ministry.

No surprise then that when feeling himself in a fathomless and swirling hole of depression and rejection, Nouwen turns to the tragic Dutchman for solace and company.

> Do not allow me to sink back into my own dark pit, O Lord, but let your warm, gentle, life-giving light lift me from my grave. Vincent van Gogh painted you as the sun when he painted the resurrection of Lazarus. In so doing, he wanted to express his own liberation from a dark, imprisoning past....In your light all becomes new. Let me be fully yours. Amen.[9]

Van Gogh was the artist *as* priest for Nouwen, irrespective the unconventional—nay, tumultuous— nature of his life, and he would return to him many times over the years, teaching a graduate course on his art and spirituality, constructing a solo performance of the man and his genius for both admiring and perplexed audiences, and using him as a defining figure in his own theological aesthetics.

It was Merton, however, who provided Nouwen with the opportunity to *see* differently, who provided him with an artist's validation and a mystic's seal of approval: *attend* to the holy wisdom revealed in art.

In 1962, Merton published his prose poem *Hagia Sophia*, the result of a correspondence he had with his close friend Victor Hammer. A typographer, bookbinder, and calligrapher, in addition to his teaching duties in lettering, drawing, and painting, Hammer was the consummate artist and craftsman. On one occasion when Merton was visiting Victor and his wife, Carolyn, Hammer showed his guest a triptych he had been working on. The central panel showed a woman crowning a young boy, and Merton asked aloud who the woman was. Hammer had initially conceived of the woman and the young boy as a Madonna and Child, but no longer knew who she was. Merton then responded, "I know who she is. I have always known her. She is Hagia Sophia [Holy Wisdom]."[10]

In a letter dated May 2, 1959, Hammer invited Merton to come and bless the triptych and explain in greater detail what he meant by Hagia Sophia. This latter request Merton met in a twofold manner: in a subsequent letter dated May 14 and in the prose poem of the same name.

Merton's poem is an eloquent meditation on and celebration of wisdom. He observes,

> There is in all things an inexhaustible sweetness
> and purity, a silence that is a fount of action and

joy. It rises up in wordless gentleness and flows out to me from the unseen roots of all created being, welcoming me tenderly, saluting me with indescribable humility. This is at once my own being, my own nature, and the Gift of my Creator's Thought and Art within me, speaking as Hagia Sophia, speaking as my sister, Wisdom.[11]

Merton also conceived of wisdom as the *point vierge*—the enlightened awareness at the juncture of despair, the very center of the soul—and in so doing the portal that leads us back to our sweet innocence. In his "reading" of the Hammer triptych, Merton articulates David Foster's hermeneutic process outlined in his *Contemplative Prayer: A New Framework*. When we look at a picture initially,

we just see it and recognize it, as if that were that. What strikes us initially may well be something that says more about us than about the picture, something in the way it reflects our experience or aspirations. Our attention has to move beyond our personal preoccupations; it needs to engage with the picture itself. We might ask ourselves what strikes us and how, and let the work itself teach us how to look at it. That may mean a change of attitude, a conversion of mind and heart. We have to let the picture be. What matters is how the picture "works;" we need to enter the world the picture creates and try to see it as a whole. It is a gradual process, and it is a process more like a conversation than a speech, but that is how a picture "speaks to us." In the process we have learned to pay attention.

This is a hermeneutic process. Once we have begun to pay attention, dispassionate looking does not leave us untouched. It lets the object of our experience take the initiative, as it were, in disclosing itself. It works in the way in which we are able to let ourselves be surprised and challenged by what we see. We find ourselves invited to new ways of looking, and to new ways of learning to look at everything in the light of that experience. In this context, it is also uncontroversial, however strange it is to reflect on, that what works for one person will not for another; a painting can have different "conversations."[12]

The key ideas in Foster's art/prayer framework were already adumbrated in Merton's seasoned reflections on art, on the making of art, and in his own art—literary and visual. This art Nouwen would have known, read, seen, and responded to. Nouwen had already mined his own various responses to art and knew in the words of novelist and essayist Marilynne Robinson "that the aesthetic should be an aspect of human nature that reveals our affinity to God."[13]

Nouwen's interest in the visual arts and in the pure seeing that defines one's attention was nurtured by his appreciation of the monk-poet but not wholly dependent upon it. His articulation of his own aesthetic, its very modality of expression, was more typical of the art critic—refined, sensitive, and insightful—than the executor of art per se. In a letter to James Luther Adams, a Harvard faculty friend and Unitarian theologian, Nouwen defined the special, if not salvific, quality he found in art:

The works of Rublev, Rembrandt and van Gogh have often given me ways to communicate the mystery of God's presence among us, when words proved so inadequate. A few weeks ago I was in the Louvre and saw Rembrandt's *Pilgrim of Emmaus*. I stood there for half an hour and was so overwhelmed by the ecstatic as well as intimate look of Jesus and the splendid light on his hands breaking the bread that felt as if I was present at the celebration of the Eucharist. The many tourists and talkative guides had vanished from my consciousness. I truly was in church![14]

Whether teaching a course on spirituality and art in the life and work of van Gogh, writing his spiritual masterpiece on a Lucan parable rendered with compelling compassion in Rembrandt's *The Return of the Prodigal Son*, writing an introduction to the calligraphies of the Japanese artist Yushi Nomura (*Desert Wisdom: Sayings from the Desert Fathers*), tracing the beauty and searing mystery of icons with Robert Lentz, or standing transfixed by a painting at the Art Gallery of Ontario, Nouwen was engaged in fresh seeing, as Canadian artist Emily Carr names it, cleansing the doors of perception, as William Blake would call it, and doing all of this *as* prayer.

The concentration, the *attention* he learned from mystic-philosopher Simone Weil, and the simple adoration he accorded the revelatory quality of art defined Nouwen's approach to art. He viewed art as the mirror of the soul—the artist's soul and the viewer's soul. It is a form of communion, a sacrament of encounter with God.

Art could feature Christ directly, as in this reflection on a fourteenth-century sculpture he discovers in the Augustiner

Museum in Freiburg, *Christus dem Esel ("Palmesel")*, or
Christ on the Palm-Donkey:

> Christ's long, slender face with a high forehead,
> inward-looking eyes, long hair, and small forked
> beard expresses the mystery of his suffering in a way
> that holds me spellbound....His unfocused eyes see
> what nobody around him can see; his high forehead
> reflects a knowledge of things to come far beyond
> anyone's understanding.
>
> There is melancholy, but also peaceful acceptance.
> There is insight into the fickleness of the human heart,
> but also immense compassion....Every time I look at
> this Christ on the donkey, I am reminded again that I
> am seen by him with all my sins, guilt, and shame and
> loved with all his forgiveness, mercy and compas-
> sion.[15]

Or it could feature elements revelatory of the character of
the artist that are either consonant or dissonant with the
sensibility of the viewer, that is, Nouwen. In a surprisingly
frank examination of the personality—hence, the soul—of
American artist Edward Hopper, Nouwen interprets the
art through the biography, in what is his consistent critical
approach as we see in his writings on Rembrandt and van
Gogh. What he sees confirms what he reads: an artist in
retreat from intimacy, who is cruel toward his wife of forty
years, Josephine, a man who led

> a chilling life, frightfully reflected in his chilling
> art....The soul of the artist cannot remain hidden.
> The bitter, isolated, and mean soul of Hopper and

the restless but love-hungry soul of van Gogh are both revealed in their works. Vincent van Gogh was and remained a minister, always trying to bring people together, even though he failed miserably. Edward Hopper was and remained a man who was only interested in himself, and he lived and died in splendid isolation.[16]

What he saw in both Hopper and van Gogh were qualities of the soul—quickened or dead—that spoke to him personally. To the degree that Hopper repelled him, another American artist appealed to him, an American artist who spoke to him in the same way as his beloved van Gogh: Georgia O'Keeffe: "Just as Vincent's story and his art cannot be separated, so Georgia's story and her art belong together. It's not just her paintings that hold me in her grip; it's also this most remarkable woman, whose intense search for intimacy and solitude is part of the art she created. *Seeing her art is seeing her life, and seeing her life is helping me see my own.*"[17]

What he discovered in O'Keeffe is what he most yearned for in himself: "a new integration of solitude, intimacy, and creativity in the decades ahead of me."[18] There is a special poignancy in this 1996 diary entry and in the close emotional connection he was developing with O'Keeffe: he didn't have decades left for him; he had months only.

Nouwen's phenomenological aesthetic owes much to his reading of Merton. The monk of Gethsemani validated his approach. Merton would write of his Rorschach-like illustrations or abstract markings—calligraphies—that accompanied his prose collection *Raids on the Unspeakable* that there was "no need to categorize these marks. It is better if they remain unidentified vestiges, signatures of someone who is not around."[19] When one "reads" them one discovers new possibilities of awareness, prods that alter perception, rich consonances that reverberate throughout one's life. Merton saw these drawings or signs, as he subsequently did with his astonishingly rich photographs of both animate and inanimate realities, as signs, sacraments, "transcending all logical interpretation," their very raison d'être as "summonses to awareness."[20]

The "hidden wholeness" to be found in the visual art of Thomas Merton is a reminder that "all matter, all life, is charged with *dharmakaya* [the essence of all beings] and that everything is emptiness and everything is compassion."[21] That "hidden wholeness" that he saw in the Hammer triptych is the "hidden wholeness" that readers discovered in his own art—literary and visual.

That very "hidden wholeness" for Nouwen was best realized in the brokenness of our humanity. This is the scandalizing mystery of Christianity, the shattering reason of Blaise Pascal's heart, the resplendent truth of Golgotha. It is the wisdom of the broken chalice.

Nouwen saw brokenness under the rubric of blessedness in a scene from Leonard Bernstein's 1971 music/theatre work, *Mass*, which he recalled a decade later when he wrote,

> Toward the end of this work, the priest, richly dressed in splendid liturgical vestments, is lifted up by his people. He towers high above the adoring crowd, carrying in his hands a glass chalice. Suddenly, the human pyramid collapses, and the priest comes tumbling down. His vestments are ripped off, and his glass chalice falls to the ground and is shattered. As he walks slowly through the debris of

his former glory—barefoot, wearing only his blue jeans and a T-shirt—children's voices are heard singing, "Laude, laude, laude"—"Praise, praise, praise." Suddenly the priest notices the broken chalice. He looks at it for a long time and then, haltingly, he says, "I never realized that broken glass could shine so brightly." Those words I will never forget...they capture the mystery of my life... and now, shortly after his death, of Bernstein's own splendid but tragic life.[22]

In this observation Nouwen underscores his conviction that art, whatever its medium, is the mirror of the soul, the soul of the creator/artist and the soul of the viewer/listener. Both are tied together in an act of pure seeing, in a moment of co-sympathy, in a metaphysical conversation grounded in beauty.

Merton and Nouwen were one in their belief that the spiritual is best mediated in the arts, that the cleansing of perception and pure seeing are the aperture to the divine, and that contemplation and solitude are the breeding ground, fecund territory, for the imagination.

Although Merton anticipated the Second Vatican Council through his work on returning to the biblical, patristic, and monastic sources, and through his exploration of various ecumenical and interfaith convergences, he survived the Council by barely three years. Nouwen, by contrast, was very much a product of the Council and its wisdom, shaped by its teaching and custom-changing dynamic.

For Nouwen, Merton recovered the contemplative tradition for the larger church, he reclaimed interiority and meditation as crucial ingredients of any meaningful humanist philosophy or anthropology, and he embodied for him, to an unprecedented degree, a theological and spiritual extra-territoriality that he wished to emulate in his own life and ministry.

Although Nouwen was Merton's disciple, his influence persisting through upheavals personal and ecclesial, there were many points where their lives were in alignment:

- they were both children of the twentieth-century (Thomas Merton: 1915–68; Henri Nouwen: 1932–96);

- they were enthralled by the fields of psychology and psychiatry, included numerous experts among their friends, drew on the work of pioneers in each of the disciplines both to write about and to employ for their own benefit (Merton experienced a period of depression in the monastery, and Nouwen was diagnosed with clinical depression and sent for treatment in Winnipeg);

- they both struggled with their sexuality, a constitutive dimension of their respective spiritual journey to maturation and integration;

- they both experienced the dynamic and often torturous tension between solitude and community;

- they both developed a "spirituality of peace-making" that was both all-pervasive and controversial;

- they experienced at its core the exacting demands of compassion in a time—personal and global—of dissolution;

- they feared the soul-destroying power of the cult of celebrity; and

- they remained throughout their writing lives quintessentially autobiographical.[23]

The centrality of contemplation in Merton's life was a key marker of Nouwen's attraction to the poet-monk. He recognized in Merton's christocentrism and devotion to prayer a kindred spirit. Contemplation for Merton is at the heart of the making of the fully human. Contemplation brings the subject into a rare intimacy with the Transcendent, allows for the casting off of the shackles of self-delusion, and ensures our true freedom. His understanding of contemplation was sophisticated, highly nuanced, historically flavored, and spiritually expansive. Merton knew that the revivifying springs of authentic contemplation nurture a deepening dialogue among all faiths, helping to build connections in an increasingly pluralistic world, valuing religious diversity and yet seeking new commonalities.

Nouwen read Merton with care and insight. He sought to pray as Merton would pray, sought to report on his spiritual life the way Merton reported on his, and struggled to balance the contraries of solitude and community.

But he also learned something from the sage of Gethsemani, and this is the Trappist twist that gave him validation: an epistemological and aesthetic openness that rooted him in the new realities revealed when one *sees* through cleansed doors of perception. In other words, it wasn't simply the cloistered contemplative who appealed to Nouwen. It was the artist in him, the Mozart in Merton, that shored up Nouwen's own identification with the artistic sensibility, freeing him to work outside the conventional constraints of academic discourse, the ratiocinative hegemony illustrative of William Blake's "Single vision."

As much in their anguish as in their self-honesty—sometimes searingly forthright—Merton and Nouwen shared corrosive bouts of self-doubt, compassion for the conflicted and the confounded, irrepressible energy, and almost pathological restiveness.

They were also surprised by their deaths: Merton's accidental electrocution in Thailand and Nouwen by heart attack in Holland. In a way, the drama of their passing only in part explains our fascination with their lives. After all, it is the drama of their spirituality that compels us to *attend*.

Nouwen's priestly life was enriched, nay, grounded, in Merton's *via contemplativa*. His universal pastorship, as he conceived it, would have him ministering in places far from the bucolic setting of a monastic cloister, and his counseling skills and homiletic genius deployed in ways that could never be fully exploited in an enclosed religious environment. Nouwen's spirit was regularly replenished by reading his beloved mentor, by spending two extended retreats in a Trappist community, and by imitating the art of the master diarist. In the end, however, the consecrated life of the institutional monastic was not to be his calling, reluctant though he was to admit it.

Nouwen was a Trappist wannabe. Though more important still, he was a conduit of Merton's insights to the larger world, integrating them with his own reflections, a foundational pillar of his life as a priest. The other priest pillar was John Henry Cardinal Newman, whose "distinction between real and notional assent set me on the mystical path."[24] The contours of that serpentine path were, however, best negotiated by Merton. In the end he remained the preeminent model surpassed, if at all, by Vincent van Gogh, an abiding priestly presence in his own right.

As the possibility of monastic life faded, another form of priestly ministry presented itself: priest as missionary.

THE LIBERATIONIST CRITIQUE

So Many and Such Grievous Outrages

In 1992, the conflicts generated by a centuries-old theological debate found its way to the stage and screen. *La Controverse de Valladolid*, originally a play written by Jean-Claude Carrière, was adapted for television and then distributed as a commercial film. Carrière's film credits illustrate the range of his interests: *The Unbearable Lightness of Being*, *Cyrano de Bergerac*, *The Discreet Charm of the Bourgeoisie*, *Swann in Love*, and *The Tin Drum*—works that tackle complex characters and challenging ideas. In this film about a sixteenth-century debate, Carrière explores the devastating consequence for indigenous peoples when Christian colonizers set about deciding who does and who does not possess a soul.

From the first frames of the film, Bartolomé de Las Casas has the look of someone suffering post-traumatic stress. He barely suppresses rage as the memories of the violence and injustice he has observed ever since his first crossing from Spain to the New World in 1502 continue to overwhelm him. On the other side of the courtroom, Juan de Sepulveda is unmoved by such displays of emotion. He has the collected works of Aristotle and St. Thomas Aquinas at the ready. At the slightest misuse of a word, he pounces. Sitting above these two opponents, the papal legate reminds them that he is not a referee, but the judge whose decision will be taken to the Vatican to become irrevocable papal policy.

Carrière presents a much-studied historic debate about slavery, theology, moral responsibility, and economics as a courtroom drama. The film was shot in the immense and shadow-filled chapel of the Cistercian abbey (now museum) of Le Thoronet in Provence. Carrière adapted the evidence from documents written by the Dominican and bishop of Chiapas, Bartolomé de Las Casas (1475/85?–1566), and the philosopher Juan Ginés de Sepúlveda (1494–1573). He distills the debate to a single question with consequences. Are indigenous people genuine descendants of Adam and Eve and therefore in possession of an immortal soul? If so, then what?

De Sepulveda uses visual aids to put this matter to the test. He arranges for a large Mayan stone-carved serpent to be hauled into the court to compare it with the elegant statuary and fine filigree stonework of the abbey where the debate is taking place. Then he brings in four indigenous people from Mexico, each dressed in traditional clothing. A woman holds her baby. Two adult males, not related to her, stand beside her. None can understand a word that is being spoken. On de Sepulveda's command, one of the guards snatches the baby from the woman's arms and threatens to kill it with his sword. The woman fights back ferociously as the men stand immobilized in fear. The baby cries for its mother as de Sepulveda asserts that the men's inaction proves their lack of humanity and thus their possession of a soul. He introduces a second test. Since laughter, he asserts, is universal, de Sepulveda invites clowns to perform for the panic-struck Mayans. The clowns' antics are in the tradition of *commedia dell'arte*, filled with playful overstated violence and sexual innuendo. The note-taking monks in the gallery laugh at their antics as the indigenous adults watch in confusion and silence, another obvious demonstration of their lesser humanity.

When it is his turn, the fictional de Las Casas begins to build his case, citing events he has observed on the island of Hispaniola, where he says with remorse that he was, briefly, a slave owner. He concedes this was an error, and then, after a conversion experience, he decided to establish a different kind of community in Venezuela, one based on tolerance and understanding, rather than on slavery and exploitation. The actual de Las Casas did manage an estate and owned slaves before concluding this was immoral. He returned to Spain, where he entered religious life and, in 1515, was ordained, later joining the Dominicans. The on-screen de Las Casas describes the centuries-old cultures of the indigenous peoples he has met, their firm religious beliefs and practices, their strong family bonds, and how some had already converted to Christianity. There could be no doubt, he says, about their full humanity.

After deliberating on what he has seen and heard, the celluloid legate/judge concludes that indigenous peoples do indeed have souls and are worthy of just and human treatment and liberation from slavery. Then he adds a "but" that will have catastrophic consequences for centuries. Aware that releasing slaves will disrupt the colonial economy, he adds a codicil to his decision. To allay the potential labor shortage throughout Spain's extensive colonies, it would be appropriate to bring "lesser" slaves to replace any liberated indigenous peoples. There was one place in the world where they could be found. Slaves from Africa could be transported and exploited without difficulty, since unlike the indigenous peoples of the Americas whom he had just confirmed were indeed fully human, the status of those captured in Africa had yet to be determined. As the courtroom empties, out of the shadows enters an African man who begins to sweep away the dust.

The encounter with "strangers who had never heard the gospel was a challenge to the church's self-understanding," writes a current fellow Dominican brother of de Las Casas, Timothy Radcliffe.[1] Such an encounter, he says, forced the question: What kind of community is the church? "This is a drama which we are still living through today, as the church is becoming, for the first time, truly global, the most profoundly global institution in existence."[2]

The "real" Bartolomé de Las Casas is celebrated as a "defender of the Indians."[3] In 1975, the editor of his collected works, Angel Losada, argued that de Las Casas was ahead of his time because of his insights into basic human rights. His calls for "the mutual respect of race, religion and culture" made him "a forerunner of the modern concept of racial, cultural, political and religious pluralism."[4] It is hardly surprising, then, that de Las Casas has a recurring presence in the work of the Peruvian priest and liberation theologian Gustavo Gutiérrez, whose 1971 book, *Teologia de la liberación, Perpectivas*, rapidly attained international classic status.[5]

In *¡Gracias! A Latin American Journal*, Nouwen explains that his 1981 post-Yale move to Bolivia and Peru was his response to a fundamental question he had about his vocation: Was God calling him to live and work in Latin America in the years to come?[6] In a now-familiar pattern in his career, the only way was for him to go and take a look and find someone—a living human document—who might help in this discernment. He had already taken a few small steps in this direction with short-term "excursions" and "piecemeal involvements and limited commitments" as he called them, in Mexico, Chile, and Paraguay.[7] These experiences haunted him for a decade, he said, and that was why, during his stay at the Abbey of the Genesee, he began a more systematic preparation. After consulting with the Maryknoll Fathers and Brothers, the American-based missionary order founded in 1911 by Father James Anthony Walsh and Father Thomas Frederick Price, he took a three-month language training program in Cochabamba in Bolivia. Nouwen's subsequent travels in Latin and South America were coordinated through and supported by Maryknoll.

Nouwen struggled through Spanish classes for three months and in January 1982, traveled to Peru for a twelve-week immersion experience of contemporary missionary activity, including an experience of living with a family in Pamplona Alta, a rough-and-tumble area of Lima. In addition to the usual shocked observations typical of North American and European professionals witnessing extreme poverty, Nouwen writes in his journal something that reveals a consequence of his exclusive formation and career to date. He was shocked by the "new" experience of being in a family where children, parents, and grandparents interacted daily. From the age of eighteen his "family" had been his fellow seminarians, his priest colleagues, and then the university with its "worlds of young adults, worlds in which children and old people hardly entered."[8] At almost fifty years of age, he confesses that this is his first genuine encounter with children, "affectionate, open, playful children who are telling me about love and life in ways no book was ever able to do."[9] This is a telling confession in the people-before-books spirit of Anton Boisen, who preferred turning first to living human documents before reaching for theories.

In Lima, he joined the hundreds of participants in the annual courses given by Gustavo Gutiérrez. In addition to these church-run courses, Gutiérrez founded an independent center in 1974, which he named after de Las Casas. His *Instituto Bartolomé de Las Casas* was a research and training center for the promotion of inclusive democracy and social justice, as well as the principles and practices of liberation theology.[10] The course put Nouwen in the company of students from Chile, Brazil, Colombia, Paraguay, Uruguay, Argentina, Panama, and Nicaragua who were preparing to become "active pastoral agents in the process of liberation."[11] Most of them had been born and raised in barrios. Their social justice work required them to think "with one eye on the gospel and one eye on the painful reality they shared with the people."[12] In addition to these students were visiting priests and religious, mostly from the United States, Great Britain, and Ireland. This annual program alternated its focus each year from theology, to Christology, and to spirituality. After lectures, each afternoon, there were discussion groups, and Gutiérrez was the star attraction.

Toward the end of his time in Peru in March of 1982, Nouwen visited *Instituto Bartolomé de Las Casas*, hoping to meet with Gutiérrez. He was surprised to learn that this symbol of the liberation theology movement was a simple house in a Lima suburb. Unfortunately, Gutiérrez was not there that day. Nouwen spoke with members of the research staff instead, sociologists and theologians. He asked them how they did their research into popular religious practices, about the life experiences of the poor, and the role of the poor as active agents in their own history. They discussed the complex dynamic of the relationship between the church and society in Latin America. He was impressed by the center's commitment to stay close to the Peruvian poor and its method of work that begins with solidarity that might lead to conversion. The discussion touched on the process of liberation and how it is born from an individual's and a community's experience of injustice.[13] What he heard and saw at the *Instituto* confirmed "one of the oldest of truths: that *theologia* is not primarily a way of thinking, but a way of living. Liberation theologians do not think themselves into a new way of living but live themselves into a new way of thinking."[14]

Two possible scenarios emerged. First, Nouwen arranged to meet with Bishop Herman Schmidt, an auxiliary bishop of Lima to discuss the possibility of returning to Peru for a much longer visit to learn more about working with the poor. This initial stay had not been long enough. He told the bishop that seeing the children had given him a rare glimpse of God. The pragmatic bishop explained that what he needed was help in the promotion of spiritual growth and formation in the communities where people lived. The annual Lima courses required people to take time off, travel from the country to the city, and find accommodation. It would be up to the cardinal of Lima to approve any such arrangement. Nouwen left the meeting with the sense that something was "becoming visible that might prove to be more than just a fantasy."[15]

The second option involved Gutiérrez, a potential mentor whom Nouwen was keen to meet. He arranged a formal meeting with him. Gutiérrez was supportive of Nouwen's proposal to return to Peru for an extended stay to do pastoral work, live in a parish, and get to know the poor and their conditions of life in the barrios. Nouwen's academic experience gave him the potential to become a valuable member of the teaching staff at the *Instituto*. Nouwen says he still felt like a "lonely bystander" and was noncommittal about the prospect of teaching during the meeting. He felt the nature of his vocational call in the South was still not clear to him.

On the last day of the program, Gutiérrez gave a presentation that focused on the example of the archbishop of El Salvador, Oscar Romero, who was assassinated as he celebrated Mass in the chapel of the Divine Providence Hospital in San Salvador on March 24, 1980. In his early career, Romero was a cautious cleric who "sought to temper the stridency of some proponents of liberation theology," but who eventually managed "to overcome the limits his own conservative instincts might have placed on his perspective and field of operation."[16] Romero became both "a touchstone of hope for the oppressed of El Salvador and lightning rod of resentment among its ruling elite."[17] Nouwen writes that Gutiérrez used the example of Romero to explain a larger historical process. The Christians of Latin America, Gutiérrez said, had undergone a major shift from a traditional to a revolutionary understanding of their faith. Such a transition typically involves an intermediary phase of modernization, but this had not been the case in Latin America. The way that Romero made the shift from former "traditional" churchman to "true revolutionary" was the same process because it was brought about through direct contact with the poor all around him, without an intermediary process in between. Whenever there is a dramatic shift from one paradigm to another—in this case traditional to revolutionary—the challenge is invariably one of trust. Both sides are naturally suspicious about the motives underlying such dramatic change. Is this a flirtation or a fully committed embrace of an idea? Romero's example proved that past actions are not impediments to new ways of thinking and being. This was also "true of most Latin American Christians who joined the movement for liberation. Their traditional understanding of the teachings of the Church was never a hindrance to their conversion. On the contrary, it was the basis for change," reported Nouwen in his notes.[18]

Robert Ellsberg describes Romero, whose cause for beatification soon ran into difficulties, as someone who "continues to walk ahead of the church," albeit a church that has struggled with the implications, both symbolic and political, in any canonization process. "What is the gospel message that his life proclaims? What significance does it hold for the Church of our time and for the future?"[19] For some, the Romero message was embroiled in divisive church and state politics, and for others, it represented an unwavering, uncompromising faith. What mattered to the poor of El Salvador was that many of them had been taught by a living saint who spoke to them directly in his frequent radio broadcasts. They acclaimed him "San Romero de los Americas" even as his funeral was taking place in 1980. The official process to promote his cause began in 1993. Pope John Paul II declared him a Servant of God in 1997, and then the process stopped, caught in a debate as to whether Romero was killed "in hatred of the faith" (*odium fidei*), the essential criterion for using of the term *martyr*. During an in-flight media conference in 2014, while traveling back to Rome from South Korea, Pope Francis explained the delay:

> The process was at the Congregation for the Doctrine of the Faith, blocked "for prudential reasons," so they said. Now it is unblocked. It has been passed to the Congregation for Saints. And it is following the usual procedure for such processes. It depends on how the postulators move it forward.

This is very important, to do it quickly. What I would like is a clarification about martyrdom *in odium fidei*, whether it can occur either for having confessed the Creed or for having done the works which Jesus commands with regard to one's neighbour. And this is a task for the theologians. They are studying it....For me Romero is a man of God, but the process has to be followed, and the Lord too has to give his sign....If he wants to do it, he will do it. But right now the postulators have to move forward because there are no obstacles.[20]

In February 2015, Pope Francis issued the decree of martyrdom for Archbishop Romero, clearing the path to his beatification, and three months later, the finally acknowledged martyr Oscar Romero was beatified in a ceremony in San Salvador. It was attended by an estimated 260,000 people, as large a gathering as attended his funeral, thirty-five years earlier. The prefect of the Congregation for the Causes of Saints, Cardinal Angelo Amato, read a letter from Pope Francis on the nature of Oscar Romero's priestly vocation:

In times of difficult coexistence, Archbishop Romero knew how to lead, defend and protect his flock, remaining faithful to the Gospel and in communion with the whole Church. His ministry was distinguished by particular attention to the most poor and marginalized. And at the moment of his death, while he celebrated the Holy Sacrifice of love and reconciliation, he received the grace to identify himself fully with the One who gave his life for his sheep.

On this feast day for the Salvadorian nation, and also for the neighboring Latin American countries, let us give thanks to God because He granted the martyred Bishop the ability to *see* and *hear* the suffering of his people, and molded his heart so that, in His name, he could direct them and illuminate them, to the point of making of his work a full exercise of Christian charity.[21]

Finally, on October 14, 2018, Pope Francis officiated at the canonization of St. Oscar Romero in a celebration of seven blesseds, including Pope Paul VI and five others. The crowd was much smaller that day, estimated at seventy thousand. The Catholics of El Salvador had already claimed their saint. In his homily, Pope Francis said that Romero "left the security of the world, even his own safety, in order to give his life according to the Gospel, close to the poor and to his people, with a heart drawn to Jesus and his brothers and sisters."

In a reflection on Romero's enduring example to Catholics around the world, Mary Jo Leddy, one of the founders of Romero House in Toronto, wrote, "The Catholic Church has often suffered from poor leadership and from the sins of the clergy and laypeople. Yet, mysteriously, it continues to summon people of courage and grace who bear witness to the many and varied ways of holiness."[22]

In his pilgrimage-like journey into the lived experiences of liberation theology, Nouwen continued to struggle with his own many and varied ways of holiness. Before returning to New York state, he attended a liturgical celebration to mark what was the second anniversary of Romero's murder. He described it as a mysterious experience "in which grief and joy, gladness and sadness merged."[23] Then, reconciled with his decision to return to the more familiar church in North America, on March 29, 1982, he took an overnight flight from Lima to Miami, then Washington, and finally Rochester, New York, to drive to the Abbey of the Genesee the following afternoon.

A few years later, when Nouwen was living in the L'Arche Daybreak community, he returned to the example of Romero. He has been asked to write an introduction to an anthology of Romero's essays and homilies. "His words are a clear call to conversion and action," he writes, "and I am called to confess my role in the violence that Oscar Romero condemns, to ask for forgiveness for my sins against the people who are exploited and oppressed, and to be converted."[24]

Meanwhile, back in the Genesee guesthouse, he was invited to live with the community as a "family brother." He left Peru with an invitation to return. It was not in the form of a printed document, but rather a strong feeling that he understood was his "true invitation" to find a way to return to Peru for a much longer stay. This is a potential conversion and action moment in his career though there is ambiguity about it in the pages of ¡Gracias! Although the book takes the form of a journal recording events and thoughts as they arise, it is also a structured and crafted literary work that takes the reader on a journey with a destination, in this case the conclusion that the question about the next phase in his vocation is a matter that is settled. He will go back because his career path has only ever been directed by his own interests and the invitations he has received. Unlike many priests, he has not been the recipient of directives from the archdiocese's Vicar General concerning his next posting.

He was back in the United States, seemingly preparing for a radical refocusing of his ministry. But that did not happen, and it would take him several years to express clearly his reasons for not returning to Peru. He eventually conceded that he had felt incapable of doing effective ministry and pastoral work in a Spanish-speaking country. He regretted that his need for "more emotional support than my fellow missioners could offer" was also a factor. He also acknowledged that the complexity of what he had seen in Latin America had left him feeling "discouraged and dispirited."[25] He does write about these issues in the pages of *¡Gracias!*, but he does not raise the issue of nonreturn. What he does reveal clearly in this book, however, are his serious experiences of depression and his recurring states of anxiety. This was more than awkward restlessness, it was a crippling uncertainty that seemed to have cast an increasingly dark shadow on his career thus far. It was his belief that whatever direction he chose to pursue and wherever he chose to try and live it, he would invariably discover his inability to translate the experience into a feeling that he had finally found his "home"—or, in the language of Thomas Merton, discover his true self. Merton explored this concept in his 1961 book, *New Seeds of Contemplation*, published when Nouwen was still deep in psychological research in the Netherlands:

> Every one of us is shadowed by an illusory person: a false self.

> The secret of my identity is hidden in the love and mercy of God.

> Our vocation is not simply to be, but to work together with God in the creation of our own life, our own identity, our own destiny.

In order to become myself I must cease to be what
I always thought I wanted to be, and in order to
find myself, and order to live I have to die.[26]

These ideas certainly resonate in the decisions that
Nouwen made once he was back in North America, where
his immediate and temporary home was the abbey guesthouse, from which he also participated in the daily routine of
prayer, work, and reading according to Trappist practice. It
was a routine that enabled him to catch up with innumerable
letters, phone messages, requests for retreats and speaking
engagements, as well as for polishing the final manuscript
that would become ¡Gracias! One of the requests came from
Lima. In We Drink from Our Own Wells: The Spiritual
Journey of a People, Gustavo Gutiérrez turns to Bernard of
Clairvaux for the title of his book, and to Henri Nouwen for
an introduction to the English edition. Gutiérrez took his title
from a line in De Consideratione, St. Bernard's commentary
on what it takes to become a good pope. Gutiérrez chose a
phrase from the Cistercian book about the tension between
contemplation and action that Thomas Merton thought was
"a profound and succinct handbook on meditation and mental prayer."[27]

In his introduction to the Gutiérrez book, Nouwen
adapts some material from ¡Gracias! and comments on what
he has learned from Gutiérrez and how it forced him to reas-
sess his own ideas about spirituality, contemplation, and
action. Nouwen identifies the comfortable spirituality that is
distinctly different from spirituality that is born of struggle.
He confesses he has been made aware "how individualistic
and elitist my own spirituality has been" and characterizes it
as "spirituality for introspective persons who have the luxury

of the time and space needed to develop inner harmony and quietude."[28] In contrast, the spirituality of liberation is not a personal but "a truly biblical spirituality that allows God's saving act in history to penetrate all levels of human existence. God is seen here as the God of the living who enters into humanity's history to dispel the forces of death, wherever they are at work, and to call forth the healing and reconciling forces of life."[29]

With the introduction complete, Nouwen then turned his attention to some healing and reconciling acts of his own. Having lived the life of an ordained priest for a quarter of a century, he wanted to mark this anniversary with an event that could bring colleagues past and present, students past and present, advisors, and especially his many friends under one big tent that he rented for the occasion. The celebration was held on the grounds of the abbey, and the guest list expanded to more than two hundred people. Robert Ellsberg was on that list. He had recently converted to Catholicism and was editing Dorothy Day's *Catholic Worker* newspaper in New York. Ellsberg had met Nouwen a few years earlier on a visit to Yale. He invited Nouwen to write some pieces for the newspaper. "It's a long journey that our friendship took. It had dry spells and difficult turns as well," explains Ellsberg.[30] "I have to say that in the beginning I was a little bit wary of his enthusiasm. I know that he had a way of responding very deeply and genuinely and often overwhelmingly to opportunities for friendship, particularly with young people and where he recognized some sort of spark or promise of connection and understanding. I was a little surprised, at least, that this rather eminent person should show so much deep interest in me."

In advance of this large-scale celebration, Nouwen also arranged for a more intimate preparatory retreat with a smaller group of participants who were invited to spend a week in prayer and reflection. Ellsberg was also on that list. "He also wanted to show off the monastery and introduce us to the abbot, John Eudes Bamberger," he recalls. "I had been very affected by Thomas Merton and Trappist spirituality, and it was very attractive to me as a recent convert. It was a wonderful few days. I remember Henri Nouwen making a speech in which he thanked the abbot for offering this kind of home to him. He said, 'I've been wandering for many years and finally, here at Genesee, I feel I've found my true home.'"

A week later, Ellsberg received a surprising phone call from Nouwen. "He said, 'I've been offered this job at Harvard Divinity School, and I think maybe I should take it. What do you think?' I said, 'Well, I thought Genesee was going to be your true home now.' And he said, 'Well the abbot says maybe it's not such a good idea for me to do that.'"

Nouwen had decided to join the faculty of the Divinity school in the 1983–84 academic year. He was appointed professor of divinity and Horace Lentz lecturer, a teaching position that required his presence on campus for only one semester each academic year. Once again, Nouwen demonstrated his skill in the art of the deal. This arrangement gave him time for travel, discernment, research, and perhaps an opportunity, finally, to settle the question of his vocational focus. His initial courses were on Christian spirituality and liberation theology. He arrived at Harvard as a popular author with a large international following, an extensive publishing history, and with a distinctly theatrical teaching style, one that the *Harvard Gazette* explained was his "unusual ability to enable persons to enter in the Scriptures, theological reflection and prayer, so as to discover their own deeper spirituality and its relationship to the needs of the modern world."[31] He served as a member of faculty for three turbulent years and in addition to limited teaching responsibilities, and sometimes writing, and a great deal of public speaking, all the while trying to finally identify the direction and shape of his priestly vocation.

Something about intentional communities attracted his attention. What Nouwen had experienced in Peru was a mix of examples of community life that exuded "joy, peace, and true love" that grew naturally from a theological perspective and approach to community-building that was decidedly countercultural.[32] This resonated with what he had seen while "clowning" in Rome (the San Egidio Community), and in France (the Taizé Community), and in the example of Mother (now St.) Teresa's Missionaries of Charity. In 1979, in *Clowning in Rome*, he included another example. He wrote that he found great hope in the kind of work that the Canadian humanitarian Jean Vanier was doing. At the time, the two had not yet met.[33] Reading that line in Trosly-Breuil, the village in northeastern France where he had established the first L'Arche community, Jean Vanier asked one of the L'Arche community leaders in the United States to contact Nouwen to see if a meeting might be arranged. Vanier saw an opportunity when, in 1981 he planned to attend a silent Ignatian retreat in Indiana. "I suggested that we meet in South Bend. So that's where it really began," explains Vanier.[34] "I met Henri there and we talked. Every morning we would meet before breakfast and right after breakfast, and we talked together."

Their conversations led to an invitation from Nouwen for Vanier to come and speak to his classes in Harvard. There,

the highly intuitive Vanier sensed that something was seriously wrong with Nouwen. "He had amazing success there, I
mean, he was deeply appreciated, deeply loved. We must have
shared quite a bit, and he talked quite a bit about his dissatisfaction at living as a professor, with lots of students but no
real pastoral ministry, no real bonding. Students come and
students go."

Then he made an offer.

"I invited him to come and spend time in Trosly-
Breuil."[35]

In 1983, during a sabbatical, Nouwen flew to France to
spend six weeks observing the living human documents of a
L'Arche community established for people living with intellectual and other disabilities. That invitation planted as seed,
one that Nouwen says gave him the first inkling that his
"prayer to follow Jesus more radically was being heard."[36]
He watched, listened, prayed, and spoke with Vanier whenever he could. Although L'Arche gave him a tantalizing sense
of what might be called "at-homeness," some seeds fail to
thrive, others take a little longer to germinate.

Sabbatical over and back in Cambridge, Massachusetts,
Nouwen had teaching responsibilities and commitments at
the Divinity School. The next summer, there was also an invitation that arrived from a friend to return briefly to Latin
America, to a Maryknoll mission in Guatemala. He accepted
the invitation.

There was something poetic about the timing of
Nouwen's ten-day visit to the Mayan community of Santiago
Atitlán in the volcano-ringed southern interior of Guatemala.
That summer, the prefect of the Congregation for the Doctrine
of the Faith, (then) Joseph Cardinal Ratzinger (later Pope
Benedict XVI), issued a document on liberation theology.[37] It

stated that "the aspiration for justice often finds itself captive of ideologies which hide or pervert its meaning" (II 3), that the diverse positions of liberation theologies have frontiers that are "badly defined" (III 3), that its uses of Scripture are reductionist and contain "a disastrous confusion between the 'poor' of the Scripture and the 'proletariat' of Marx" (IX 10). And then the Instruction becomes geographically specific:

> In certain parts of Latin America, the seizure of the vast majority of the wealth by an oligarchy of owners bereft of social consciousness, the practical absence or the shortcomings of a rule of law, military dictators making a mockery of elementary human rights, the corruption of certain powerful officials, the savage practices of some foreign capital interests constitute factors which nourish a passion for revolt among those who thus consider themselves the powerless victims of a new colonialism in the technological, financial, monetary, or economic order. The recognition of injustice is accompanied by a pathos which borrows its language from Marxism, wrongly presented as though it were scientific language.[38]

The reason for Nouwen's decision to return to Central America was someone he had never met, a murdered missionary priest from the Catholic Archdiocese of Oklahoma, Stanley Francis Rother, killed by a Guatemalan death squad in 1981. The priest who elected to replace him at the mission was in the seminary with Rother and had also become a friend of Nouwen. John Vesey, born in Brooklyn, was, like Rother, a priest from the Archdiocese of Oklahoma. He and

Nouwen had studied Spanish together in the Maryknoll language school in Cochabamba, Bolivia, in the early 1970s and they had stayed in contact. Vesey had willingly taken on this extremely dangerous assignment in war-torn Guatemala, and he encouraged Nouwen to visit, observe, and pray with him and all the members of the mission community as they continued to try and come to terms with the murder of a charismatic and popular leader. The civil war in Guatemala that began in 1960 gave little hope for a peaceable ending, and the mission was increasingly vulnerable.

Founded under its official name, Micatokla, by the Diocese of Oklahoma and Tulsa in 1964, the mission was a response to Pope John XXIII's appeals for help, beginning with paragraph 56 of *Princeps pastorum*, his 1959 encyclical on Missions, Native Clergy, and Lay Participation:

> We exhort all the bishops, the clergy, and the faithful of the dioceses of the whole world, who are contributing to relieve the spiritual and material necessities of the missions by their prayers and offerings, to increase voluntarily their badly needed contributions. Despite the scarcity of priests which besets even the pastors of the oldest dioceses, there should be no hesitation in encouraging missionary vocations and in releasing the very best and most useful laymen, that they may be placed at the disposal of the new dioceses; heavenly consolations will soon be derived from this sacrifice, made for the furtherance of God's cause.[39]

In August of 1961, Monsignor (later Cardinal) Agostino Casaroli, who was then serving as undersecretary of the

Sacred Congregation for Extraordinary Ecclesiastical Affairs (the Vatican's foreign ministry), challenged the Catholic Church in America directly. Speaking on behalf of John XXIII, he proposed that Catholic dioceses and religious orders in the United States should send one-tenth of their priests and their male and female religious to support missionary work in Latin America.[40]

The Archdiocese of Oklahoma and Tulsa heeded that call. By 1964, it was ready to send one of its priests, Ramon Carlin, to Guatemala to set up a mission team of religious (local Carmelite sisters) and laypeople to work with the Tzutuhil and Ladino (mestizo) communities in the village of Santiago-Atitlán. Carlin's model involved the creation of a multidisciplinary missionary team offering four distinct programs: worship (focusing on the local language), catechetics (focusing on popular education techniques including training for radio production), public health (starting with the creation of a clinic at the mission, which was eventually replaced by a larger hospital) and agricultural development (starting with model farming practices).

Carlin eventually turned his focus exclusively on the Tzutuhil language and left the mission to work on translation at an indigenous language institute in Antigua, Guatemala. Enter Stanley Rother. Born in Okarche, Oklahoma, in 1935, he prepared for the priesthood in San Antonio, Texas, and Mount St. Mary in Maryland, where he met John Vesey. He was ordained a priest of the Diocese of Oklahoma City and Tulsa in 1963 and served in various Oklahoma parishes until 1968, when he took over from Ramon Carlin. Rother was tall, physically strong, and used to hard manual work. During his time at the mission, in addition to the usual liturgical and pastoral duties, he completed reconstruction work on the rectory and church, added a well and a water pump, and managed, in time, to get a hospital built to replace the mission's small clinic. Like Carlin, Rother understood the importance of indigenous languages and helped in the translation of portions of the New Testament into Tzutuhil. From 1973 onward, he celebrated Mass in that language. All this work was carried out under the shadow of the escalating violence of a civil war where the "sides" were not always obvious, though the mangled corpses of those caught up in the conflicts were found in the ditches every day.

In his 1980 Christmas letter to his Oklahoma supporters, Rother wrote, "The shepherd cannot run at the first sign of danger."[41] Within weeks, he learned that his name was on one of the militia's death lists. Typically, targeted victims were kidnapped, tortured for any names and incriminating information they might provide, and then killed, their shattered bodies dumped at the side of the road, usually miles away from where they were abducted. The diocese determined that Rother should return to the safety of Oklahoma, and for the next four months he did as he was advised. Then he returned once more to the mission, where once again he was warned, this time by a government source, that he should leave immediately if he wanted to get back to the United States alive. Rother chose to stay with the people he had come to serve.

On July 28, 1981, three masked and armed men entered the mission's rectory with the intent of kidnapping him. Rother was not going to become a victim of torture. He put up a ferocious fight. Realizing that they were not going to be able to drag him away as they had planned, they shot him in the head twice and ran away. He was one of ten priests murdered that year in Guatemala.

When John Vesey arrived at Santiago-Atitlán, he had to address the difficult question of what to do with the still-bloodstained room where Rother had been murdered. "I could not understand why for three years the room had remained empty and unused," he told Nouwen.[42] He decided to convert the room—a bullet hole still unrepaired in the floor—into the community chapel.

Nouwen spent only ten days in Guatemala, six of them at the mission with his friend Vesey.[43] It was an intense immersion in mission practices amid armed conflict and an oppressive, violent, unstable government. It was a challenge to a primary element of his vocation: the psychological impact on all those involved in this kind of work. What does a psychologist and writer on contemporary spirituality offer amid such violence and vulnerability? Nouwen's Jesuit exposure offered some wisdom, the result of the Society's long history of mission work, often in the context of violence, and especially in the Americas and Asia. Writing from India to a fellow Jesuit in 1544, St. Francis Xavier captures the timeless and irreconcilable tension of wanting to be of service and, at the same time, being aware of your inability to address the root causes of an issue. It is a timeless and contemporary challenge, though Xavier's language reinforces the paternalistic condescension of his time and culture. (At least the indigenous people he speaks of here are considered children rather than soulless slaves.)

Show the people you are with...very great kindness and charity, and aim at making yourself beloved in return. Be quite sure that if you are beloved by them, you will be able to turn their hearts whatever way you wish. Bear with moderation and wisdom all their weaknesses and infirmities, and say to yourself that if they are not yet all that you desire, in time at least, they will become so. If you cannot get out of them all the good you ask, take what you can get. You know this is my way.

...If you cannot do all you wish, be glad to do what you can, since it is not your fault that all the progress which you might desire has not been made. If you sometimes find yourself distracted by a number of duties that you cannot manage at all, do as much as you can and be content with that, and even give thanks to God for the particular blessing that He has led you to work in a place where there are so many sacred duties to be performed that you cannot be idle, however much you might wish it, for this is in truth one of the greatest blessings that God bestows.[44]

Xavier concludes by turning to the unresolved anger that grows out of helplessness:

I tell you plainly, I am sometimes weary of my life, and think I had better rather die for religion than live in the sight of so many and such grievous outrages upon the majesty of God, especially when I cannot help seeing them and yet cannot prevent them.[45]

Nouwen describes his time in Guatemala as another turning point in his lifelong conversion process. He says it gave him a glimpse of a form of deep friendship within religious life.[46] He had known Vesey for more than a decade, and it was clear they had much in common, as the descriptors

Nouwen uses for his friend illustrate: "He is moving, talking, calling, planning, organizing, teaching, and preaching all the time. He laughs, and teases whenever he has a chance."[47] Then there's a major difference: Vesey "hides little and shows his heart to anyone who wants to see it." Despite the autobiographical tone of many of his published works, Nouwen's personal disclosures are highly selective. The two friends shared a common approach to an intensive form of prayer, and Nouwen observed that Vesey "belongs to his prayer. Prayer is living in unceasing communion with God and God's people."[48] Vesey saw how important it was for Nouwen to join the parish community in prayer the moment he arrived at Atitlán. Nouwen believed that Vesey thought that prayer was a matter of "letting one's heart become the place where the tears of God and the tears of God's children can merge and become tears of hope."[49]

Vesey possessed a quality that Nouwen found disarming, a childlike directness about his faith and easy laughter that served to prevent Nouwen from becoming "too introspective or melancholy" in his company. Vesey thought that Nouwen seemed to consider himself a less strong individual than Vesey had observed. In Vesey, Nouwen saw an attractive model of an integrated and focused priestly vocation: "John is a fine example of someone who is able to grow and mature by loving people around him so sincerely that they are eager to give him their best. This makes him an excellent priest. He helps people discover how much they are worth, not only in his eyes, but in God's eyes."[50] Vesey demonstrated what Nouwen called spiritual alertness, a "rare gift of discernment in the midst of his highly complex and often ambiguous political and socioeconomic context."[51] In these spiritually based judgments, Nouwen says he found hope, courage, and confidence, both personally and professionally.

It was important to Nouwen that they were friends and not mere colleagues, because he had come to believe that friendship was at the core of his own spiritual journey. "God has given me many friends, and each of them has played a significant role in my thinking, feeling, speaking, and acting. Some of these friendships have been intense, painful, and marked by turmoil, while others have been calm, steady, and gentle."[52] This particular friendship gave him challenging insights into his own evolving vocation as a priest. He used this newly acquired hope, courage, and confidence to talk with Vesey about some of the issues he was trying to come to terms with. "I started to share with him more of my own joy and sorrow and let him see my struggles."[53] A reluctant return to Harvard topped the list.

At the end of their short time together, Vesey asked Nouwen if he would consider writing about Stanley Rother, perhaps produce something to help the Archdiocese of Oklahoma in its effort to promote the cause for his recognition as a martyr, his beatification, and eventual canonization. Nouwen stunned him with his answer. He confided in Vesey that he had not been able to write anything for the past year and a half.

"And with my request," says Vesey, "his cross only grew heavier."[54]

The magic realist novelist António Antunes describes the state of disorientation faced by explorers, colonists, missionaries, and idealists who are forced to return to the place where their journeys began. In *The Return of the Caravels*, he reimagines strangely distorted versions of Vasco de Gama, Francis Xavier, and dozens of other characters from centuries of Spanish and Portuguese colonial history and has them react to life in Lisbon during the 1970s. When they arrived, their only baggage "was a small bundle in their hands and incurable sourness in their breasts...like angels who've lost the skill of flight and were ruffling their earthbound feet through the saddest districts of the city, made up of slopes that led nowhere."[55]

Nouwen's own ruffled earthbound feet led him back to Cambridge, Massachusetts, the home of Harvard's Divinity School.

8

THE HARVARD YEARS

A Crisis of Identity

It was the end, the end. It was the beginning of the voyage, the quest of new lands." After attending the small provincial college of Pulpit Hill, Eugene Gant was on his way, finally, to Harvard University in *Look Homeward Angel: A Story of the Buried Life*, Thomas Wolfe's 1929 grandly sprawling novel about restlessness and growth.[1] By 1983, a decade-and-a-half of university teaching behind him, Henri Nouwen described his journey to Harvard not as a quest but as a "reverse mission." He believed that by accepting the invitation from Harvard Divinity School, he would be able to continue working in the familiar milieu of academic life in North America, while at the same time, find ways to serve the Latin American church by drawing attention to its circumstances in his classes and frequent public presentations across the United States. He negotiated a contract that required him to teach only one semester in each academic year, an arrangement that would allow him to return regularly to the world that the Maryknoll Mission movement had opened up for him in Latin and South America.[2] This decision surprised many who had assumed that his next port of call would most likely be somewhere in Latin America, given his recent travels to Bolivia, Peru, Nicaragua, Mexico, and Guatemala. Nouwen explained the decision to one of his readers who was curious and described it as a determination to remain open to his

165

calling. He wrote that God often changes people in ways that "we were not planning on and that sometimes we do not have eyes to see or ears to hear these changes in ourselves. I deeply believe that God is always active in us and always moulding us into new people."[3]

Nouwen's "reverse mission" began with a ten-week speaking tour across North America talking about his experiences in Latin America and directing attention to the enormous challenges that poor and indigenous people were facing in so many politically unstable and war-torn conditions. Then, from his new position at Harvard, he would be able to switch the conventional direction of mission activity and continue his commitment to serve the church in the South, making it his mission to inform the North about the conditions of their brothers and sisters in the South. As with his previous university position at Yale, this one was undertaken with the (seemingly endlessly patient) support and approval of his seventy-four-year-old archbishop in Utrecht, now Johannes Cardinal Willebrands, who, as required by canon law, would have to resign that position in 1983.

After two frustrating years at Harvard, Eugene Gant, in *Of Time and the River: A Legend of Man's Hunger in His Youth*, Wolfe's sequel to *Look Homeward Angel*, felt uncomfortably trapped. He realized that his career and life decisions had been shaped and imposed on him. It was time now for him to make his own decision about moving on from Harvard. "With the old feeling of groping bewilderment, he surveyed the history of the last two years and wondered why he had come, why he was here, toward what blind goal he had been tending: all that he had to 'show' for these years of fury, struggle, homelessness and hunger was an academic distinction which he had not aimed at, and on which he placed small value."[4]

It took Nouwen three years to realize why he ought to leave Harvard, despite its initial enthusiastically welcoming embrace.

Nouwen began his "reverse mission" with public lectures and retreats that were crowded with students and many people from off and on campus who were drawn to see this famous author and his energetic and impassioned style of presentation. With Nouwen a kind of circus had arrived at Harvard Divinity School. "I was so taken with him," recalls Robert Jonas, who was then a Harvard graduate student in Educational Psychology. He attended one of Nouwen's presentations in the basement of St. Paul's Church in Harvard Square, home of Harvard's Catholic Center. "Henri came on and he started kind of slowly, speaking about God and our relationship with God, and our belovedness in God, and about Jesus."[5]

Fascinated by Nouwen's "long, lanky body, long fingers, his prancing around the room with this incredible physical, spiritual energy," Jonas realized that the Jesus Nouwen was speaking about reminded him "of the Jesus I had met as a [Lutheran] kid. When Henri used the name Jesus, he didn't mean the historical person, Jesus. He meant the eternal presence of God that appeared in Jesus but is everywhere, in all time, in everyone's heart, *that* 'Jesus.' I had a feeling, a gradual, increasing feeling that Jesus was in the room—or the spirit of Jesus was in the room. He was making something real that was invisible."[6]

Jonas and his friends agreed that they were watching a phenomenon. He approached Nouwen at the end of the session and asked if he would consider becoming his spiritual director. They agreed to meet for lunch later that week to discuss this further, and a complex but enduring friendship began.[7] Robert Jonas has written extensively and movingly about the ebb-and-flow of this relationship that resulted, eventually, in Nouwen moving into the house where Jonas and his wife, Margaret Bullitt-Jonas, lived in order to write.[8] It was a difficult relationship that encapsulates the story of Nouwen's Harvard years. It began well, but soon ran into difficulties, of a personal and professional nature. At the time, Nouwen was trying to redefine expectations about his far-from-traditional presence in the academic world. He felt challenged by the constraints of long-established modes of practice in academic life and in the "delivery" of pastoral ministry.

The initial problem between Jonas and Nouwen began with psychology.

"I realized that Henri was very interested in psychology and I was being trained as a psychologist, so we had that common ground. And we both loved God, so we had that common ground," explains Jonas. "Our conversation kind of tacked, like a sailboat tacks in the wind, back and forth from psychology to spirituality."[9] As they discussed the possibility of Nouwen becoming Jonas's spiritual director, the tables began to turn. "We sort of framed it where instead of him being my spiritual director, I was his therapist in a way. We tried it out. It was sort of play and sort of serious."

Ethical alarm bells were no doubt sounding given their psychology background and Nouwen's pastoral counseling expertise. Then, after six months of regular meetings that confused the roles of therapist and spiritual director, they realized they could not continue. "Let's keep it simple. Let's just be friends," was their agreement. Their relationship shifted from regular meetings to occasional letters and phone calls. "I think I had some special insight into Henri at that time," explains Jonas (the Scripture-quoting Nouwen always enjoyed calling him "Jonas"). "He felt most comfortable being in some kind of community. He was as restless and uneasy and dissatisfied and unhappy at Harvard as he had been at Yale. But what made it easier for him was to feel part of a community."[10]

How does a professor create community in one semester each academic year? When Nouwen first arrived in Harvard, he lived in a university-owned apartment on the southern side of the campus and worked out of a small office on the top floor of Andover Hall, the Divinity School's Gothic center-piece at the northern edge of the campus. This arrangement changed the following August when Dean George Rupp invited Nouwen to take up residence in a small building closer to the Divinity School, The Carriage House. Before long, Nouwen had converted an upstairs room into a chapel and an informal drop-in venue was beginning to take shape. Peter Weiskel was Nouwen's administrative at Harvard and was an undergraduate at Yale when Nouwen arrived there. Weiskel also traveled with Nouwen from Harvard to Guatemala on his short visit to John Vesey. He describes Nouwen's transformation of the Carriage House with couches, chairs, and a large dining table, making it "a place of meeting, celebration, and prayer for a small, yet diverse community of students and local residents."[11] There was a constant stream of visitors and Nouwen eventually hired a cook to make sure they were all fed. "It was a time of great excitement, possibility, and more than a little chaos," recalls Weiskel, as the Carriage House was transformed into a kind of laboratory for Nouwen to "practice his unique style of hospitality."[12]

In the 1980s, Andover Hall's Sperry Room was a stuffy lecture theatre with creaky fold-down wooden seats. It was the venue for what became Nouwen's most popular course at Harvard: "An Introduction to the Spiritual Life." Michael O'Laughlin, another graduate assistant and eventual Nouwen biographer, says this course grew into "the largest class at the divinity school in living memory....It was like being part of a huge happening."[13] Nouwen was at his best, he says, in these large classes with overflowing attendance because of his ability "to hold the rapt attention of a huge group by transmitting a level of personal excitement and engagement that was something straight out of a revival tent. His hands were constantly in motion, and he would even throw out his arms, flail the air, or arch forward on his tiptoes—still flailing away—as he built to a crescendo of inspiration."[14]

It wasn't all theatre. Nouwen also had "a self-deprecating way of framing his personal insights that made most people feel he was completely authentic and just like them. Here was someone talking truth, not just mouthing nice-sounding phrases," adds O'Laughlin.[15] It wasn't only large-scale, high-performance presentations. There were small-group courses, seminars, and small-group discussions. Here, O'Laughlin says he saw Nouwen "shrivel up" and get lost in the group's own dynamics, letting the group take over his leadership of sessions. But Nouwen would shine when talking to individual students or two or three people, where he could be more personal and pastoral—perhaps more the psychologist—because he was able to listen intently and share openly.

Like many faculty members in universities around the world, past and present, Nouwen encountered the often-fractious practices under the guise of collegiality that Thomas Wolfe was so biting about in his 1935 fictional depiction of Harvard. Eugene Gant, no longer looking homeward, is on a teaching contract at Harvard and describes the highly competitive colleagues he encountered:

> The air about them was webbed, cross-webbed, and counter-webbed with the dense fabric of their million spites and hatreds. They wasted and grew sick with hate and poison because another man received promotion, because another man had got his poem printed, because another man had eaten food and swallowed drink and lain with women, and lived and would not die.[16]

Robert Ellsberg recalls Nouwen's brief Harvard period as an especially unhappy time because he was attempting to challenge the traditionally accepted academic order:

> He was a person who wanted to generate community, who wanted to stimulate a deeper spirituality in the students, and who wanted to talk about growing close to Jesus, and this was a time at Harvard when people were talking more about hermeneutics, and post-structuralism, and feminism and these kinds of things. I think a lot of them thought Henri was some sort of nut, or an evangelist. "What is this guy doing at Harvard? He's not a scholar, he doesn't write scholarly books, he's teaching books about scripture but doesn't speak Greek or Hebrew. Who is he? He doesn't have rigorous standards for grading in his classes." And

there he was, attracting these standing-room-only audiences for his lectures. People came from all over Boston to hear him.[17]

Some of Nouwen's students also had concerns. He often handed out cards during his courses and asked students to identify issues that he would attempt to integrate into the course as it progressed. One of James D. Smith's tasks, as a teaching fellow, was to collect these cards and compile their contents into a digest for Nouwen. "As he acknowledged dozens of themes and issues, many welcomed his openness as a gift," explains Smith. "Others were offended if he didn't endorse their suggestions, suggesting, 'if you don't agree, you haven't heard me.' He was hurt, but persevered, as responses from student journaling and the class's subgroups shaped his presentations."[18] Other students accused Nouwen of "spiritual imperialism" because of the unconventional way he spoke about Jesus.[19]

Robert Jonas, describing a typical Nouwen university class that would often begin with a Taizé chant, said, "This was something pretty unheard of in most academic classes," and something that Nouwen did

because he wanted first to create community, in a sense of the Holy Spirit's presence. That would be the foundation of any good learning that was to happen. If people were going to be in their heads in their individual seats nothing could really happen, and he wanted something to happen. He wanted the Holy Spirit to show up, even at Harvard. That's probably why they weren't very comfortable with him there.[20]

Despite the aggravations and tensions from whatever "this guy" was trying to do at Harvard, Nouwen was certainly capable of putting on a good show. "Everyone was saying that I was doing really well, but something inside was telling me that my success was putting my own soul in danger," commented Nouwen as he looked back on this period a few years later.[21] The recordings of some of his Harvard classes in the Nouwen archive in Toronto give little hint of such difficulties. He was a high-performance lecturer, and the students and others in the room listened intently and responded enthusiastically. When he taught at Yale, ideas and images formulated during his classes ended up in the books that were published on a regular basis. At Harvard, this was not the case. His writing stalled, as he confided in John Vesey in Guatemala. The two books that were published during his Harvard years, 1983 to 1985, have a focus elsewhere. They are about his experiences before he arrived at Harvard (his Peruvian journal, *¡Gracias!*, 1983), and his book about the murdered Stanley Rother (*Love in Fearful Land*, 1985). Whatever was percolating between 1983 and 1985 would only surface in his writing once he left Harvard. Then he would look back at his Harvard experiences and describe the challenge of feeling driven to achieve something while at the same time knowing that he was putting his soul at risk, to the extent that it was becoming difficult for him to see anything clearly. The term *burnout*, he wrote, "was a convenient psychological translation for a spiritual death."[22]

Although Nouwen framed his difficulties as something related to his soul, the problem, as Robert Ellsberg understood it, was situated elsewhere. Nouwen was "struggling with his own restless heart, his own tendency to cling to a false and 'needy' self. He was describing his own compulsion 'to be seen, praised, and admired.' That struggle would continue...until the end of his life."[23]

What Nouwen was not ready to introduce into his autobiographical writing was an example of what Kierkegaard describes in *The Sickness unto Death* as "this thing in the background that might again emerge."[24] Deep within the cluster of tensions that Nouwen was experiencing at Harvard was the matter of his sexual orientation. Some close friends were aware of this. "Henri was gay, and I knew that from the beginning of our relationship," recalls Jonas. "And I'm a heterosexual man, so there was never anything sexual between us." He asked Nouwen what the "history" of this was. "And my memory is that he said: 'Jonas, I knew very early I was gay. As a boy I was never attracted to women.' So that tells me, yes, he was aware from the time he was very young that he was gay, and also aware from the time that he was very young that he was meant to be a priest."[25] The more they talked about his struggles of being gay, Jonas suggested that Nouwen consider becoming more open about this in his ministry and perhaps find a way of coming out publicly. "Many of his friends wanted him to lead the movement to a more open and gay-friendly Roman Catholic church, but I felt that his identity was so deeply that of a Roman Catholic priest that he could not survive any other way of life."[26]

Peter Naus recalls a conversation in 1978. Nouwen talked to him about the extent of his struggles with his sexual orientation. "What I remember very well is his agony, and my deep compassion for the situation in which he found himself because I already knew that at that time it would be extremely difficult for him to 'come out of the closet,' so to speak."[27] Naus identifies Nouwen's primary reasons for keeping this issue private. First, he was very concerned "about anything that would distract from what he saw as his spiritual message, or messages."[28] Second, "I think Henri had an aversion to any kind of scandal in the church. He was a very faithful servant, and he was very afraid of being engaged in anything that would cause a scandal."[29]

In *Persona humana*, the 1975 Declaration on Certain Questions Concerning Sexual Ethics, the Congregation for the Doctrine of the Faith makes a distinction between homosexuals "whose tendency comes from a false education, from a lack of normal sexual development, from habit, from bad example, or from similar cases, and is transitory or at least not incurable" and those who are "definitively such because of some kind of innate instinct or a pathological constitution judged to be incurable" (no. 13).[30] In either case,

> In Sacred Scripture they are condemned as a serious depravity and even presented as the sad consequence of rejecting God. [Rom 1:24–27] This judgment of Scripture does not of course permit us to conclude that all those who suffer from this anomaly are personally responsible for it, but it does attest to the fact that homosexual acts are intrinsically disordered and can in no case be approved of. (no. 13)

When that document was published, Nouwen had been in ordained ministry for eighteen years. Immediately prior to his Harvard contract, he had celebrated twenty-five scandal-free years in the priesthood. A quarter-century into his career as a priest, he was being challenged to examine his own living human document concerning the issue of an "intrinsically disordered" orientation. What was the implication of this "disorder" not only for his ministry but for his vocation itself? There would be a great deal of prayer and reflection, some guarded statements, much intentional silence, and more than a decade of unresolved anguish.

It is a "mysterious truth," said Carl Jung as he delved into the ways unresolved conflicts put pressure on the body and the spirit. He wrote that "the *spirit* is the life of the body seen from within, and the *body* the outward manifestation of the *life* of the spirit—the two being really one."[31] A tension encountered within will reveal itself externally, and a tension experienced externally will exert pressure on the interior life. In the same article, Jung stated that "the body cannot tolerate a philosophy that denies it in the name of the spirit." Applying this to Nouwen, he turned his attention to prayer and contemplation, trying to keep the focus on his interior well-being. All the while, that Kierkegaardian "thing in the background" was creating unbearable physical tension and restlessness. "I began to ask myself whether my lack of contemplative prayer, my loneliness, and my constantly changing involvement in what seemed most urgent were signs that the Spirit was gradually being suppressed. It was hard for me to see clearly."[32]

Peter Naus believes that Nouwen's anguish over his sexual orientation was inextricably linked with what he considered was "his incredible—I call it insatiable need—for emotional intimacy." This, says Naus, is the recurring theme in Nouwen's books. "You will find that theme. And he himself sees that as the basis of his restlessness. It's also at the basis of his disappointment in friends for not being attentive enough, for not always giving him the affirmation that he needed or that he thought he deserved."[33]

Unhappy at Harvard and feeling unable to write, at the end of the 1984 fall semester, Nouwen arranged a second visit to France for a month-long retreat at L'Arche in Trosly-Breuil. There, in silent contemplation, he could ponder on what had become an unorthodox priestly career. His chosen path of psychology and pastoral counseling in North America had isolated him not only from clinical practice, but also from the traditional networks that support most diocesan priests in their local deaneries and dioceses. His experiments in community building in his university classes had created some tensions, and for the first time in his prolific literary career, his writing had stalled. He had become a lonely and itinerant loner.

When Jean Vanier welcomed Nouwen to L'Arche this second time, he observed a talented yet needy individual. He already knew about Nouwen's remarkable power to attract attention, "with all the intelligence of a charismatic."[34] In addition to noting an individual who was evidently at a critical moment in his career, Vanier also thought that such a charismatic presence might somehow benefit the long-term interests of L'Arche, but only when the time was right and Nouwen had addressed whatever it was that was troubling him.

"I sensed maybe it would be important *in* L'Arche, or *for* L'Arche, because we didn't have any people in the United States who really knew L'Arche. There were no important theologians who knew L'Arche and I thought it was important to get to know him, and for him to get to know us better," said Vanier.[35] He sensed in Nouwen "a man deeply imbedded in a desire to bring people closer to Jesus, and [to do that] with his deeply charismatic personality."[36] He did not want to rush any decision concerning the kind of relationship that

Nouwen might have with L'Arche. Besides, Nouwen's brief return to L'Arche was not an internship of any kind. He had arrived to pray and think about his vocation, and especially why he was reconsidering his decision to make Harvard his vocational home.

It had something to do with community, and if in between his prayers and long walks at L'Arche Nouwen spent time rereading the papal documents concerning the priesthood that appeared the decades following his ordination, he would note how the word *community* appears with increasing frequency. In 1950, there is a single use of it by Pope Pius XII in *Menti nostrae*, his Apostolic Exhortation to the Clergy on the Development of Holiness in Priestly Life. Here, *community* refers to the desirable custom of priests living together, wherever possible, because it "nourishes the spirit of charity and zeal among the priests," and serves as an example "to the faithful of the detachment of the ministers of God from their own interests and from their families. Finally, it is a testimony of the scrupulous care with which they safeguard priestly chastity" (no. 3).[37]

In 1965, in the section on ministry in *Presbyterorum ordinis*, the Decree on the Ministry and Life of Priests, Pope Paul VI uses the word eight times in the following four paragraphs, which have particular resonance, not only for communities of priests, but also for intentional communities such as L'Arche:

> The office of pastor is not confined to the care of the faithful as individuals, but also in a true sense is extended to the formation of a genuine Christian community. Yet the spirit of the community should be so fostered as to embrace not only the local church,

but also the universal Church. The local community should promote not only the care of its own faithful, but, filled with a missionary zeal, it should prepare also the way to Christ for all men. In a special way, catechumens and the newly-baptized who must be educated gradually to know and to live the Christian life are entrusted to his care.

No Christian community, however, is built up unless it has its basis and center in the celebration of the most Holy Eucharist; from this, therefore, all education to the spirit of community must take its origin [2 Cor 12:15]. This celebration, if it is to be genuine and complete, should lead to various works of charity and mutual help, as well as to missionary activity and to different forms of Christian witness.

The ecclesial community by prayer, example, and works of penance, exercise a true motherhood toward souls who are to be led to Christ. The Christian community forms an effective instrument by which the path to Christ and his Church is pointed out and made smooth for non-believers. It is an effective instrument also for arousing, nourishing and strengthening the faithful for their spiritual combat.

In building the Christian community, priests are never to put themselves at the service of some human faction of ideology, but, as heralds of the Gospel and shepherds of the Church, they are to spend themselves for the spiritual growth of the Body of Christ. (no. 6)[38]

In his 1975 Apostolic Exhortation on Evangelization, *Evangelii nuntiandi*, Pope Paul VI uses the word *community* twenty-seven times and pays particular attention to evangelization within small intentional communities, or *communautés de base*. Ideally, these communities of "hearers of the Gospel...will soon become proclaimers of the Gospel themselves" (no. 58).[39] They come in all shapes and sizes:

> In some regions they appear and develop, almost without exception, within the Church, having solidarity with her life, being nourished by her teaching and united with her pastors. In these cases, they spring from the need to live the Church's life more intensely, or from the desire and quest for a more human dimension such as larger ecclesial communities can only offer with difficulty, especially in the big modern cities which lend themselves both to life in the mass and to anonymity. Such communities can quite simply be in their own way an extension on the spiritual and religious level—worship, deepening of faith, fraternal charity, prayer, contact with pastors—of the small sociological community such as the village, etc. Or again their aim may be to bring together, for the purpose of listening to and meditating on the Word, for the sacraments and the bond of the *agape*, groups of people who are linked by age, culture, civil state or social situation: married couples, young people, professional people, etc.; people who already happen to be united in the struggle for justice, brotherly aid to the poor, human advancement. (no. 58)

So far, so good. The problem is the shadow-side of communities that emerge from an oppositional perspective and come together in a spirit of bitter criticism of the Church, which they are quick to stigmatize as "institutional" and to which they set themselves up in opposition as charismatic communities, free from structures and inspired only by the Gospel. Thus their obvious characteristic is an attitude of fault-finding and of rejection with regard to the Church's outward manifestations: her hierarchy, her signs. They are radically opposed to the Church. By following these lines their main inspiration very quickly becomes ideological, and it rarely happens that they do not quickly fall victim to some political option or current of thought, and then to a system, even a party, with all the attendant risks of becoming its instrument. (no. 58)

The exhortation contains a general warning and a precise reminder. It warns the episcopate, all clergy, and all the faithful of the entire world (to whom the document is addressed) to not think about "the universal Church as the sum, or, if one can say so, the more or less anomalous federation of essentially different individual Churches" (no. 62). Then it reminds every priest what is at the core of his vocation: "What identifies our priestly service, gives a profound unity to the thousand and one tasks which claim our attention day by day and throughout our lives, and confers a distinct character on our activities, is this aim, ever present in all our action: to proclaim the Gospel of God" (no. 68).

By the mid-1980s, Nouwen's experience of community had been limited. He chose to live independently wherever he taught. There was no rectory with a housekeeper for this parish-free priest. The closest he came to community life was his various "drop-in" experiences for relatively short periods of time, his retreats and then residency with the Trappists, and this second retreat at L'Arche. Five years earlier, he discovered the Sant'Egidio Community.

When Nouwen was presenting a series of lectures in the North American Pontifical College in Rome, during the five months he spent "clowning" there in 1978, he observed the work of the community that had been founded by Andrea Riccardi in 1968. The Sant'Egidio Community is built on a four-part program of "works." The first is prayer, with daily prayer sessions for the community and its visitors; the second is preaching and communicating the gospel, formally and informally; the third is befriending and serving the poor, the disabled, and the excluded; and the fourth is a commitment to ecumenism.[40] In his book on new movements within the Roman Catholic Church, Michael A. Hayes describes this community and its "border-dissolving charisma" that has led its members to work "in peacekeeping and mediation in conflicts worldwide, as well as a campaign against the death penalty, and a nationwide AIDS treatment program in Mozambique. The community also organizes the world's largest annual interfaith meetings: a task entrusted to it by the Pope [John Paul II], following the world prayer for peace in Assisi in 1986."[41] The Sant'Egidio Community is now an international movement with some sixty thousand members in seventy-three countries. In 2002, Pope John Paul II focused on the word *friendship* in the speech he gave to the members of the community when he met with them:

> One could say that friendship stamps every dimension of the life of the Sant'Egidio Community. Friendship lived with sensitivity of the Gospel is

an effective way of being Christian in the world: it makes it possible to cross frontiers and to shorten distances, even when they seem insurmountable. It is a question of a real art, the art of encounter, of careful attention to dialogue, of loving passion for communicating the Gospel. This friendship becomes a reconciling force; it is really needed in our time, so tragically famous for wars and violent clashes.[42]

Then there were Nouwen's experiences with another form of community, Taizé. As noted earlier, he often began classes at Yale and Harvard by getting the students to sing Taizé's simple, modal, repetitive chants. These contemporary chants are used in the candle-lit liturgies of the community that was founded in 1940, in Burgundy, France, by the Swiss-born, Protestant pastor in the Reformed tradition Roger Schütz. As Brother Roger, he sought to reconcile Christians of all denominations as the violence of the Second World War showed no sign of ending. He created what he later described as an ecumenical "parable of community" built on the great monastic traditional practices of prayer, work, and liturgy.[43] The community's Rule appeared in 1954 and was amended slightly in 2005:

> You are afraid that a common rule may stifle your personality, whereas its purpose is to free you from useless fetters, the better to bear responsibility and exercise all the boldness possible in your ministry. Like every Christian, you need to accept the tension between the total freedom given by the Holy Spirit and the impossibilities in which you are set

by human nature—both your neighbour's and your own.[44]

The original Taizé community in France now has a hundred brothers, Protestant and Catholic, from thirty countries, and it continues to attract thousands of visitor/pilgrims, especially those of university age, to its ecumenical liturgical celebrations. Pope Francis singled out Taizé in his homily in the Patriarchal Church of St. George in Istanbul during his apostolic journey to Turkey in 2014. He described it as a positive force in the lives of young adults because of its inclusiveness:

> New generations will never be able to acquire true wisdom and keep hope alive unless we are able to esteem and transmit the true humanism which comes from the Gospel and from the Church's age-old experience. It is precisely the young who today implore us to make progress towards full communion. I think for example of the many Orthodox, Catholic and Protestant youth who come together at meetings organized by the Taizé community. They do this not because they ignore the differences which still separate us, but because they are able to see beyond them; they are able to embrace what is essential and what already unites us.[45]

In between his courses in 1984, Nouwen attended Taizé's European gathering in Cologne and, before returning to Harvard, spent a few days with the brothers of the Taizé community in France.[46]

The models of L'Arche, Sant'Egidio, and Taizé may have informed Nouwen's approach to activities inside the Carriage

House and Andover Hall, but as far as the university was concerned, he was responsible for teaching credit courses with consistent standards and grades, rather than building a version of Sant'Egidio or Taizé in their midst. At Harvard, Nouwen arrived with an essentially countercultural teaching and learning style that grew out of his interest in empowerment and community formation, a style of teaching and learning that was markedly different from the one he experienced in the seminary in the Netherlands. He was not imparting research-driven information or testing his students' recall of it, or for that matter, their conformity with it.

There are elements in Nouwen's teaching and his public presentations that are consistent with the ideas and practices of the influential Brazilian philosopher and educator Paulo Freire, whose work Gutiérrez had long championed. In the 1960s, the Catholic-trained Freire developed an approach to education that he called the "pedagogy of the oppressed," which, through a process of conscientization, enabled adult learners to move from a naïve or passive awareness of issues to a more critical awareness of their root causes. Freire reenvisioned the practice of education that was as radical in its interpretation of power and control as the theology of liberation, to which it was closely linked.[47] Freire was a visiting professor at Harvard in 1969–70,[48] and that year he wrote for the *Harvard Educational Review*, and again in 1985 and 1995.[49] In his later work (he died in 1997), Freire wrote about how he struggled with the consequences of his faith. It is not easy to have faith, he said, "due to the demands faith places on whoever experiences it. It demands a stand for freedom, which implies respect for the freedom of others, in an ethical sense, in the sense of humility, coherence, and tolerance."[50]

Those three words—*humility, coherence,* and *tolerance*—were at play when it came to an assessment of Nouwen's presence at Harvard. His tolerance was being stretched as he continued to seek coherency in his vocation. In humility, he conceded that the discernment of his true vocation should continue somewhere else. "I was not really happy there, found myself somewhat sulky and complaining, and never felt fully accepted by the faculty or students. The signs were clear that I still had not found the way."[51]

In his 1961 book, *The New Man,* Thomas Merton describes the spiritual damage that occurs when someone begins drifting away from their true way or identity. Incidentally, this is one of the few books that Merton places on his list of "better" works,[52] though it is a title that Nouwen does not reference in his 1972 work on Merton, *Pray to Live.* Merton writes that identity gets lost when we become overwhelmed by self-awareness and guilt.

> Instead of being perfectly actualized in spirit, integrated and unified in the selfless ecstasy of a contemplation that goes out entirely to the "other," man is literally "dis-tracted"—pulled apart—by an almost infinite number of awarenesses. He is conscious of everything trivial, remembers everything except what is most necessary, feels everything that he should not feel, yields to demands that he should never even hear, looks everywhere, pays attention to every creaking board and shutter in his haunted house. For his soul and body, created to be a temple of God, cannot but seem a haunted place after the desecration that has evicted its only rightful dweller.[53]

Nouwen was certainly aware of his distractedness, and not only at Harvard. He might find fraternal support in the words of Thomas Merton as he continued to struggle with the nature of his vocation and the kind of priest he was still in the process of inventing. Merton includes a key line about that, as well: "The vocation to charity is a call not only to love but to *be loved*. The man who does not care at all whether or not he is loved is ultimately unconcerned about the true welfare of the other and of society. Hence we cannot love unless we also consent to be loved in return."[54]

Merton adds that we cannot set about searching for what we already "expect" to find, that is something only God will reveal.

> It has to be "given."...We do not know God and we do not know ourselves. How then can we imagine that it is possible for us to chart our own course toward the discovery of the meaning of our life? This meaning is not a sun that rises every morning....We must learn that life is a light that rises when God summons it out of darkness. For this there are no fixed times.[55]

What had been revealed to Nouwen during this opportunity to think and pray and listen and watch at L'Arche was a feeling of "at-homeness" and the experience of a way of life that was decidedly noncompetitive and ungradable. At L'Arche, the core members he lived among had no idea about his books or his reputation.[56] Being in their presence destabilized the hierarchical rank and credential structures that characterize religious and academic careerism. Nouwen was not at L'Arche as a visiting professor or as a cleric on the rise; he was there to experience community life. So far, his brief stays in the L'Arche community had offered him more of those fleeting momentary glimpses of God's presence. "I could hear the gentle invitation of Jesus to dwell with him," he wrote.[57]

In fact, it was Jean Vanier who sent his invitation. "Maybe we can offer you a home here," is what he proposed, shortly before Nouwen had to return to the United States.[58] Nouwen told him that this was indeed what his heart desired. The invitation grew from Vanier's observation of Nouwen during his second retreat. It was apparent to him that Nouwen "had come to a brick wall." Vanier said he didn't know what that brick wall was and that he chose not to ask for any explanation. "I didn't want to know, particularly. But it just couldn't go on at Harvard. I felt that for him, L'Arche was a salvation. From what I didn't know, but from a brick wall. Was it the whole teaching situation? Was it that he didn't have the right relationships? Whatever it was, to come here, I think, was a saving situation."[59] Vanier did not impose any particular expectations. "Coming to L'Arche he would have a nice room, he'd have time to write. Everything in a way just fell into place."[60]

Loose arrangements such as this rarely appeared in Nouwen's contract, though of course this was not a traditional employment relationship. It was an open-ended invitation to return to the L'Arche community in Trosly-Breuil to really get to know community life with people who are intellectually disabled. He could observe and participate in the bustling, noisy ambiance of a L'Arche *foyer*—the name used by L'Arche to identify its community homes. In French, the word can be linked, depending on the context, to "home," "hearth," "homestead," "hostel," and sometimes "source."

"I'm not sure he had any particular agenda, except to have space to write and to be in L'Arche. And to have occasion to meet me," recalled Vanier.

All that was left for Nouwen to do was to seek the approval of his new archbishop, (soon to be cardinal) Adrianus Simonis, to resign his position at Harvard and return to France, where he planned to spend August 1985 to August 1986 at L'Arche. After that, who knew?

Nouwen returned to the United States, conceding that his stated goal of a "reverse mission" from Latin and South America to North America had finally come to an end. This "probationary" year when he returned to France would allow him to reframe what he now thought his mission might become. Instead of advocating on behalf of the poor to the rich, the oppressed to the liberated, those on the periphery to those at the center, he was about to enter an intentional community founded by a celibate layperson in the wake of the Second Vatican Council. Vanier established L'Arche "in the spirit of the Gospel and the Beatitudes that Jesus preached," and "on covenant relationships between people of differing intellectual capacity, social origin, religion and culture." Those relationships aspired to be "signs of unity, faithfulness and reconciliation."[61] At L'Arche, Nouwen was closing in on Gustavo Gutiérrez's conviction, expressed in *A Theology of Liberation*, that change takes place when something recognizable and familiar is reinterpreted in a radically liberating new way and with "a new attitude—ever more lucid and demanding—suggestive of a qualitatively different society and of basically new forms of the Church's presence in it."[62]

Except for occasional short-term teaching engagements, Nouwen's university days were over once he left Harvard.

In the final section of Wolfe's *Of Time and the River*, Eugene Gant has traveled to the south of France, his difficult Harvard days a distant memory. In Arles one day, he is shocked at the experience of noticing something he believes he has seen before. He suddenly realizes he is standing in front of the very trees that Vincent van Gogh painted in his 1889 painting, *The Road Menders*. They were the same, and they were also different. The trees in front of him had tall, straight, symmetrical trunks, whereas he remembered that the tress in the painting "had great, tendoned trunks that writhed and twisted like creatures in a dream—and yet were somehow more true than truth, more real than this reality. And the great vinelike trunks of these demented trees had wound and rooted in his heart, so that now he could not forget them, nor see this scene in any other way than that in which Van Gogh had painted it."[63]

At L'Arche, Nouwen would encounter a way of life that was strangely familiar and impossibly strange at the same time. In a series of remarkable books written in this last decade of his life, based at a L'Arche community in Canada, Nouwen would paint in words an enduring series of portraits that capture the truth, the reality, and the significance of this mission-driven approach to creating community. In doing so, he would also discover, finally, the vocation that had long been "wound and rooted" in his heart.

During Nouwen's previous visit to L'Arche, in 1983, he was working in the small archive and noticed a poster behind the archivist's desk. It was a painting he had not seen before. He knew it was not the work by his favorite artist, van Gogh, something he would have recognized immediately. The archivist explained that the painting was much older, and the work of another Dutch painter.

Rembrandt's shadow-filled, dream-like painting was "imprinted on my soul" as he would later write.[64] In the years that remained, he reflected deeply on the painting and what it revealed about the parable. His interpretation matured over time, resulting in his celebrated 1992 book about fathers and sons, jealously and forgiveness, and the discovering of where home is. The book was just one in a series of remarkable final works that are rooted in Nouwen's longed-for integration of his self-image as a gay celibate man and the "impressively free" priest he might finally become.[65]

Harvard was the departure point and L'Arche would be the final destination in Nouwen's creative transformation of his vocation. The journey was one of light—"We are called to follow Christ on the downwardly mobile road, tempted to choose the broad path of success, fame, and influence, and challenged to subject ourselves to spiritual disciplines in order to gradually conform ourselves to the image of our Lord Jesus Christ."[66] It was also a journey of shadow—"We will never know for sure where we are being led. We are tempted at every moment of our day and night and we will never know precisely where our demons will appear."[67]

9

A GRACED
RECONFIGURATION

Where True Living and
True Seeing Are One

The allotted function of art is not, as is often assumed, to put across ideas, to propagate thoughts, to serve as an example. The aim of art is to prepare a person for death, to plough and harrow his soul, rendering it capable of turning to good."[1] This is how the exiled Russian filmmaker Andrei Tarkovsky explained his approach to filmmaking, an approach that was clearly evident in his 1966 film about the monk and iconographer Andrei Rublev (ca. 1360–ca. 1428). Rublev's "Holy Trinity" icon depicts the three angels encountered by Abraham in Genesis, chapter 18. Rublev's approach to iconography was declared the obligatory model for subsequent church-based artists in the Russian Orthodox tradition. In 1988, Andrei Rublev was canonized by the Russian Orthodox Church. His "trinity" icon remains one of the most reproduced images of religious art.

Tarkovsky was born the same year as Nouwen and graduated from the famed Russian State University of Cinematography, founded in 1919 in the fervor of the early days of Soviet Russia. *Andrei Rublev* (Tarkovsky's original title for this film was *The Passion According to Andrei*) is a complex sequence of scenes that follow the artist/monk during a time of turmoil and Tatar invasion and when Muscovite princes bribed, married, and fought their way, ruthlessly, to power.[2] The film's focus on political, economic, and religious motivations, and the role of the artist when creating commissioned works with a specific purpose, created problems for Tarkovsky. He encountered production difficulties and funding delays, censorship, and finally interference with distribution. He made all his subsequent films in Europe, after negotiating international coproductions in order to reduce the degree of state interference. In 1983, after completing a film shoot in Italy, Tarkovsky declared that he would never return to the Soviet Union. Despite his cancer diagnosis, he managed to shoot one final film, *The Sacrifice*, but he died shortly after in Paris in 1986. This final film, filled with silences, is about a reclusive writer who, as a nuclear war is about to begin, bargains with God for peace, with terrifying personal consequences. Sounding remarkably like Nouwen on the concept of the wounded healer ("by hiding our pain we also hide our ability to heal"[3]), Tarkovsky identified the recurring theme in his art: his firm conviction that it is "always through spiritual crisis that healing occurs....The soul yearns for harmony, and life is full of discordance. This dichotomy is the stimulus for movement, the source of our pain, and our hope: confirmation of our spiritual depths and potential."[4]

Nouwen had hardly settled into his new, though temporary, home at Trosly-Breuil when he encountered yet another period of discord and dichotomy in the form of a spiritual crisis, "a hard period...in which verbal prayer had become nearly impossible and during which mental and emotional fatigue had made me the easy victim of feelings of despair and fear."[5] He sought healing comfort, sitting and praying in front of a print of Rublev's trinity icon, the subject of

Tarkovsky's *Andrei Rublev*. Deep in contemplation, Nouwen heard an inner voice and sensed that some form of healing could, perhaps, at last, begin and that he could now start writing once again, as he did so freely throughout his decade at Yale.[6] And he does. The writing flows, beginning with the journal eventually published as *The Road to Daybreak*.

On the surface, this is a breezy account of a busy transitional year of meetings, travel, greeting visitors, and preparing for what will be a complete break from the "institutional rivalry, intellectual competition," "competitive ambitious career-oriented life," and "the race for achievement" of university careerism. Nouwen presents himself as a reenergized, eager learner who has returned to France to determine if serving L'Arche in some way or other will be the next development within his far-from-conventional career. He is fascinated by what he sees and experiences, and comments on the daily routines, the noise, Jean Vanier's wise and insightful comments, and the ability of the young assistants who work so effortlessly with the core members of the community, who face so many challenges with even the most ordinary details of daily life. He takes long walks and finds that he is also able to pray once more. He makes a quick visit to Canada to meet the staff at L'Arche Daybreak in Richmond Hill, Ontario, where it seems he will most likely be headed, after this initial immersion experience in France.

Beneath the surface, things were more turbulent. As 1985 turned into 1986, some familiar demons and vulnerabilities returned, and he set them out in print for all to read. Bouts of depression. Anger at friends who didn't show up, as well as some who did. Frustration over wanting to write once more but at the same time feeling lost for words when trying to write about Andrei Rublev's icon. Away from university life, he was still overly busy, and restlessness was his constant companion. His move to France would be a new beginning, even as the ploughing and harrowing of unfinished life business continued. He hoped for something that would feel like integration as he identified fault lines in the landscape of his vocation in this, his first post-university journal. Before his year in France was over, these would heave and fracture and shift inconveniently and dangerously as he entered the final and highly creative decade of his life.

In France, Nouwen learned the L'Arche ropes while welcoming visiting friends from Yale and Harvard. He traveled back and forth to Paris, Strasbourg, Freiburg, Rheims, and the closest town to L'Arche, Compiègne. He took notes when Jean Vanier spoke, and he received regular and helpful spiritual direction from L'Arche's Père Thomas, and Ignatian guidance from a Jesuit, Père André. He was a highly motivated student, and when the formal invitation arrived from L'Arche Daybreak in Richmond Hill, Ontario, he needed approval from Cardinal Simonis. They planned to discuss this, face-to-face, during the Christmas break when Nouwen would visit his family in the Netherlands.

Nouwen did not like what he saw in the Netherlands of the 1980s. He felt the culture had become hedonistic and had somehow moved on from God. At his meeting with Cardinal Simonis, their relationship sustained a hairline fracture. Nouwen experienced his cardinal as "distant and pragmatic" because of his focus on the nuts-and-bolts issues of pension and insurance. After being wrapped in the pastoral blanket of L'Arche, this caught him off guard. Simonis advised Nouwen that he would let him know his decision in due course.

Then, amid a family celebration, another hairline crack suddenly surfaced, as they so often do at such gatherings. For his father's eighty-third birthday celebration, Nouwen prepared a "life-giving message" for him but was upstaged by his brother (he doesn't say which one) who offered a toast, improvising on their father's astrological sign and linking it to his personality. This received much laughter and applause and Nouwen was miffed that his brother knew better than he did what the family audience would appreciate. He left the room to call Cardinal Simonis. The cardinal told him he had permission to relocate to L'Arche Daybreak, in Richmond Hill, Canada, for a three-year term, after which time he hoped that Nouwen would, at long last, return to the Archdiocese of Utrecht.

Early in 1986 and happy to be back at Trosly, Nouwen continued to immerse himself in the L'Arche approach to community life. He wrote about constantly moving from darkness to light, and back again. In the light, he was inspired by the example of the Jesuit saint, Francis Xavier, who, among other things, reassured him that he was not the only one to be disappointed by a university life that seemed to be focused on honors and privilege above faith and sacrifice. In the light-and-shadow world of Rembrandt, specifically his 1648 painting in the Musée du Louvre, *The Pilgrims of Emmaus*, he realized that a gallery is a kind of church, and that great artists minister through art, just as priests do through creative liturgy.[7] In the life and writings of martyred Charles de Foucauld, briefly a Trappist and then founder of the Little Brothers of Jesus, he is challenged to "See Jesus in all people."[8] Nouwen cites de Foucauld in this journal, as he will in several subsequent books, especially de Foucauld's prayer about surrendering "without reserve and with boundless confidence."[9]

Reading the poet Rainer Maria Rilke writing about himself, he encountered three words that resonated with his own life: unfinished, unable, and distracted. When Rilke first encountered the art of Paul Cezanne, he writes that he felt transformed because he had encountered an artist who was a mystic and a saint, and whose life and work were somehow united to God. It was after reading this in Rilke that Nouwen began to explore the paintings of Cezanne, in whose work, he discovered a place where "true living and true seeing are one."[10]

Despite such solace, an interior darkness was never far away, a darkness that took away his courage to name things "by their true names."[11] Whatever names these might be given at this stage of Nouwen's life, these were the same issues that he brought with him when he entered the seminary in Holland, and that also accompanied him when he left it in 1957 as an ordained priest. There was one major difference now. He had convinced himself that when he got to his new home at L'Arche Daybreak, he would arrive there with a renewed sense of freedom, the experience of "belonging to God and free to be wherever we are called to be."[12]

Nouwen populates *The Road to Daybreak* with the words "friend," "friendship," and "community." He returned often to the importance of friends, acknowledging how difficult it is to nurture genuine friendships. "It is hard for me to speak of my feelings of being rejected or imposed upon, of my desire for affirmation as well as my need for space, on insecurity and mistrust, of fear and love," he writes.[13] Nouwen's language of friendship was a theme with many variations. When he describes welcoming and discussing things with his friend Jonas, his language is professional and unambiguously clear, what you might expect when two professionally trained psychologists go back and forth. Similarly, when his Harvard assistant Peter Weiskel arrived at L'Arche for a short visit, there was the comfortable ease of colleagues discussing projects and deadlines. When Nathan Ball arrived from Canada, the language suddenly shifted. Nouwen had discovered "a new companion in life, a new presence that will last wherever I go," someone whose absences made him "aware of a real affection for him that had grown in me,"[14] and the person who had become "one of the most sustaining and nurturing aspects of my stay at Trosly." What they felt for each other, he pronounces is "a love that is not of our own making," and he defines their friendship as "deep and nurturing," "beautiful and supportive," "the center of my emotional stability," and "a safe place in the midst of all the transitions and changes."[15]

In Tarkovsky's film *Andrei Rublev*, one of the iconographers, Kiril, is lost for words when he is asked to praise Andrei, his more experienced colleague. His superior asks what prevents him putting his feelings into words. "It seems I cannot, I cannot say it clearly. Konstanine Kostenecki put it well when he said, 'You will know the true essence of a thing if you name it properly.'" In this first flush of a new kind of emotion, Nouwen was not able to do that.

In August 1986, after his immersion experience in France, Nouwen flew to Canada to begin his new "job" at L'Arche Daybreak. His arrival was Nouwen in circus mode, with a bright-yellow moving van filled with boxes of books and papers, and a motorcade of vehicles filled with enthusiastic helpers and friends, much to the astonishment of the community leaders and the delight of the core members.[16] Sister Sue Mosteller, CSJ, who would become one of his most-trusted confidants and also his literary executrix, remembers their first exchange. "It was like hugging a board," she recalled. "I mean, he was absolutely stiff, and L'Arche is a lot about the body because we're close to people in their bodies, people who cannot wash themselves, people who need help with brushing their teeth and their hair."[17] Nouwen had some important mind and body work to contemplate.

Nouwen's first room was in the basement of the New House, one of eight houses in the Daybreak community. It was not long before he began to loosen up and, in Mosteller's words, "blew the walls down" with the remarkable energy that he brought to his work there. Within the first days of his arrival and being forced to learn (quickly if not effectively) how to cook and clean, he also bought a new car. The next day, as he was driving to Toronto's Pearson Airport (just as in France, there would be constant visitor interruptions, arrivals, and departures), he had an accident and, though unharmed, had to replace the wrecked vehicle.

Some basic "etiquette" required for life within a community eluded him. "He would bring guests, without announcing for a meal," Mosteller explains. "We're five minutes to six and he walks in with five people and says, 'I invited them for supper.' And we're scrambling and just screaming inside, 'Why did you not tell us?!'"[18]

Nouwen had two parallel careers at Daybreak: his ongoing professional activities (the Nouwen "industry" of writing, media interviews, conferences, discussions with editors and publishers, and a constant stream of visitors), and his pastoral participation and liturgical duties within the Daybreak community, a community he not only served but also lived in. This meant there were many last-minute unanticipated interruptions and activities, so typical in L'Arche communities where members live with difficult physical and intellectual needs and expectations. Not surprisingly, there were many moments of confusion and tension.

And there was Adam.

Adam Arnett was born on November 17, 1961, and during his infancy he began to experience uncontrollable seizures that resulted in his inability to walk without assistance or to speak. He was twenty-five years old when Nouwen moved in to the L'Arche house where Adam lived. He could not dress, feed, or bathe himself. That would be Nouwen's job, something he initially resisted because he was so nervous, but with fear and trembling and a great deal of support from other assistants, he took on this two-hour-a-day responsibility.[19] In time, Adam's routines became Nouwen's quiet time, "the most reflective and intimate time of the day. Indeed they became like a long prayer time….Adam was becoming *my* teacher, taking *me* by the hand, walking with me in my confusion through the wilderness of *my* life."[20]

After a year-and-a-half of trying to hold on to the complex and demanding roles of being the public Nouwen and while serving as the chaplain at L'Arche Daybreak, he suddenly realized that he had stopped sleeping, had begun to cry uncontrollably, and had lost his appetite. He found himself "flat on the ground and in total darkness."[21] He had become "preoccupied by a friendship that had seemed life-giving but had gradually become suffocating."[22] A once deeply nourishing relationship had become a source of anguish. He discovered "that the enormous space that had been opened for me could not be filled by the one who had opened it. I became possessive, needy, and dependent, and when the friendship finally had to be interrupted, I fell apart."[23]

Nathan Ball, who had arrived at Daybreak the same time as Nouwen, explains, "It became clear, as our relationship evolved, that there was a sense in which Henri was depending on me to help him find this place of belonging in the world."[24] This was an impossible task and Nouwen needed to withdraw from Daybreak. He sought psychological support and found it in Holland, not the country of his birth but the small town in southern Manitoba. This Holland is where the Trappists had relocated their original Manitoba abbey. The Trappists founded the Abbey of Our Lady of the Prairies (*Notre Dame des Prairies*) in 1892 in St. Norbert, a little village near Winnipeg. As the decades passed, St. Norbert became surrounded on all sides by Winnipeg's suburban sprawl. In 1975, the monks decided they needed a quieter, more isolated location. They chose Holland, deep in the prairie heartland, 90 miles (145 kilometers) to the west of St. Norbert.

At the monastery, within the familiar solitude of Trappist life, Nouwen began regular meetings with members of *Maisons de Croissance*, or Homes for Growth, a retreat movement established in Winnipeg in 1977 with the support of the Oblates of Mary Immaculate and the Holy Cross Sisters. This retreat method was modeled after the technique called *Personalité et Relations Humaines*, or PRH, the French initials for Personality and Human Relations. PRH is the "psycho-pedagogy" program developed in France in 1970 by André Rochais, who like Nouwen was an ordained priest and a trained psychologist.[25] At that time, PRH was being used in Canada in French-language seminary formation programs and, in the 1980s, by at least one English-speaking congregation. Some of its trainers used *The Wounded Healer* in their work. PRH "psycho-pedagogy" requires participants to write extensively about their experiences, thoughts, and feelings, and to work closely with a guide who accompanies them.

Nouwen says that his two guides held on to him "as parents hold a wounded child."[26] His posthumously published journal about this period of exile, as he called it, contains sixty-two "spiritual imperatives."

When this book was released (posthumously), some friends reassessed the Nouwen they thought they knew. Some described it as tortured self-reflection, but Richard Sipe was surprised neither by the book nor what had led up to it. He had been in communication with Nouwen ever since their days at the Menninger Clinic in Kansas. No longer a Benedictine and now married, Sipe had continued his longitudinal studies into celibacy and sexuality in religious life. He felt that Nouwen's sexual orientation was not the only issue at play, though it was his "private struggle."[27] He remembers that in the 1960s, Nouwen asked him pointed questions about the nature of homosexuality: "Was it genetic? How did it develop? How did it fit in with the spiritual life? Was it mutable? We talked around these issues, but he was not ready to deal with that."[28]

Suddenly, at Daybreak, Sipe says that Nouwen "let himself fall in love with a man. And this was absolutely new. Now many of us, we fall in love in that way when we're teenagers, and we kind of let go and idealize this man, this person, whom we think should be a friend, a very close friend. Henri had not gone through that stage, and he knew it."[29] Sipe believes that underlying this experience was a fundamental problem within formation, and not only Nouwen's. "The Catholic priesthood fosters prolonged adolescence in people, the dependency and idealization, and so on."[30]

In Sipe's view, Nouwen was, emotionally, a late developer who was forced to address a basic identity issue after a quarter-century of avoidance. Tough enough. But he was trying to do this work under extremely stressful circumstances. For Sipe, this is a familiar and recurring crisis within religious life. "There's a certain parallel between Henri and Thomas Merton. Both of them, after twenty-five years in religious life, fell in love. So here are two celibate men: Merton falls in love with this girl and really acts like an adolescent, all of his friends say so. An adolescent in a love affair...and here's Henri after twenty-five years in the priesthood, for the first time allowing himself the human feelings of falling in love. In this case he fell in love with a man, which was appropriate to his orientation."[31]

In *The Red Book*, Carl Jung writes that spirituality and sexuality should never be thought of as qualities, since neither should ever be considered as anything that could be possessed or encompassed. "Rather, they possess and encompass you, since they are powerful daimons, manifestations of the Gods, and hence reach beyond you, existing in themselves."[32] The "daimons" of sexuality and spirituality fed Nouwen's depression. Sipe thinks that "part of his depression was over his sexual loneliness, his sexual unsolved problem. He accommodated. But the spiritual life is a very difficult path and a very difficult struggle, and I think most people die with some unsolved problems. I think that there's an accommodation maybe at death that we call peace."[33]

Nouwen's psychology-trained friends remain cautious about speculating what might appear to be a retrospective diagnosis. Nevertheless, Sipe believes that the challenge Nouwen faced concerning his orientation was intensified by his unwavering commitment to his priestly vocation. "I think at base, Henri was very conservative, if you talk about it in those terms. He had to align himself, at least externally, with the Roman Catholic Church, and so, in a sense, he had to toe the line. Not that he wasn't integrated. He was an honest guy, and he was certainly a celibate practicing person, at a great, great, great, great price to himself. His sexual orientation was that unfinished business that he took to the grave with him."[34]

Peter Naus describes this issue as Nouwen's "dark night of the soul," and at the same time an inner force that made his books so appealing. "He was honest enough to indicate, or to say clearly, 'I have trouble living that which I write about or that which I preach.' People said, 'That's very authentic. That is something I recognize. This is not a guy who is trying to tell me a nice story or who represents himself as holier than thou.' On the contrary, he is pretty clear in saying he has trouble living in accordance with what he thinks is spiritually important."[35]

Naus cautions that even his best friends could never know "what Henri felt in the deepest moments of that darkness of the soul."[36] The focus of Nouwen's work, he says, remained constant, neither theology nor church policy, but ministering to the many hundreds of thousands of people who were attracted to his books and who heard him speak, "helping them to realize their relationship with their God, and later on in his life that became very specific: helping people to experience in their own life the reality of being God's beloved."[37]

Seven healing months later, Nouwen was able to return to Daybreak, not to the New House, but to an apartment in Dayspring, then a fledgling retreat center that had been set up in 1985 for the ever-increasing number of L'Arche members, friends, and visitors. Renovated and expanded under Nouwen's leadership, and with the untiring support of Sue Mosteller, Dayspring grew into a very busy retreat center. The first work to appear from within this new setting was

Heart Speaks to Heart, the book he dedicated to Jean Vanier's mother, Pauline Vanier, widow of Canada's Governor General, Georges Vanier (1888–1967). Madame Vanier and Nouwen spent a lot of time together in prayer and conversation during his year at Trosly, and she suggested that Nouwen should "write something" about the Sacred Heart of Jesus. He delayed and delayed until his 1988 arrival in Holland, Manitoba, where he wrote a series of prayers during the triduum, prayers that became the book. "I simply prayed as I wrote and wrote as I prayed....The words just flowed out of me," he writes in the prologue.[38] Read alongside the tortured lines of *The Inner Voice of Love*, in *Heart Speaks to Heart*, Nouwen manages something serene. Although he "framed" the book around his breakdown, he managed to produce a devotional icon with words, rather than paint.

In May 1988, Nouwen was invited by Emmett Cardinal Carter to preach at St. Michael's Cathedral in Toronto, during the Marian year. The homily he gave was the basis of his next book, *Finding our Sacred Center*. Like the "Sacred Heart" book, this one is also based on the prayers and reflections written during his mostly uninterrupted time with the Trappists in Manitoba. "I know that to be truly faithful to my vocation, I must go to Mary," he writes. "Jesus has given her to me so that I can be a truly compassionate priest."[39]

Nouwen's return to Daybreak was characterized, initially at least, by a new energy for writing with an overtly traditional Catholic focus on prayer and Scripture in daily life. These works were by "Father" Nouwen rather than the more inclusive "just Henri" books that would emerge in this final decade of his life. After adapting prayers and homilies into books, he turned next to letters. He adapted *Brieven aan Marc*, written and published in Dutch in 1987, as *Letters to*

Marc about Jesus: Living A Spiritual Life in a Material World.
Marc Van Campen is the son of Nouwen's sister, Laurien,
who was nineteen years old at the time that Nouwen sent him
the letters that comprise the book. These seven letters are
Nouwen's encouraging, homiletic reflections on the experience of living a faith-driven life and are intended for a larger
audience beyond his nephew. Nouwen explained the letters
as a form of logbook of the spiritual discoveries he was making and that influence how his faith informed his daily life.
His primary intention, he said, is to convey a helpful message
with enthusiasm.[40]

With this renewed enthusiasm and clarity of focus—and
now with confirmation from his archbishop that his original
three-year term at Daybreak could be extended indefinitely—
Nouwen had become a reenergized Catholic "celebrity." He
received countless invitations, requests, fan mail, and other
letters that kept pulling his focus away from the daily routines of Daybreak and the retreat activities of Dayspring. He
somehow managed to answer many of the letters in elegant
longhand. Although they required time and thoughtful attention, Nouwen saw all these requests as invitations to "look in
a new way at my identity before God."[41] One request was
nearly fatal.

Early one icy winter morning in 1990, Nouwen's services were requested. Would he help a core member with
bathing, dressing, and breakfast in the Corner House, one of
the L'Arche Daybreak houses in downtown Richmond Hill as
two assistants were away on a course? Usually, to get there
from his apartment in Dayspring would be a five-minute
drive, but with snow accumulating on an already icy road,
Nouwen decided to walk instead. Cars passed him as he
struggled and fell several times, all the while becoming

increasingly anxious about arriving late. Suddenly, a passing van struck him with its wing mirror, throwing him to the ground where he lay motionless with five broken ribs, and in great pain.

After initial tests at York Central Hospital, his condition deteriorated because of internal bleeding. He was quickly moved to the intensive care unit where further tests revealed that his spleen had been so damaged by the impact of the van that it had to be removed immediately before he bled to death. In his book about this experience, *Beyond the Mirror: Reflections on Death and Life*, published the same year as the accident, Nouwen managed to do three things simultaneously. First, unlike the preceding works with their overt Catholic piety, he crafted a thought-provoking exploration of the spiritual experience of a sudden encounter with death, regardless of the reader's religious tradition. Second, he turned his reflections into a parable about human vulnerability based on his experience of letting himself become totally dependent on others. Third, he articulated what he sees as a clarification of his vocational orientation that is reminiscent of the words of Charles de Foucauld who asserted that a vocation is not about making a choice but "doing all we can to hear the divine Voice calling us, to make sure what he is saying."[42] Nouwen achieved all of this in just seventy-four pages.

"I could suddenly also see what my deepest vocation had always been to be a witness to the glimpses of God that I have been allowed to catch," he says.[43] Throughout his career these rare fleeting "glimpses" of the sacred enabled him to finally trust that now he could be "*free in the world—free to speak* even when my words are not received: *free to act* even when my actions are criticized; *free also to receive love* from people and to be grateful for all the signs of God's presence in the world."[44] The remaining six years of his life reveal the extent to which this short book marked an intentional shift within his vocation far distant now from anything remotely recognizable in conventional diocesan, institutional, or university settings. His reframed role as a priest was nothing less than a commitment of service to a dispersed and fluid community.

Peter Naus places this new vocational insight at the center of Nouwen's work:

> The core theme of his writing is: Am I lovable? Am I valuable? Am I worthwhile? Spiritually interpreted, for Henri, God has declared that you are, because you are "My beloved." And Henri's spiritual insight was that we can only ever come to grips with psychological questions of our own value if we can believe and hopefully experience that there is a "prior love," as he calls it, which is that God loves us, and God's love means that it doesn't matter what you do, whether you do something that is good, or something that is bad, something that is valuable or something that is not valuable. You are lovable in My eyes.[45]

Naus also puts Nouwen's insights into biographical context:

> I have to tell you something that is also very seldom said, but Henri told me, I don't remember when, "Peter, what is sometimes very difficult for me, especially because I write about it all the time, is that I have never really experienced God's presence

in my life." Think about that. This man, I believe, strongly believed that he was God's beloved, but he really never had even what is called a numinous experience, if I have to take him at his word.[46]

The key word in Nouwen's phrase "never really experienced" appears to be *never*, but the evidence in his published works suggests that the key word is *really*. Nouwen's glimpsed experiences of the Divine were, as he records them, limited and rare. Nevertheless, these meaningful glimpses suddenly appeared, like the word *glimpse* itself, in so many of his published books, including *Beyond the Mirror*. In explaining such fleeting experiences to his friend, Nouwen was speaking from deep within the contemplative awareness of the desert of spiritual aridity.

In April 1991, having escaped death and after a full recovery from surgery, Nouwen returned briefly to the Netherlands to spend time with his aging father. After decades of feeling injured by the way his father related to him as a child and seminarian, Nouwen had begun to make more "concessions," to accept him as he was, and to "try harder to relate lovingly with him."[47] This trip combined business and father-and-son time. He invited his father to accompany him to Freiburg, home of his German publisher, Herder. One evening, after a day of discussing German editions of his books, Nouwen decided to take his father to see Circus Barum, one of the largest traveling circuses in Europe, which happened to be in town that week. Recalling the evening in one of his public presentations, Nouwen explains what happened: "I went to the circus four years ago with my father, who was eighty-eight years old. I said, 'Dad, let's go to the circus.' And there were lions, and tigers, and elephants, and there were clowns. And I was quite bored."[48]

Although today circuses are imagined more than they are experienced, a circus can still be a surprising place. Robert Lax, the poet, hermit, and lifelong friend of Thomas Merton, who once traveled across North America with the Cristiani Brother's Circus, explains in the poem "Circus Days and Nights" what really happens under the big top:

> By day from town to town we carry
> Eden in our tents and bring its wonders to the
> children who have lost
> their dream of home.[49]

Nouwen's boredom started to fade when the Flying Rodleighs entered the ring and began the slow ascent to their trapezes. Literary historian Linda Simon writes that for centuries, circuses have enticed members of the audience "with the possibility of reinvention, especially of reinventing and perfecting one's body. Aerial and acrobatic acts, central to the circus experience, present us with bodies magnificently strong and controlled, performing feats ever more daring and death defying....Our empathy for the performers' peril reflects, at the same time, our desire to inhabit those amazing bodies."[50]

Nouwen's response was immediate:

> I said, "Dad! Now I know what my real vocation is. I want to be a trapeze artist!"
> And in the intermission, I didn't want to go and look at the lions and tigers, I wanted to go and see these trapeze artists.
> And I did.

I said, "You guys are great."

And they said, "Well, do you want to come tomorrow to our practice session?"

And I did.

And then they said, "Do you want to come for dinner in our caravan?"

And I did.

And they said, "Do you want to travel with us for a week and have your own caravan and join us?"

And I did.

And I became a close friend of them and I travelled all over Germany with these trapeze artists.

They told him how dependent they were on each other:

There are three flyers and two catchers and they are called the Flying Rodleighs. And one day I was sitting in the caravan with Rodleigh Stevens, and he said, "Henri, let me tell you something. I am the flyer and I make all these triples. But you know who is the real hero? The catcher."

And he said, "Henri, the greatest temptation for me is to try and catch the catcher. If I go there saying, 'Where are you?' then we will break each other's wrists. I have to make my triple and fly down this way, eyes closed, knowing that I have to trust the catcher."[51]

Rodleigh Stevens remembers that first meeting with Nouwen, though he did not know what to make of this overly enthusiastic "old guy" whom he eventually discovered was a Roman Catholic priest. "It was a very unusual first encounter," he says, because of Nouwen's "insatiable fountain of questions that he kept wanting to ask us."[52] The troupe invited Nouwen to observe them rehearse and perform the following day and to sit in during their post-performance discussions.

"He spent a lot of time with each team member and interviewed each team member for his books, and eventually for the television documentary that we did with him," says Stevens. "It made me wonder what this very learned man would want to do with this flying trapeze team that he found in a circus in Germany. How is he going to fit our story into a religious context?"[53]

Stevens would eventually find out in 1996, when he attended both of Nouwen's funerals.

Although Nouwen did not complete the "Rodleighs" book that he researched so intently, he did publish a two-part diary in the *New Oxford Review* that hints at what it might have looked like. Nouwen was clear that there is more than escapist entertainment taking place under the big top—"the myth of the world within the world," as Linda Simon characterizes the circus.[54] The image of the flyer and the catcher, with their "on" days of dazzling synchronicity, and their miserable "off" days of botched timing, grabbed Nouwen's imagination. He saw the flyer/catcher relationship as a defining metaphor. Although there's a definite childlike sense of wonder in his enthusiastic responses to the Flying Rodleighs, he realized that what he was watching in their performance was nothing less than an affirmation of his faith. When the time would come to make that final journey from life to death, he was confident that the Divine "catcher" would be there, waiting with perfect synchronization.

Dear friends, we are called to do a lot of flying. You and I are called to do a lot of triples, a lot of jumps, and take a lot of risks. But finally, you have to say, "Lord, into your hands I commend my spirit and trust."

And when it really comes down to it, He'll be there and pull you right up.[55]

Nouwen gave subtitles to his circus diary excerpts: "Finding the Trapeze Artist in the Priest" and "Finding A New Way to Get a Glimpse of God." The diary reveals Nouwen's attention to the smallest of technical details concerning every aspect of the troupe's work, from rigging to rehearsal, from diet to transportation. He saw the Rodleighs as a community that was also a family and a team of creative artists. They stirred something else, something to do with his body and spirit that he knew he was still not able to express.[56] Even if he tried, he would need to use new forms of writing that he had never tried before. He toyed with the idea that the book might take the form of a novel.[57] He conceded that despite his commercially successful publishing record, he had never studied the craft of writing. Accordingly, he went in search of writing guides (Jon Franklin's *Writing for Story: Craft Secrets of Dramatic Nonfiction* and Theodore Rees Cheney's *Writing Creative Non-Fiction: Fiction Techniques for Crafting Great Nonfiction*) and packed them the following year, when he returned to Germany to tour with the Rodleighs for their sixteen-day tour with Circus Barum.

I am convinced that I have been sent to the Rodleighs to discover something new about life and death, love and fear, peace and conflict, heaven and hell....I am not dismissing my earlier writing as no longer valid, I feel that something radically different is being asked of me....This new way includes not only content but form....I know I have to write stories. Not essays with arguments, quotes, and analyses, but stories which are short and simple and give us a glimpse of God in the midst of our multifaceted lives....I want to steal little fragments of conversation from real life. That's new for me.[58]

In his circus diary, Nouwen also returns, in passing, to the life-changing "glimpse" of God's presence that he experienced when a Rembrandt poster caught his attention at Trosly. He explains how this compelled him to travel to Russia to visit the Hermitage Museum in St. Petersburg to learn more about the work itself. In contemplation of it, he made his first entrance into "the great event that Rembrandt's painting portrays."[59] The painting and parable are inextricably linked together and with his decision to move to L'Arche Daybreak. Now, older and wiser, he studies the painting once more. "When I first saw Rembrandt's painting, I was not as familiar with the home of God within me as I am now....I have a new vocation now....I am called to enter into the inner sanctuary of my own being where God has chosen to dwell. The only way to that place is prayer, unceasing prayer."[60]

Like Nouwen, Ron Rolheiser is a celebrated author of books about spirituality and a Roman Catholic priest. They met only a couple of times, but Rolheiser was greatly influenced by him and he continues to study his work and how people respond to it. Rolheiser says that he changed the direction of his own vocation after reading Nouwen's 1975 book, *Reaching Out: The Three Movements of the Spiritual Life.*

"It was like being introduced to myself. And, from that day on, Henri had a huge influence on my life. In fact, it was partly him who led me into spirituality, to move away from teaching philosophy and dogmatics, to teaching and writing in spirituality."[61]

The Return of the Prodigal Son is Nouwen's masterpiece, says Rolheiser, because of the complexity of its content and the ease with which he presents it in a story-filled, multilayered narrative. "That book is utterly simple and really deep," he says. "His books speak to the heart, and they speak at a certain depth, and so precisely. He worked at this continuously to try to eliminate technical terms. Where he could use a smaller word, he'd use a smaller word. This was part of his genius. He was able to be deeply personal without being exhibitionistic."[62]

Over the years, the psychological language that Nouwen used in his early books gradually disappeared, observes Rolheiser. "His psychology was just one of his tools that gave him deep insight into human nature. He introduces you to yourself, to some of your deeper parts, your deeper nobler self, but also to your deeper chaotic pathological struggling self."[63]

Nouwen's gift was to "enter deeply into human experience. And he was able to articulate that. A lot of people can enter deeply into experience, but they can't articulate it. He could take a flashlight into the human psyche and into the human spirit and say, this is what's happening, and this is the way you're going to feel. And this is why you feel this way."[64]

Nouwen charted his autobiographical journey as he aligned himself with the different characters in the parable, beginning with the kneeling young son, the angry brother, and then the aging father. He moved from "the place of being blessed to the place of blessing."[65] Nouwen arrived at Daybreak disheveled and dependent and, in time, he grew more confident in his emerging vocational role as the one who offers blessing while also being blessed.

Carolyn Whitney-Brown was a member of the Daybreak community during the decade that Nouwen lived there. They often spoke about the effects on the community of the time he spent away because of all the demands on his time. She says he certainly talked about "the conflict within, of wanting to be traveling, wanting the stimulation, being excited about the people he met." At the same time, he yearned for home, "feeling that he was missing that comfortable feeling of being right in the fabric of the community. Feeling like he had to reinsert himself and then wrench himself out again. And yet if he stayed too long in the community, he did get restless."[66]

When he returned from yet another trip, core members often complained that he was away for too long. "People were no-nonsense," says Whitney-Brown. "Henri fit very well into L'Arche. He was wounded and handicapped himself. He needed affirmation. He wanted to know that he was loved. It was as simple as with any other human being: he wanted to know that he was valued for who he was, not for what he did, not for what he wrote. But people knew him and loved him for himself. And in that way, it was an excellent fit for Henri."[67]

L'Arche Daybreak gave Nouwen the opportunity to travel freely whenever he wished and to accept speaking invitations that allowed him to experiment with including core members in his presentations. "No one had really done that before," says Whitney-Brown. "He could be quite innovative within L'Arche and very intuitive." L'Arche gave Nouwen a genuine sense of home that he had not experienced before, she says.

> You see that in his writings. He isn't trying to prove anything to an audience anymore. I mean, he always liked affirmation, being human, but it seems that his later books are less academic. He's not trying to write from an academic institution. He's simply trying to write from his heart, and from his community, to say things he thinks will be helpful for people. And what he thinks will be helpful is to share his own journey so that people can claim their own journeys. If he can expose and love his journey to some degree, then maybe other people will be able to do the same with their lives.[68]

Whitney-Brown also reminds us that Nouwen learned about community within the particular circumstances of L'Arche, amid

> worlds and lives he had never imagined before: the lives of people who had grown up in institutions, the lives of people who lived huge amounts of social ostracization, the lives of people who had lived with a great deal of rejection and violence. But these are also the lives of people who had taken all of that and chosen to grow in maturity, become wise in community, who had become fully and deeply connected to others, who had taken the pieces of very difficult, painful lives, and really grown into being very, very fruitful members of the

community. I think for Henri, that gave him permission to do the same kind of thing.[69]

When, in his 1992 Apostolic Exhortation, On the
Formation of Priests in the Circumstances of the Present Day
(*Pastores dabo vobis*), Pope John Paul II observed that "the
older priest has a sort of interior fatigue which is dangerous"
(no. 77), he could have been talking about Nouwen at this
time in the exercise of his ministry as a "conscious, free, and
responsible person" (no 25).[70] In the document, the pope
identified several simultaneous dilemmas for the Catholic
Church, which if it were a business, might be categorized as
issues needing critical path analysis related to human
resources, environmental scanning, and marketing.

Who gets into the seminary and what they do when they
get there is scrutinized in the document since formation is not
an apprenticeship that is intended "to make the candidate
familiar with some pastoral techniques," but a full initiation
in the "sensitivity of being a shepherd" (no. 58). The seminarian "will affirm in the most radical way possible his freedom to welcome the molding action of the Spirit" (no. 69).
Those already in ministry are reminded of St. Charles
Borromeo's advice from the Reformation era to "not give
yourself to others to such an extent that nothing is left of
yourself" (no. 72).

The pope identified the 1990s as "a new period of history," a time of religiosity without God (no. 10) and also a
time of widespread seeking out the divine (no. 6), even though
much of it was being carried out by gratification-seeking
"prisoners of the fleeting moment" (no. 7). This new historic
period was also time where family breakup was more frequent
and human sexuality more distorted, a time of confusion and

relativism, and where many who belonged to the church, did so with a commitment that was "ever more partial and conditional" (no. 7) amid a "persistent indifference toward and almost unacceptance of the magisterium of the hierarchy" (no. 10).

Since every life is "a constant path toward maturity," all priests require constant formation, regardless of their age or prior experience (no. 70). Every priest has a unique vocation "within" his priesthood (akin to what St./Mother Teresa of Kolkata described as "the call within a call"[71]) that reveals God's "saving plan in the historical development of the priest's life" (no. 70). The priest's ministry should never be "activism which becomes an end in itself," or a "businesslike function which he carries out on behalf of the Church" (no. 72). John Paul II concludes with the affirmation, "God promises the Church not just any sort of shepherds, but shepherds 'after his own heart.' And God's 'heart' has revealed itself to us fully in the heart of Christ the good shepherd" (no. 82).

Although Nouwen's formation was from an earlier era, within each stage of his own ministry (thirty-five continuous years by 1992) it is clear how in freely welcoming the molding action of the Spirit, his sense of vocation "within" his practice of priesthood kept inviting him to enter new challenging situations. The living human documents he encountered changed over the years (clients, students, people with disabilities, spiritual seekers), as did his practice of ministry. The core component of that evolving ministry was writing books that spoke directly to particular audiences and to offer inclusive eucharistic liturgies wherever possible. Most of his books succeeded, and the evidence is the large number of them that remain in print today. He identified one notable failure: *The Life of the Beloved*, a book that he opens with a scene that could be from a novel.

An irritated secular Jewish journalist arrives to interview a Catholic writer and professor at Yale for a newspaper profile. Their exchange is perfunctory until the journalist puts away his notepad and the interviewee asks his own question: "Tell me, do you like your job?" The journalist's answer is what inspires Nouwen to write a book for people who feel disconnected from religious tradition, but who still seek something that is greater than themselves. After this dialogue-filled prologue, Nouwen switches styles to a form with which he is much more comfortable. The remainder of the book is an extended, personal letter from a friendly pastor to the inquisitive secular writer, Fred Bratman, who once interviewed him at Yale.

Before sending the manuscript to his publisher, Nouwen sent it to Bratman for his opinion. Bratman traveled to Daybreak with the bad news. "You are not aware of how truly secular we are," he told Nouwen.[72] Deeply disappointed and initially considering a rewrite, Nouwen eventually decided that this 1992 work should still go to press, unrevised. The 2015 edition shouts out on its cover "Over 200,000 Copies in Print!" and like most of Nouwen's more popular works, it has gone through several editions and remains in print. The "failure" of this book was not commercial. It may not have given Bratman and his friends answers to their questions about the spiritual life, but it confirmed Nouwen's reputation as a major and accessible writer on Christian spirituality whose readership crosses denominations and includes many who would not classify themselves in that way. As Rolheiser points out, Nouwen's language is confessional without being denominational. It catches people by surprise, and I think he needs to be credited for that. He, more than anybody else, got a lot of Protestant schools of theology—including Yale—into spirituality, and they have been interested ever since. He doesn't write as some secular analyst. He's deeply committed, and he doesn't hide the fact that he's a priest, a Roman Catholic priest, but that's not the voice he uses. It's always "Henri." In fact, very few people call him "Father Nouwen." He's "Henri" and Henri is speaking as a human being and, in that sense, he's deeply theistic, and Christian, and committed, and even speaks from a clear denominational stance, but it's not what you hear. It's faith-filled without being denominational, without being churchy. It's pure art.[73]

As he approached his tenth anniversary at Daybreak, the subject of death took up more space in his talks and in his books, especially *Sabbatical Journey*. "My body will lose its strength, my mind its flexibility," he writes. "I will lose family and friends: I will become less relevant to society and be forgotten by most; I will have to depend increasingly on the help of others; and, in the end, I will have to let go of everything and be carried into the completely unknown."[74] Helping people to prepare for death is now a priority within his ever-expanding vocation. Death should not be allowed to lurk in silence in the shadows but should be acknowledged as an ever-present companion to be befriended. "Our great challenge is to discover this truth as a source of immense joy that will set us free to embrace our mortality with the awareness that we will make our passage to new life in solidarity with all the people on the earth."[75]

Between 1990 and 1996, the annual death rate for people with AIDS in Western and Central Europe and North America increased from 42,000 to 70,000. Globally, the death rate from AIDS in 1990 was 310,000, and 960,000 in 1996. The death rates in Europe and North America began to decline from 1997 onward, but increased sharply in the rest of the world, especially Africa. In 2016, the European and North American death rate from AIDS was 18,000, and in the rest of the world, slightly more than one million.[76] AIDS was at once a public health catastrophe and a profoundly complex theological and pastoral care challenge.

At the 1994 gathering of the National Catholic AIDS Network at Loyola University in Chicago, Nouwen ministered in the way he knew best, not with a political or theological critique, but with a personal pastoral reflection about community and isolation. "I'm well embraced, well-held, well kept by my friends, then suddenly, by the very intimacy of that embrace, I know that I am alone in a very deep way, in a loneliness that I didn't know before. It is precisely the love and intimacy of the other that reveal my deepest loneliness, which I couldn't get in touch with before I entered into community."[77]

Nouwen remained reluctant to take public stands that might appear overtly political. "I love the church," he wrote in his journal. "I do not want to write about the church as a problem, a source of conflict, a place of controversies, but as the Body of Christ for us here and now."[78] At the 1995 AIDS conference, as the health crisis worsened, his approach was slightly less oblique: "You have thousands of people who went before you....You have to embrace them as saints. Yes, those who were born and died long ago struggled like me and were anguished like me. They had their sexual struggles as I have, and they were lonely and depressed and confused. They went through the Black Plague. They are part of my human family."[79]

It was the "community piece" that kept tripping Nouwen up. His 1994 meditation on the eucharistic life, *With Burning Hearts*, addresses this as a flaw in his ministry. Despite living in a L'Arche community for nearly a decade, he acknowledged, "I am deeply aware of my own tendency to want to go from communion to ministry without forming community."[80] He stated that his core vocational task was to teach, heal, inspire, and to offer hope. He wanted to communicate to the world an "expression of our faith that *all we have to give comes from him who brought us together*."[81] This was his creative adaptation of the "reverse mission" concept that he brought back from Latin America. Mission is only possible, he said, "when it is as much receiving as giving, as much being cared for as caring."[82] Burnout in ministry is inevitable "if we cannot receive the Spirit of the Lord from those to whom we are sent."[83] Charles de Foucauld, that other impressively free spirit of a live-it-don't-just-speak-it approach to slow, progressive evangelization seemed to be praying over his shoulder as Nouwen articulated the major themes of his ministry.[84] At the center is gratitude, and for Nouwen this was more than the willingness to say an occasional polite "thank you." This requires "a completely new look at our lives, a look not from below, where we count our losses, but from above, where God offers us his glory," and to have the courage to welcome the stranger, in gratitude, as we allow our own lives to become part of the "mysterious work of God's salvation."[85]

After ten years at Daybreak, an increasingly exhausted Henri Nouwen needed a performance review before either leaving for his next career move or for a sabbatical. This discernment exercise included the participation of Jean Vanier. Whitney-Brown describes it as "a working process with Henri to decide whether this was a good fit, whether the way in which he lived in community was healthy, good for him, good for the community, how the next few years would look."[86] Nouwen's presence in the community often created difficulties of scheduling and other challenges. "People warped their lives out of shape so he wouldn't feel disappointed," she says. Life with a prolific and eccentric artist became the focus of an evening of skits, proposed by Vanier and performed by core members and assistants, as a way to close the exercise and, to Nouwen's relief, the invitation for him to stay.

"We really sent Henri up in all sorts of ways: life in the community, his anxieties, the stress he caused the community, the amusement, his travels, his teachings, his spiritual leadership....We had to demonstrate that we really did know him and loved him and wanted to live with him, and that these eccentricities were fine. We understood them really well, better than Henri himself in some ways. They were lovable to the community," she explained. He was both surprised and delighted. "I think in that moment he really got something deep, received it deeply that he was loved."[87]

The appraisal gave him much to ponder during his sabbatical year away from Daybreak. This kind of impressively free vocation risks being so open-ended that it overwhelms through its lack of defining boundaries. Nouwen struggled to determine and contain boundaries. The journal he kept throughout this sabbatical notes his travels and his ideas for future books. In his first week away from Daybreak, September 8, 1995, he set himself an additional goal. He would become more of a storyteller, using different ways to present the story of his faith and how it guided and sometimes misdirected his focus. Even at this late stage in his career, he was a work in progress as he continued to give shape to his vocation. Early in February 1996, he explained why he must interrupt his sabbatical and rush back to Daybreak.

Adam Arnett, now aged thirty-four, had suffered a heart attack combined with a seizure, and was not expected to survive. Nouwen joined the family at his bedside. The wordless person who had taught him so much did not survive. As he grieved the loss of his friend, he began to shape the story of their friendship and how it empowered him to say, "I believe."

To give shape to the book, Nouwen turned to a project that Robert Ellsberg, publisher of Orbis Books, had commissioned, a book about the Apostles' Creed. He would interpret the Creed through Adam's life story. "He had written a kind of treatment of what became the book *Adam: God's Beloved*," explains Ellsberg,

> and he told the story of Adam as a kind of a figure for the story of Christ, the episodes in the life of Jesus—his hidden life, his baptism, his ministry, his mission, his suffering, his death, his resurrection—as episodes. A kind of Way of the Cross, through the life of Adam, and it was quite remarkable. It really was Henri's creed, a summary of everything he'd learned, a synthesis of everything that had converged in his experience at L'Arche that would have taught him about the Gospel, about what it means to be a child of God. And he

was working on this. It was the last book he was
working on, as it turns out.[88]

Adam: God's Beloved was published in 1997.

As the sabbatical year drew to a close, Nouwen visited
the Rodleighs once more as they were touring Germany with
Circus Barum. The Rodleighs conceived of a plan whereby
they would position him on the trapeze, he would be held up
by Rodleigh Stevens himself, the founder of the troupe, and,
secured by safety lines, he would swing and swing, and at the
right moment he would drop into the net. He was transported
by the experience. He lay in the net for several minutes,
immobile, silent, "frozen in the moment" as Stevens described
it, at peace with himself. This was the way the Flying
Rodleighs could thank him for his friendship, express their
love for him, and seal their shared love for their art. Rodleigh
Stevens recalls his final encounter with Nouwen:

> I drove him to the Frankfurt railway station and he
> was about to take his train back to Holland, and then
> go from there to Canada. He was a little bit distracted.
> He was about to embark on this trip to Saint Peters-
> burg where he was going to do a television program
> about his favourite painter. He was concerned about
> the trip and the writing. He wasn't exactly agitated,
> but, for the very first time, Henri became concerned
> about a different side of our personality. My wife had
> become pregnant and we were told by the German
> government that due to her age we had to take an
> amniocentesis test to make sure that the child she was
> bearing was a normal child. Henri was very concerned

about this. "What if the child is not normal? What are you going to do?" he asked.

This was the first time that he showed us that he was kind of parenting us in a way, and we really understood and accepted his concern. We said there was nothing to worry about. Although we did the test, we knew that we would not have changed anything if the child was abnormal. We would have loved him as our own. Unfortunately, Henri did not live long enough to see our son, Bradley, who was born on December 28, 1996. I'm sure he would have been very pleased to see my son growing up.[89]

Back in Canada, Nouwen rushed to complete his Adam book before racing back to Europe in September 1996 to record the documentary about Rembrandt's *Return of the Prodigal Son* and its depiction of a father and his sons, a homecoming, and the tenderness of a final embrace. Nouwen's other favorite Dutch artist, Vincent van Gogh, was similarly inspired by Rembrandt's ability to capture "the tenderness in the gazes of human beings...that heart-broken tenderness, that glimpse of the superhuman infinite, which appears so natural."[90]

On Monday, September 16, 1996, Nouwen arrived in the Netherlands with his 1992 book about the parable and a new set of notes. Shortly after, he suffered a heart attack and was rushed to a hospital where his condition, although critical, stabilized. Friends and family gathered around his bedside and arranged a roster to ensure that someone would be with him round the clock. He improved enough to get out of bed and take a few steps. Although the Russian portion of the trip had been cancelled outright, his doctors suggested that he might be well enough to return to Canada within a week or so. The roster was suspended. Early in the morning of September 21, with no friends or family at his bedside, Henri Nouwen did not survive a second series of heart attacks.

The first of two funerals was arranged in Utrecht, with Cardinal Simonis officiating. This is where Rodleigh Stevens finally learned about "this old guy" who had so enthusiastically befriended his troupe. Given Nouwen's assertion that he had finally discovered his true "home" at Daybreak, the Nouwen family agreed to fly his body to Canada for burial. On September 28, the Daybreak community held a grief-filled yet celebratory second funeral event, entitled "Coming Home." The largest church in the vicinity, the Slovak Greek Catholic Cathedral of the Transfiguration in Markham, Ontario, was still not large enough to hold all those who wanted to attend.

In his book *Rembrandt's Eyes*, Simon Schama explains that "The Return of the Prodigal Son"—one of Rembrandt's final paintings begun as his health was failing—was one of thirteen that were left scattered in the rooms of his house after he died at the age of sixty-three in 1669. Schama believes that Rembrandt's final pupil, the teenaged Arent de Gelder, likely touched up some unfinished details in the original to try and give them more definition, and suggests that he added the "oddly wooden bystanders" who are not mentioned in the parable and who, on the canvas, stand in the shadows staring at the father and his son.[91] Attempted improvements aside, Schama describes the painting as "the dying, phosphorescent flare" of Rembrandt's "deathbed vision in its proper incandescence."[92] Drawn from the gospel of Luke, the patron saint of healers and of painters, the painting is Rembrandt's attempt, as he was dying, "to say something to those close to him and to all of us...so that we could not fail to comprehend him. But his utterance is broken, the message choked off; the hand strong at moments, at other times wavering, the clarity of the line ragged."[93] Flyer and catcher, father and son, priest, these "melt together in a single form, the pathetic shred of humanity returned to the boundlessly encompassing compassion of his creator."[94]

At the age of sixty-four, Nouwen died, a reconfigured, though still unfinished work, the phosphorescent flare of his first impressively free vocation interrupted. His second vocation was about to begin.

CONCLUSION

The Gift of Blessing

Tom Galvin, the protagonist of priest-novelist William King's *A Lost Tribe*, is quite simply a survivor. The novel is a *roman á clef*, a wide canvas of ecclesiastical types that define the Irish church over the last century with the title of the book illustrating the primary focus: the swan song that is the clerical tribe.

The novel is episodic, fractured like so many of the characters that people its pages, the chronology sometimes confusing, the structure occasionally inchoate. The list of players, the *dramatis personae*, is both broad in its range and specific in its treatment.

We have seminarians desperate for the career path; seminarians who stomach the mindless rules for the greater good; seminarians who mock the regime but conform for the prestige of their family; seminarians who expend their racing sexual energy in the rough and tumble of the playing fields or pitches; seminarians who glory in the bric-a-brac of devotional art, statuary, relics, and raiment; seminarians who find themselves "disappeared" in the clerical manner (that is, they are expelled in the middle of the night without explanation given to their remaining confreres); and seminarians who only minimally check their libidos and find that they need to negotiate new diocesan jurisdictions. Finally, there are those seminarians who simply don't know why they are where they are but who can't quite muster the fortitude and courage, or even imagination, to be somewhere else.

Set variously in the national pontifical seminary of the country—historically known as St. Patrick's, Maynooth, but in the novel identified as St. Paul's—and then in locations spanning both urban and rural parishes throughout the many dioceses that make up the north and the south of Catholic ecclesiastical Ireland, King highlights the turmoil, the travails, and indeed the traumas, that have marked, and continue to mark, the lives of priests in a country that was once the premier priest-producer on the planet.

And so, we meet priests wrestling with their vocation; priests who are sexually active and leave their ministry; priests who are alcoholic, manipulative of their curates, disposed to follow their own bookkeeping rules; priests who sublimate their erotic energy into their career ambitions; priests who lust for power at the same time feigning humility; priests who struggle with the bitterness of having made the wrong decision in their lives, electing for a vocation that was not their authentic choice; and priests, the majority as it happens, who try to make the best of an unanticipated upheaval in their professional status and personal job satisfaction.

Galvin, the key figure of the novel, is at first a reluctant priest, unsure that he is on the right track, open to self-examining his motives but propelled by the system to put the deeper reflections at bay. He is collegial to the core, inspired by the reforms of the Second Vatican Council—reforms that are changing the face of the church—a sound friend to other priests who succumb to their demons, and a decidedly unambitious cleric who finds himself secretary to an autocratic bishop at the height of his waning powers and influence.

Just prior to his ordination, Galvin hears a *ferverino* from the archbishop who will ordain him and his classmates. It represents in concise form the ruling theology of priesthood and its exalted state that would have been heard by all soon-to-be priests throughout the Catholic world, Galvin's Ireland and Nouwen's Netherlands, at the time.

The archbishop devoutly intones,

You have responded with great generosity to the call of our Divine Master. Very soon, by virtue of your ordination, you will have the power to transform the elements of bread and wine into the body and blood of Our Lord and Saviour. You will raise your hand in absolution and forgive sin in the sacrament of penance. Not the greatest potentate on earth, the most able leader—the President of the United States even— has the power to forgive sin. Reverend gentlemen, if the Lord were, in His wisdom, to call you to Himself, just after saying your first mass, your decision to follow in His footsteps would have been worth more than anything you could achieve in worldly terms.

Some of you here had the opportunity to become doctors, lawyers, or to distinguish yourselves in the world of banking; some of your families come from such noble professions. You might have accumulated riches in the marketplace, but all that would be as flotsam and jetsam in the rich ocean of sanctifying grace, which will be yours when you exercise your ministry as an *alter Christus*. The reward that is stored up for you is beyond description after a life of service in the Lord's vineyard.

Bear this in mind, gentlemen, and you are to be this year's *ordinandi*: As soon as you are ordained for the priesthood, you will, from then on, be set aside from all men. Ordination will have conferred on you that ontological change that Divine Grace has effected in your souls.[1]

These eloquent and confident words of a prelate the clerical corps calls the High Command would have been very much the same, in content if not in tone, as those delivered by the ordaining bishop who anointed Henri Nouwen and his confreres. The theology of the priesthood at the heart of the High Command's holy disquisition underscores the exceptionalism of the clerical state, the exalted calling to a life of spiritual leadership grounded in the power of the sacraments, and the clear acknowledgment that, however configured and explained, an essentialist change occurred, an ontological adjustment, further demonstrating the singularity and dignity of one's new status.

From the day of his ordination onward, Nouwen was a member of the clerical caste, a group set apart, intermediaries between the divine and the secular, bridges between the holy and the mundane, God's special workers. But this highly romanticized and rarefied view of the priesthood, though normative and culturally unassailable at the time of Nouwen's priestly rite of passage, would in the subsequent decades come tumbling down with a vengeance.

The world as pictured both in the early chapters of King's *A Lost Tribe* and in the Holland of Nouwen's priesting was a world in which the stable, revered, and cultic qualities of clerical life provided a consolation or antidote to the sexless life of isolation, male camaraderie, and exaggerated athleticism that was typical of parochial living in the concrete and not in the holy abstract.

Within a short chronology—the turbulence of postwar Holland, the shock waves of the Second Vatican Council, the social crisis precipitated by the rapidly deteriorating status of the priest in modernity, the radical overturning of the centuries-long cultural norms by an accelerated and pitiless secularizing of the Netherlands, and the tempest of change and experimentation, revolution and reaction, characteristic of U.S. Catholicism—all these factors would play determinative roles in reshaping Nouwen's own self-understanding of his priesthood.

The young candidate kneeling in front of Bernard Alfrink, archbishop of Utrecht, in July 1957, having his hands anointed with chrism, surrounded by his classmates and his family and relatives, basked in the glow of an admiring social acceptance, and buoyed by the belief and high expectations of the congregants. He was primed to enter a world—known, secure, untroubled by doubt—that would reward him a hundredfold for his ministry as another Christ. He would change as that world crumbled, would grow in spiritual wisdom, even as all the social pillars that held him aloft collapsed around him.

The fictitious Tom Galvin and the very real Henri Nouwen had that in common.

The rapid spread of secularization and the growing disenchantment with religious institutions presented substantive threats to Catholicism. Caught in the crossfire were the priests, hitherto untouchable objects of respect if not veneration, and now shiftless shamans trying to find meaning in what they do.

American sociologist and popular novelist Andrew M. Greeley tracked the fluctuating fortunes of the Catholic priest in his opinion surveys and in his fiction. He saw the priest as a bellwether for the seismic structural and conceptual changes occurring within postconciliar Catholic life. Distrustful of clerical power yet fascinated by its exercise, Greeley explored the different priest paradigms that emerged after the Council, the crumbling self-esteem of the ordinary parish priest, the radical altering of parishioner perceptions of the local pastor, the breakdown of trust between the bishops and their priests, their diminishment as ministers of the sacrament in a culture indifferent to the power of symbols and mystery, and the often woefully caricatured portraits of priestly sexual dysfunction.

Greeley tried to capture the angst, turmoil, and misdirected eroticism of his priestly cadres in ways that were empathetic and nonjudgmental, despite the often soap opera-like timbre of much of his clerical fiction.

Nouwen knew Greeley's work and could sympathize with his efforts to explore the social and ecclesial pathologies that as much confined as they defined the way priests lived their ministry in a once cohesive and now irreparably torn mythology, a shattered narrative of meaning.

American archbishop Daniel Edward Pilarczyk, in an address to the National Conference of Bishops in 1986, spoke to the image of the priest universally current when he formally began his own seminary formation at the age of fourteen, just after the Second World War:

The priest dealt with sacred matters in a sacred language. He was versed in the mysteries of faith. He was holy by the mere fact of being a priest. He was highly educated and wise, and had unquestioned authority in every facet of the parish. It did not matter much if he could not preach well. The real important thing was that he could celebrate Mass. The specifics of his personal life were shrouded in mystery. He seemed happy, and he seemed to live better than most of his parishioners....To be a priest was the highest life a boy could aspire to. It meant being a real Christian, it meant being called to serve Christ and his church, it meant being respected and revered almost as Christ himself.[2]

It doesn't get much more exalted, romantic, or idealistic than that. All you had to do was survive the antiquated seminary curriculum, self-censor to an alarming degree, defer to higher authority in all matters, cultivate a holy demeanor, adopt a devotional stance devoid of theological querying, wear distinctive garb, sublimate your sexual instincts, and pose in public as a model of Christian rectitude if not perfection.

Although new theologies of priesthood emerged during and after the Council, with different pastoral emphases and cultural perceptions, they remained within the larger historical framework and drew more substantially than in the post-Trent period (the ecclesiastical universe for four centuries that preceded the Council) on patristic and early Christian sources. They also took seriously the insights of the social sciences. The Oxford-trained priest theologian James J. Bacik observed the new identities of the priest after the Council and highlighted vertiginous shifts in both function and image. The priest, he writes, "went from pedestal to participation; from classical preacher to contemporary mystagogue; from the lone ranger style to collaborative ministry; from a monastic spirituality to a secular spirituality; from saving souls to liberating people."[3]

Secularism—the boogeyman of Catholic apologists—was chipping away at the sacred identity of the priest as rampant individualism undermined their function in the community. The proliferation of the "helping professions" (psychologists, therapists, social workers, credentialed marriage counselors) eclipsed the multiple roles of the priest. Then, the image of the Catholic priest faced the catastrophic impact of clerical sex abuse scandals that unfolded in cataract-like speed in many countries throughout the 1980s and 1990s.

The sheer breadth and range of the crisis was, and remains, staggering. Prominent predators and the bishops who shielded them—regardless their rationale—have entered the books of infamy. Of special consequence, given the comprehensive media coverage, are such figures as Frs. Gilbert Gauthe, Lawrence Murphy, Paul Shanley, John Geoghan, and Joseph Birmingham in the United States; Bishops Hubert O'Connor and Raymond Lahey, Frs. James Hickey, Barry Glendinning, and Bernard Prince in Canada; Cardinal Hans Hermann Groër and Bishop Kurt Krenn of Austria; Frs. Peter Hullermann of Germany, Marcial Degollado of Mexico, and Fernando Karadima of Chile, and Frs. Brendan Smyth and Malachy Finnegan of Ireland. These are merely a fraction and represent a limited number of national jurisdictions.

The perfidy of clerical sex abuse affects the universal church, its personnel, its leadership, and its reputation and credibility. All have suffered; none have been spared.

In his stunningly fair, nonvindictive, and insightful novel *The Long Run*, Newfoundland author Leo Furey re-created the immediacy and the terror of the Mount Cashel Orphanage scandal in St. John's, Newfoundland, which is fictionalized as Mount Kildare in the novel. Although the institution was under the care of the Irish Christian Brothers—a nonclerical order of religious whose mission is to educate young people caught on the margins of society—what happened in the orphanage presaged the later revelations around Canada's residential schools and indeed the clerical scandals in the Archdiocese of St. John's. The sins of clericalism are not limited to clerics.

In a scene, the only one of its kind, where the devastating pathology of sexual predation is portrayed with gripping intensity, the impact on the reader is magnified by the comparative economy of expression. Aiden Carmichael, the novel's narrator, paints the scene:

> The next morning at breakfast we tell Blackie [the leader] what happened, and he says he isn't surprised there's a night walker. And he isn't surprised that he stopped at Nowlan's bed either. He said he knew as much. "Nowlan's goin to the infirmary a lot. Always sick. No, not sick, sad."
>
> "But if Nowlan isn't sick, if he's just sad, why does he go to the infirmary all the time? Does he always get the spells?" I ask.
>
> "Nowlan's always sad," Oberstein [the savant] says. "That's a kind of Sickness, always being sad."

"It's deep...deep inside him," Blackie says. "It's soulful, a different kind of sickness, the sadness sickness."[4]

Furey's "sadness sickness" has penetrated the very pores of the church and it has spread extensively.

Nouwen, priest and psychologist, was never implicated in any act of predation, any allegation, any complicity, any omission or cover-up. He was certainly aware of the visceral upheaval caused by the revelations, the loss of faith in the structures, the flood of departures by morally outraged Catholics stunned to discover the hidden iniquities of many of their priests, the profound sense of betrayal by parents, the suppressed anger and hopelessness of the victims, and the enervating humiliation experienced by countless innocent priests.[5]

Although the clerical abuse crisis did not originate the reputational decline of the priesthood, it exacerbated it, coarsened it, devalued it, and derided it to a degree not seen since the persecutions of Revolutionary France.

The very emotional climate, sociocultural context, and theological environment into which Nouwen had been ordained no longer exists. It imploded throughout the decades of his ministry, and he was not unaware of its deleterious aftershocks. It was clear that a new model of priesthood was necessary, a radical revisioning of the very structures of ministry imperative for the future.

Characteristic of the Nouwen modus operandi, he did not campaign for the immediate reformation of the seminary, the jettisoning of imposed celibacy, the relaxation of the rules around chastity, the scouring of the clerical leadership to oust administrative malfeasance, the public excoriating of bishops slow to discipline and deceptive in their public communications, the rousing of the laity out of their moral stupor to fight against the institutional church in a desperate effort to reverse its decline.

There was, and is, a place for such action. But it was not the way Nouwen worked; it was not the way he defined his priestly presence and certainly not the way he lived his vocation.

Key to understanding Nouwen's priesthood is his vigilant fidelity to his ministry. This fidelity was defined by his spiritual interiority, belief in communion, joy in celebrating Eucharist, personal attachment to the spiritual efficaciousness and psychologically therapeutic qualities inherent in the sacrament of reconciliation (confession), the joy taken in the liberating dimensions of meaningful ritual, the rich and often unpredictable epiphanies of grace that dot the highway to holiness.

Nouwen's postconciliar world is encapsulated by a former seminary rector and author who understood the changing face of the priesthood from the inside:

> For the neo-conservative Catholic, any dark night the priest might be suffering was traced to the Church's infidelity to the pre-conciliar structures and practices that resonated with such surety and clarity amidst the social chaos and moral relativity of modernity. For other Catholics, however, and for most priests, I believe, the dark night was the work of the Spirit, leading priests through dark valleys only to bring them to a point where they could see new horizons. The darkness was necessary to bring about a conversion of mind and heart,

to effect a new way of seeing and listening, an *aggiornamento*. In the midst of the dark night priests stood in a fire of transformation and conversion. Stripped of the cultural supports and roles that shaped their identity and mission, they were pressed to ask, as if for the first time, what it meant to be a priest; what it meant to be *one of the faithful* and their servant-leader; what it meant to be a tender of the word.[6]

Donald Cozzens sees the priest, partly through a heroic and romantic lens, but mostly through the lens of raw reality. The priest—broken among the broken, naked before a mocking world, or at least a dismissive one, unsupported by the historical-cultural props of the past, a conduit of hope in a darkening landscape but not inured to that darkness, and longing for new vistas of the spirit—has the capacity to be a genuine *alter Christus*, not above or beyond the laity but in their very midst and as one of them.

Shorn of his ersatz reputation, no longer dependent on the easy deference of the pious, operating in an intellectual universe where symbol, sign, and sacrament are seen as archaic, exotic, or residual cave memories, the priest must become the servant-leader that inspires by lived witness, not cultic authority, the figure whose own suffering and struggles become a cipher for a troubled humanity. The priest's spirituality is no longer a variant of the monastic *contemptus mundi*.

He has become the world's lover and "a tender of the word."

He is the wounded healer at the nexus of an anguished world.

Nouwen understood the centrality of the priest as mediator, the priest as cosufferer, the priest as celebrant of the broken offering at the table. His empathy—as amply demonstrated in his voluminous correspondence—was an empathy without discrimination. No matter who sought him out, how close the friendship, how distant the connection, how arbitrary the contact, Nouwen responded and with a compassionate intensity.

Take the case of Rebecca Jonas. Rebecca's father, Robert, and her mother, Margaret, were friends of Nouwen's. They had met at Harvard, bonded, and found their lives interconnecting at key moments: Robert's struggles with his Catholicism, the collapse of his first marriage and his refusal on conscience grounds to proceed to get a decree of nullity from the Catholic juridical authorities. Nouwen blessed but did not witness the subsequent marriage of Margaret and Robert. Nouwen and Robert worked in a symbiotic relationship that was part therapeutic and part spiritual counseling (though discontinued after a while because it didn't work). They found common academic and pastoral cause in their shared interest in the untapped relationship of spirituality and psychology. The Jonases would come by way of personal tragedy to see the priestly Nouwen at his most comforting and insightful.

Carrying their first child in 1992, Margaret went into premature labor and was rushed to a Boston hospital for an emergency caesarian. Rebecca was delivered, but her lungs were insufficiently developed. She died within four hours of her birth. Devastated, they called out for Nouwen's help. Although he was in England at the time, Nouwen took immediate leave of whatever he was doing, flew to Massachusetts, spent several days with the grieving and uncomprehending parents, presided at many eucharistic celebrations with them in their home, and listened, listened, listened, and attended.

At one point, Nouwen mentioned to Jonas that Jesus too lost Rebecca, instantly decentering his grief, shifting the focus from his ego to a larger reality outside himself. He didn't minimize Robert's pain, he situated it within the redemptive narrative of Jesus, the High Priest. He immersed Robert's pain in Jesus's pain, and broke the paralyzing hold of grief on the ego—grief that is isolating, diminishing, anni-hilating. He went further still, understanding its potential catharsis, by advising Robert to write a book about Rebecca. And he did. Nouwen wrote the forward to *Rebecca: A Father's Journey from Grief to Gratitude*, in which he high-lighted what became a governing truth of his own ministry: the value of one's life is not dependent on its productivity, longevity, or its social acceptance. The value of life is life itself—life as pure gift, which is in no way weighed in signifi-cance and purpose by any external measuring tool, or even by its historical-cultural impact. It simply is. Rebecca's life, Nouwen argues, is just as worthy as that of a Beethoven in music, a Marc Chagall in art, and a Gandhi in politics. The book "proclaims the mystery of life by weaving a tapestry of spiritual wisdom, integrating insights from psychotherapy and prayer, Christianity and Buddhism, medieval mysticism and contemporary spirituality. Rebecca is at the center. She is Jonas's teacher in it all."

As indeed was Nouwen—Jonas's teacher in it all.[7]

The *priest as teacher* is a governing concept of Nouwen's valuation of his vocation. After all, Jesus was a teacher.

Then there is also the *priest as friend* concept that was at play throughout his entire life in ministry. His friendship with the Flying Rodleighs is illustrative of his very capacity to make friends, hold them close to his heart, enter their private world, free them to trust him with intimate disclosures regarding their lives and dreams, and stay with them throughout unanticipated ordeals.

The Flying Rodleighs mesmerized him by their performance to the extent that he became a groupie. Their athleticism, artistry, and discipline impressed him. He saw their trapeze acts as conceits, tropes, and metaphors for the spiritual life, their troupe a holy compact of human interdependence, a portal onto the freedom of the Holy Spirit. He loved their tactility, their bodily joy—the comfort with which they lived in their bodies—their invigorating sense of humor, their very wholeness. Their art was a dramatic embodiment of community, of the marriage of the aesthetic with the cerebral. As he observed them, they observed him. They saw in his dedication to them—singly and collectively—a moral earnestness that was tempered by a child's wonder. He got into their heads, their stories, their lives, and they wanted to create for him something of how they felt when performing. And they did when they secured him with safety lines so that he could swing on the trapeze and fall, safely, to the net, where he lay for several minutes immobilized, silent, "frozen in the moment," and at peace with himself.

Without preaching, he showed them that the requirements of their art—the concentration, the empathy, the resolve—constituted a form of prayer. Their art *was* prayer. And what they did through their art, a collective exercise in which no one was dispensable and in which all participated, was community-building. They were a means by which Nouwen himself could see his own prayer life as something that required the rudiments that made up their art: community, trust, and the utter abandonment that comes with placing your life unconditionally in the hands of God—the catcher.

Perhaps it was the *priest as anam cara* that proved to be his supreme concept of priesthood. The priest as soul companion—a Celtic notion revived and made popular by writer and poet John O'Donohue—speaks eloquently to Nouwen's rich sense of accompaniment, of being *with* not *beside* or *above* those to whom one ministers. Nouwen stood with all who sought his company, his counsel, his many pastoral gifts.

It was with Adam Arnett that he learned the full meaning of the "other Christ." Very quickly Nouwen discovered that Adam was *his* teacher, *his* guide, *his* friend. The tables were turned; the vulnerable taught the able bodied what it meant to love; they taught the strong why grace is mediated in weakness; they taught the confident what it means to be broken and to taste God's love.

Not despite but through his numerous infirmities and dependencies Adam opened to Nouwen his own poverty of spirit and more than any theological tome, ecclesiastical edict, legal code, ritual, or prayer manual, Adam modeled Jesus for Nouwen. He became Jesus for Nouwen.

Nouwen mused that Jesus lived centuries ago but Adam lived in his time, that the apostles had Jesus with them physically, palpably, and that he had Adam. Jesus was Emmanuel and Adam a sacred person, a sacrament of the Living God, a holy individual.

Adam was the epitome of Nouwen's compassionate caring and because of Adam, though not exclusively so, Nouwen became increasingly the catalyst of compassion for others; as Adam transformed him, so he would transform. He always did this, of course; his capacity for friendship was limitless; his ability to insinuate himself into the torment of others, an extraordinary gift. But Adam crystallized this *via pastoralis* for him, confirmed him in his priesthood, and brought him face-to-face with Jesus.

The three concepts—*priest as teacher*, *priest as friend*, *priest as anam cara*—were incarnated in Nouwen's ministry. In several of his letters, he underscored—sometimes in the very midst of personal turbulence—the critical components of his priestly spirituality: power and joy in a letter to a historian and human rights activist in 1974; his priestly life as a life of presence to others witnessing for Christ through his senses, fully sacramental in his ministry, as disclosed in a letter to a doctoral candidate in theology in 1982; and the realization that the most important spiritual direction comes from a life enveloped in prayer, the liturgical rhythms of prayer, the witness of the mystics, as revealed in a letter written to a friend a year before his death.

Nouwen would not subscribe to the thesis proposed by Catholic historian and public intellectual Garry Wills that the priesthood, "despite the many worthy men who have filled that office, keeps Catholics in a remove from other Christians—and a remove from the Jesus of the Gospels, who was a biting critic of the priests of his day."[8] He would not subscribe to any argument proposing the dismantling of the sacramental and apostolic structures that he saw integral and not inimical to the faith. And he would not advocate for the reformation of the priesthood that would leave it unrecognizable as an essential ministry of the church.

Nouwen was a priest of the church, a priest of God, and he lived the agony and the ecstasy of his often riven and always hectic life in the context of his priestly ministry. It defined him.

And his way of being priest is an incontrovertibly effective way of being Jesus for others. He is a model for the diocesan priesthood, in particular, because he was drawn to the margins and not the center, because he built bridges that united people not walls that contained them in their fears and prejudices, and because he knew that perhaps the greatest gift a priest possesses is the gift of blessing, movingly encapsulated in the concluding paragraph of his monumental bestseller *The Return of the Prodigal Son*:

> When, four years ago, I went to Saint Petersburg to see Rembrandt's *The Return of the Prodigal Son*, I had little idea how much I would have to live what I then saw. I stand with awe at the place where Rembrandt brought me. He led me from the kneeling, disheveled young son to the standing bent-over old father, from the place of being blessed to the place of blessing. As I look at my own aging hands, I know that they have been given to me to stretch out toward all who suffer, to rest upon the shoulders of all who come, and to offer the blessing that emerges from the immensity of God's love.[9]

NOTES

CHAPTER 1

1. Brendan Hoban, "On the Edge of the Abyss in Ireland," *The Tablet*, November 6, 2014.

2. "A Modest Proposal," Editorial, *America*, April 27, 2009.

3. Ronald Rolheiser, "Who Is Really to Blame for the Fall in Church Attendance?" *The Irish Catholic*, December 20, 2014.

4. Henri J. M. Nouwen, *Our Second Birth*, which integrates material from *Sabbatical Journey: A Diary of his Final Year* (New York: Crossroad, 2006), 105–6.

5. Henri J. M. Nouwen, *Life of the Beloved* (New York: Crossroad, 2002), 65.

6. Henri J. M. Nouwen, *The Road to Daybreak: A Spiritual Journey* (New York: Image/Doubleday, 1990), 224–25.

7. Interview with Rev. Dr. Denis Grecco, Stratford, Ontario, Canada, January 16, 2017.

8. Interview with Rev. Dr. Denis Grecco.

9. Henri J. M. Nouwen, *The Selfless Way of Christ: Downward Mobility and the Spiritual Life* (Maryknoll, NY: Orbis, 2007), 71.

10. Henri J. M. Nouwen, *¡Gracias! A Latin American Journal* (Maryknoll, NY: Orbis, 2007), 106.

11. Nouwen, *Our Second Birth*, 58–59.

12. Michael W. Higgins, "Greene's Priest: A Sort of Rebel," in *Essays in Graham Greene: An Annual Review* (St. Louis: Lucas Hall Press/University of Missouri-St. Louis, 1992), 23.

13. Henri J. M. Nouwen, *Love, Henri: Letters on the Spiritual Life*, ed. Gabrielle Earnshaw (New York: Convergent, 2016), 317.

14. Henri J. M. Nouwen, *Creative Ministry* (New York: Image/ Doubleday, 1971/2003), 107 (emphasis added).

CHAPTER 2

1. Jurjen Beumer, *Henri Nouwen: A Restless Seeking for God* (New York: Crossroad, 1997), 13–14.

2. From interview for *Genius Born of Anguish* documentary (*GBA* Interview hereafter).

3. Michael O'Laughlin, *God's Beloved: A Spiritual Biography of Henri Nouwen* (Maryknoll, NY: Orbis, 2004), 28.

4. Carl Jung, "The Stages of Life," in *The Portable Jung*, ed. Joseph Campbell (New York: Viking Penguin, 1971), 7.

5. Jung, "The Stages of Life," 7.

6. Jeroen Dewulf, *Spirit of Resistance: Dutch Clandestine Literature during the Nazi Occupation* (Rochester, NY: Camden House, 2010), 4.

7. John A. Coleman, *The Evolution of Dutch Catholicism, 1958–1974* (Berkeley: University of California Press, 1978).

8. Henri J. M. Nouwen, *Seeds of Hope—A Henri Nouwen Reader*, ed. Robert Durback (New York: Image/Doubleday, 1989/1997), 23.

9. Coleman, *Evolution of Dutch Catholicism*, 49.

10. *GBA* Interview.

11. Coleman, *Evolution of Dutch Catholicism*, 43.

12. A. C. Duke and C. A. Tomse, eds., *Britain and the Netherlands*, vol. 7, *Church and State Since the Reformation* (The Hague: Martinus Nijhoff, 1981), 216.

13. D. C. O. Adams, *Saints and Missionaries of the Anglo-Saxon Era* (Oxford: Mowbray, 1901), 49.

14. Henri J. M. Nouwen, *Can You Drink the Cup?* (Notre Dame: Ave Maria Press, 1996), 14.

15. Nouwen, *Can You Drink the Cup?*, 55.

16. *GBA* Interview.

17. *GBA* Interview.

18. Henri J. M. Nouwen, *Here and Now: Living in the Spirit* (New York: Crossroad, 1994), 78.

19. *De Telegraaf*, Wednesday, October 20, 1937.

20. *Provinciale Noordbrabantsche en 's-Hertogenbossche Courant*, November 20, 1937.

21. Robert Coles, "The Pilgrimage of Georges Bernanos—'The Supreme Grave Would Be to Love Ourselves,'" *New York Times*, June 8, 1986.

22. O'Laughlin, *God's Beloved*, 61–64.

23. Nouwen, *Can You Drink the Cup?*, 16.

24. Henri J. M. Nouwen, "My History with God—Notes for the Class: Communion, Community, and Ministry—An Introduction to the Spiritual Life, Regis College September–December 1994," quoted in *The Road to Peace*, ed. John Dear (Maryknoll, NY: Orbis, 2002), xviii.

25. Georges Bernanos, *Diary of a Country Priest*, trans. Pamela Morris (London: The Bodley Head, 1937), 76.

26. See the digital portal of the Bibliotheek voor de Nederlandse Letteren, http://dbnl.org/titels/titel.php?id=_gem001geme00 (accessed August 18, 2017).

27. The history of this organization is presented on the Sisters of Our Lady of Sion website, accessed August 18, 2017, www.notredamedesion.org/en/dialogue_docs.php?a=2&id.

28. Marnix Croes, "The Holocaust in the Netherlands and the Rate of Jewish Survival," *Holocaust and Genocide Studies* 20, no. 3 (Winter 2006): 474–99. Doi: 10.1093/hgs/dc1022.

29. The Viktor Frankl Institute Vienna, "Biography," accessed August 14, 2017, http://www.viktorfrankl.org/biography.html.

30. Gordon Allport, "Preface," Viktor E. Frankel, *Man's Search for Meaning: An Introduction to Logotherapy* (New York: Beacon Books/Pocket Books, 1963), xiii.

31. J. Bosmans, "Alfrink, Bernardus Johannes (1900–1987)," *Biografisch Woordenboek van Nederland* (Den Haag: Huygens ING, 2013), http://resources.huygens.knaw.nl/bwn1880-2000/lemmata/bwn5/alfrink.

32. Henri J. M. Nouwen, *The Road to Daybreak* (New York: Doubleday, 1988), 86.

33. Frankel, *Man's Search for Meaning*, 176–77.

34. Jung, "The Stages of Life," 12.

35. Jung, "The Stages of Life," 12.

CHAPTER 3

1. Henri J. M. Nouwen, *Can You Drink the Cup?* (Notre Dame: Ave Maria Press, 2006), 17.

2. Michael O'Laughlin, *Henri Nouwen: His Life and Vision* (Maryknoll, NY: Orbis, 2005), 24.

3. Michael W. Higgins and Douglas R. Letson, *The Jesuit Mystique* (Toronto: Macmillan Canada, 1995), 142.

4. Michael Ford, *Wounded Prophet: A Portrait of Henri J. M. Nouwen* (New York: Doubleday, 1999), 81–82.

5. Jurjen Beumer, *Henri Nouwen: A Restless Seeking for God* (New York: Crossroad, 1997), 177.

6. Maryann Confoy, *Religious Life and Priesthood: Perfectae Caritatis, Optatam Totius, Presbyterorum Ordinis* (Mahwah, NJ: Paulist Press, 2008), 79.

7. Translation of the transcription of a "spoken" letter by Henri Nouwen to Henk Egberts concerning the correspondent's reflections on the seminary at Rijsenburg, on the occasion of a reunion of former seminarians. The letter was recorded on tape by Henri Nouwen at Daybreak, Richmond Hill, Ontario Canada, April

1993. Note of translator, Peter J. Naus, January 2010: "I have tried to give an almost literal translation of the Dutch transcript of the tape. I only deviated from the original text, if I deemed it necessary for a better understanding of what I thought Henri meant to convey. As is often the case with manuscripts like this, the language is not always smooth. I made no effort to polish it." Transcript/translation provided, courtesy the Nouwen Archives, Special Collections, John M. Kelly Library, University of St. Michael's College, University of Toronto, Ontario.

8. Nouwen, "Spoken" letter to Henk Egberts.

9. Nouwen, "Spoken" letter to Henk Egberts, 2.

10. Nouwen, "Spoken" letter to Henk Egberts, 2–3.

11. Nouwen, "Spoken" letter to Henk Egberts, 5.

12. The academic, student-run journal founded in 1933.

13. Nouwen, "Spoken" letter to Henk Egberts, 5.

14. Nouwen, "Spoken" letter to Henk Egberts, 4.

15. Michael W. Higgins and Kevin Burns, *Genius Born of Anguish: The Life and Legacy of Henri Nouwen* (Mahwah, NJ: Paulist Press, 2012), 36–38.

16. William Thompson-Uberuaga, "Jansenism," in *The New Westminster Dictionary of Christian Spirituality*, ed. Philip Sheldrake (Louisville: WJK, 2005), 379.

17. Higgins and Burns, *Genius Born of Anguish*, 54.

18. Konrad Hecker, "Jansenism," in *Encyclopedia of Theology: The Concise Sacramentum Mundi* (New York: Crossroad, 1989), 730.

19. Higgins and Burns, *Genius Born of Anguish*, 53–54. The significant and enduring Bamberger-Nouwen relationship is further developed in chaps. 5 and 6 of this book.

20. Higgins and Burns, *Genius Born of Anguish*, 54.

21. Nouwen, *Can You Drink the Cup?*, 16.

22. Interview with Robert Jonas, Empty Bell, Northampton, MA, August 26, 2017.

23. Michael M. Winter, Letter to the Editor, *The Tablet*, July 29, 2017.

24. Rita Ferrone, "Cardinal Virtues: Why Character Matters to Francis as Much as Geography," *Commonweal*, June 16, 2017, 8.

25. Correspondence with Dr. Cathy Clifford, theologian, Saint Paul University (Ottawa), July 26, 2017.

CHAPTER 4

1. E. Fouilloux, "The Antepreparatory Phase: The Slow Emergence from Inertia (January 1959–October 1962)," in *History of Vatican II, Volume I, Announcing and Preparing Vatican Council II toward a New Era in Catholicism*, ed. Giuseppe Alberigo and Joseph A. Komonchak (Maryknoll, NY: Orbis, 1995), 122.

2. Michael W. Higgins and Kevin Burns, *Genius Born of Anguish: The Life and Legacy of Henri Nouwen* (Mahwah, NJ: Paulist Press, 2012), 29.

3. Michael W. Higgins and Douglas R. Letson, *Power and Peril: The Catholic Church at the Crossroads* (Toronto: HarperCollins, 2002), 22–23.

4. John W. O'Malley, "Vatican II: Did Anything Happen?" in *Vatican II: Did Anything Happen?* ed. David G. Schultenover (New York: Continuum, 2007), 81.

5. O'Malley, "Vatican II: Did Anything Happen?," 63–64.

6. John W. O'Malley, *What Happened at Vatican II* (Cambridge: Belknap Press of Harvard University Press, 2008), 40.

7. Yves Congar, *My Journal of the Council*, trans. Mary John Ronayne and Mary Cecily Boulding (Collegeville: A Michael Glazier Book, Liturgical Press, 2012), 169.

8. Congar, *My Journal of the Council*, 627.

9. Letter dated April 11, 1964, from Henri J. M. Nouwen to Bernard Alfrink, trans. Annemarie Kruger and courtesy of the

Nouwen Archives, Special Collections, John M. Kelly Library, University of St. Michael's College, University of Toronto.

10. O'Malley, *What Happened at Vatican II*, 73.

11. Walter M. Abbott, ed., *The Documents of Vatican II* (New York: Angelus, America Press, 1966), 575.

12. Henri J. M. Nouwen, *Love, Henri: Letters on the Spiritual Life* (New York: Convergent/Penguin Random House, 2016), 8–9.

13. Michael W. Higgins, "Gregory Baum: Journalist as Theologian," *Commonweal*, December 2, 2011.

14. Abbott, *The Documents of Vatican II*, 662.

15. Congar, *My Journal of the Council*, 756–77.

16. Michael Ford, *Wounded Prophet: A Portrait of Henri J. M. Nouwen* (New York: Doubleday, 1999), 57.

CHAPTER 5

1. Leonard Bernstein (score), Stephen Sondheim (lyrics), *West Side Story* (London: Boosey and Hawkes, 2000).

2. G. H. Gerrits, *People of the Maritimes: Dutch* (Tantallon, Nova Scotia: Four East Publications, 2000), 35.

3. Jan Raska, "Postwar Dutch Immigration through Pier 21," Canadian Museum of Immigration at Pier 21, accessed August 22, 2017, https://www.pier21.ca/blog/jan-raska-phd/postwar-dutch-immigration-through-pier-21.

4. Roger Daniels, *American Immigration: A Student Companion* (New York: Oxford University Press, 2001), 93–94.

5. Gordon Allport, *Personality: A Psychological Interpretation* (New York: Henry Holt, 1937), 549.

6. Allport, *Personality*, 352.

7. Allport, *Personality*, 352.

8. Allport, *Personality*, 360.

9. David A. Leeming, ed., "Hiltner" and "Pruyser," in *Encyclopedia of Psychology and Religion* (New York: Springer—

Science and Business Media, 2014), 1393–96 and 814–17, respectively.

10. Menninger Clinic, "Quick Facts," accessed November 12, 2018, https://www.menningerclinic.com/about/newsroom/quick -facts.

11. Menninger Clinic, "Quick Facts."

12. Christopher E. De Bono, "An Exploration and Adaptation of Anton T. Boisen's Notion of the Psychiatric Chaplain in Responding to Current Issues in Clinical Chaplaincy," Faculty of Theology of the University of St. Michael's College and the Pastoral Department of the Toronto School of Theology, doctoral thesis, December 19, 2012.

13. *GBA* Interview.

14. *GBA* Interview.

15. Anton T. Boisen, *Out of the Depths: An Autobiographical Study of Mental Disorder and Religious Experience* (New York: Harper & Brothers, 1960), 177.

16. De Bono, "An Exploration and Adaptation," 155, quoting Nouwen's 1968 article "Anton T. Boisen and Theology through Living Documents," 50.

17. De Bono, "An Exploration and Adaptation," 155, quoting Nouwen, "Anton T. Boisen and Theology through Living Documents," 56.

18. Anton T. Boisen, *The Exploration of the Inner World: A Study of Mental Disorder and Religious Experience* (New York: Harper & Brothers, 1936), 185.

19. Henri J. M. Nouwen, "Boisen," in *The Henri J. M. Nouwen Archives and Research Collection in the Special Collections and Archives* (Toronto: John M. Kelly Library at the University of St. Michael's College, University of Toronto, 1964).

20. Nouwen, "Boisen," 3.

21. Seward Hiltner, *Preface to Pastoral Theology* (New York: The Abingdon Press, 1954), 51.

22. Paul Pruyser, "Anton T. Boisen and the Psychology of Religion," *Journal of Pastoral Care* 21, no. 4 (1967): 214.

23. His works include *A Secret World: Sexuality and the Search for Celibacy* (1990), *Sex, Priests, and Power: Anatomy of a Crisis* (1995). *Celibacy: A Way of Loving, Living, and Serving* (1996), *Living the Celibate Life: A Search for Models and Meaning* (2004), *The Serpent and the Dove: Celibacy in Literature and Life* (2007). He was also a consultant to the *Boston Globe*'s Spotlight Investigative team (Matt Carroll, Kevin Cullen, Thomas Farragher, Stephen Kurkjian, Michael Paulson, Sacha Pfeiffer, Michael Rezendes, and Walter V. Robinson) during their coverage of the abuse scandal in the Catholic Archdiocese of Boston, which was also the basis of the 2015 film *Spotlight*. The team's findings were published in *Betrayal: The Crisis in the Catholic Church* (New York: Little, Brown and Company, 2002).

24. *GBA* Interview.

25. Jurjen Beumer, *Henri Nouwen: A Restless Seeking for God* (New York: Crossroad, 1997), 28.

26. John F. Dos Santos in Beth Porter and Philip Coulter, eds., *Befriending Life: Encounters with Henri Nouwen* (New York: Doubleday, 2001), 197.

27. November 17, 1965. Letter translated by Annemarie Kruger, Nouwen Archives, Special Collections, John M. Kelly Library, University of St. Michael's College, University of Toronto.

28. Jurjen Beumer, *Henri Nouwen: A Restless Seeking of God*, 178.

29. Henri J. M. Nouwen, *Seeds of Hope: A Henri Nouwen Reader*, ed. Robert Durback (New York: Image/Doubleday, 1989/1997), 25.

30. Porter and Coulter, *Befriending Life*, 200.

31. Henri J. M. Nouwen, "Anton T. Boisen and Theology through Living Human Documents" (1968), and "Boisen and the Case Method," included in a centennial celebration of Boisen's

birth published by The Chicago Theological Seminary Register in 1977 (Winter).

32. De Bono, "An Exploration and Adaptation," 114.

33. Nouwen, "Anton T. Boisen and Theology through Living Human Documents" (1968), quoted by De Bono, 116. Original is found in the Henri J. M. Nouwen Archives and Research Collection in the Special Collections and Archives (Toronto: John M. Kelly Library at the University of St. Michael's College, University of Toronto, n.d. [c. 1967]).

34. Henri J. M. Nouwen, "Boisen and the Case Method," *The Chicago Theological Seminary Register* 67, no. 1 (Winter): 20, quoted by De Bono, 125.

35. Anton T. Boisen, *Out of the Depths* (New York: Harper & Brothers, 1960), 111, quoted in Henri J. M. Nouwen, *Intimacy* (Notre Dame, IN: Fides, 1969), 46.

36. Nouwen, *Intimacy*, 47.

37. Nouwen, *Intimacy*, 123–24.

38. *Bidden om het leven* (Amsterdam: Ambo, 1970) appeared as *Pray to Live: Thomas Merton, A Contemplative Critic* (Notre Dame: Fides/Claretian,1972) and as *Thomas Merton: Contemplative Critic* (San Francisco: Harper & Row, 1981).

39. Paul Pruyser, "Religion in the Psychiatric Hospital: A Reassessment," *Journal of Pastoral Care* 38, no. 1 (1984): 7.

40. *GBA* Interview.

41. De Bono, "An Exploration and Adaptation," 146.

42. Beumer, *Henri Nouwen*, 32.

43. See his introduction to *Seeds of Hope: A Henri Nouwen Reader* (New York: Image/Doubleday, 1989/1997), 32–47.

44. Henri J. M. Nouwen, *The Wounded Healer: Ministry in Contemporary Society* (New York: Doubleday, 1972), 4.

45. Nouwen, *The Wounded Healer*, 90.

46. Nouwen, *The Wounded Healer*, 83.

47. Claire Dunne, *Carl Jung: Wounded Healer of the Soul* (London: Watkin Publishing, 2012), 119, quoting Laurens van der

Post, *Jung and the Story of Our Time* (New York: Random House, 1975), 121–22 also cited as *The Practice of Psychotherapy*, vol. 16, The Collected Works (Princeton University Press, 1966), 115–16.

48. Henri J. M. Nouwen, *The Genesee Diary: Report from a Trappist Monastery* (New York: Image/Doubleday, 1976), 15.

49. Henri J. M. Nouwen, *Reaching Out: Three Movements of the Spiritual Life* (New York: Doubleday, 1975), 10.

50. This is the list of "work" issues that Nouwen presents to Bamberger, *Genesee Diary*, 135.

51. Nouwen, *Reaching Out*, 106.

52. Henri J. M. Nouwen, *Beyond the Mirror: Reflections on Death and Life* (New York: Crossroad,1990), 12.

53. *GBA* Interview.

54. Nouwen, *Genesee Diary*, 218–19.

55. Henri J. M. Nouwen, *Out of Solitude: Three Meditations in the Christian Life* (Notre Dame: Ave Maria Press, 1974), 36–37.

56. Porter and Coulter, *Befriending Life*, 128.

57. Porter and Coulter, *Befriending Life*, 10.

58. Henri J. M. Nouwen, *The Inner Voice of Love: A Journey through Anguish to Freedom* (New York: Image/Doubleday, 1996), 33.

59. Henri J. M. Nouwen, *Home Tonight: Further Reflections of the Parable of the Prodigal Son* (New York: Doubleday, 2009), 13.

60. Henri J. M. Nouwen, "Introduction," in Cliff Edwards, *Van Gogh and God: A Creative Spiritual Quest* (Chicago: Loyola Press, 1989), xi.

61. Vincent van Gogh, *The Letters of Vincent van Gogh*, ed. Ronald de Leeuw, trans. Arnold Pomerans (London: Penguin, 1996), Letter 133, 72.

62. van Gogh, *The Letters of Vincent van Gogh*, Letter 133, 72.

63. John Franklin, "Divine Darkness and the Mystical Journey," in *Mystical Landscapes: From Vincent van Gogh to Emily Carr*, ed. Katharine Lochnan, Roald Nasgaard, and

Bogomila Welsh-Ovcharov (New York: Del Monico Books, 2016), 167.

64. Henri J. M. Nouwen, *The Living Reminder: Service and Prayer in Memory of Jesus Christ* (New York: Seabury/Crossroad, 1977), 23.

65. Nouwen, *The Living Reminder*, 24.

66. Eric R. Kandel, *In Search of Memory: The Emergence of a New Science of Mind* (New York: W.W. Norton, 2006), 10.

67. Nouwen, *The Living Reminder*, 60 (emphasis added).

68. Henri J. M. Nouwen, *Clowning in Rome: Reflections of Solitude, Celibacy, Prayer, and Contemplation* (New York: Image/Doubleday, 1979), 7–8.

69. Nouwen, *Clowning in Rome*, 2–3.

70. De Bono, "An Exploration and Adaptation," 99.

71. De Bono, "An Exploration and Adaptation," 99, quoting Pruyser's 1972 article "The Use and Neglect of Pastoral Resources," *Pastoral Psychology* 23, no. 7: 16.

72. Nouwen, *Clowning in Rome*, 110.

73. Henri J. M. Nouwen, *In Memoriam* (Notre Dame: Ave Maria Press, 1980), 56.

74. Using the timeline from the PBS "Battlefield Vietnam" website, accessed September 1, 2017, http://www.pbs.org/battlefieldvietnam/timeline/index.html.

75. Henri J. M. Nouwen, *Peacework* (Maryknoll, NY: Orbis, 2005), 20.

76. Nouwen, *Peacework*, 21.

77. Nouwen, *Peacework*, 124–25.

78. Henri J. M. Nouwen, *The Road to Daybreak: A Spiritual Journey* (New York: Image/Doubleday, 1988), 2.

79. Quoted from Georges Bernanos, *Cahiers du Rhone* (Neuchatel: Editions La Baconnière, 1949), as translated and quoted in Robert Speaight, *Georges Bernanos: A Biography* (New York: Liveright/Norton, 1974), 154.

CHAPTER 6

1. Thomas Merton, *Raids on the Unspeakable* (New York: New Directions, 1966), 17–18.

2. Henri J. M. Nouwen, *The Genesee Diary: Report from a Trappist Monastery* (Garden City: Doubleday, 1976), 64.

3. Henri J. M. Nouwen, *Love, Henri: Letters on the Spiritual Life*, ed. Gabrielle Earnshaw (New York: Convergent/Penguin Random House, 2016), 218.

4. John Eudes Bamberger, introduction, in Henri J. M. Nouwen, *Encounters with Merton: Spiritual Reflections* (New York: Crossroad, 1981), 13.

5. Nouwen, *Love, Henri*, 216.

6. Nouwen, *The Genesee Diary*, xi.

7. Michael W. Higgins and Kevin Burns, *Genius Born of Anguish: The Life and Legacy of Henri Nouwen* (Mahwah, NJ: Paulist Press, 2012), 40–41.

8. Nouwen, *The Genesee Diary*, 173–74.

9. Henri J. M. Nouwen, *A Cry for Mercy: Prayers from Genesee* (New York: Doubleday, 2002), 82.

10. A detailed commentary on Merton's layered understanding of wisdom, as well as an exegesis of Hagia Sophia can be found in chap. 5, "Urthona: The Wise One," in *Heretic Blood: The Spiritual Geography on Thomas Merton*, 233–73.

11. Thomas Merton, *Emblems of a Season of Fury* (New York: New Directions, 1963), 61.

12. Dom David Foster, *Contemplative Prayer: A New Framework* (London: Bloomsbury, 2015), 95–96.

13. Interview with Marilynne Robinson conducted by Matthew Sitman in *Commonweal*, October 20, 2017: 19.

14. Nouwen, *Love, Henri*, 111.

15. Henri J. M. Nouwen, *Road to Daybreak: A Spiritual Journey* (New York: Doubleday, 1990), 135.

16. Henri J. M. Nouwen, *Sabbatical Journey: The Final Year* (New York: Crossroad, 1998), 34.

17. Nouwen, *Sabbatical Journey*, 169 (emphasis added).

18. Nouwen, *Sabbatical Journey*, 169.

19. Merton, *Raids on the Unspeakable*, 182.

20. Merton, *Raids on the Unspeakable*, 182.

21. Thomas Merton, *The Asian Journal* (New York: New Directions, 1973), 235.

22. Henri J. M. Nouwen, *Life of the Beloved: Spiritual Living in a Secular World* (New York: Crossroad, 2002), 102–3.

23. Higgins and Burns, *Genius Born of Anguish*, 43.

24. Nouwen, *Love, Henri*, 216.

CHAPTER 7

1. Timothy Radcliffe, *What's the Point of Being a Christian?* (London: Burns and Oates/Continuum, 2005), 177.

2. Radcliffe, *What Is the Point of Being a Christian?*, 177.

3. Francis Augustus MacNutt, *Bartholomew de Las Casas: His Life, Apostolate, and Writings* (Cleveland: Arthur H. Clark Company, 1909), 210.

4. Angel Losada, "Bartolomé de Las Casas: Champion of Indian Rights in C16th Spanish America," *Unesco Courier*, June 1975, 4–10.

5. Gustavo Gutiérrez, *A Theology of Liberation: History, Politics, and Salvation*, trans. Caridad Inda and John Eagleson (Maryknoll, NY: Orbis, 1973, revised 1988).

6. Henri J. M. Nouwen, *¡Gracias! A Latin American Journal* (New York: Harper & Row, 1983).

7. Nouwen, *¡Gracias!*, xiv.

8. Nouwen, *¡Gracias!*, 122.

9. Nouwen, *¡Gracias!*, 122.

10. Nouwen outlines the program he took in his introduction to Gustavo Gutiérrez's, *We Drink from Our Own Wells* (Maryknoll, NY: Orbis, 1984, revised 2003), i–vii, adapted from 132–55 of *¡Gracias!*

11. Nouwen, introduction in Gutiérrez, *We Drink from Our Own Wells*, i–vii.

12. Nouwen, introduction in Gutiérrez, *We Drink from Our Own Wells*, i–vii.

13. Nouwen, introduction in Gutiérrez, *We Drink from Our Own Wells*, v.

14. Nouwen, *¡Gracias!*, 159.

15. Nouwen, *¡Gracias!*, 154.

16. Kevin Clarke, *Oscar Romero: Love Must Win Out* (Collegeville: Liturgical Press/Toronto: Novalis, 2014), 13 and 5.

17. Clarke, *Oscar Romero*, 10.

18. Nouwen, *¡Gracias!*, 175.

19. Robert Ellsberg, "Raised to the Altars: One Who Fell for the Poor," *The Tablet*, May 21, 2015, http://www.thetablet.co.uk/features/2/5595/raised-to-the-altars-one-who-fell-for-the-poor.

20. "In-Flight Press Conference of His Holiness Pope Francis from Korea to Rome," August 18, 2014, accessed September 17, 2017, http://w2.vatican.va/content/francesco/en/speeches/2014/august/documents/papa-francesco_20140818_corea-conferenza-stampa.html.

21. Letter to José Luis Escobar Ala, archbishop of San Salvador, May 23, 2015, accessed September 14, 2017, https://w2.vatican.va/content/francesco/en/letters/2015/documents/papa-francesco_20150523_lettera-beatificazione-romero.html.

22. Mary Jo Leddy, "A New Saint for the Suffering, and an Enduring Leader for the Catholic Church," *The Globe and Mail*, October 12, 2018.

23. Nouwen, *¡Gracias!*, 180. In 1988, two years into his Daybreak experience, Nouwen wrote a five-page introduction to an anthology of Romero's writing, *The Violence of Love: The*

Wisdom of Oscar Romero, originally published by Harper & Row and republished by Orbis in 2004.

24. Henri J. M. Nouwen, foreword to *The Violence of Love: The Wisdom of Oscar Romero*, ed. James. R. Brockman, originally published by Harper & Row in 1988 and republished by Orbis in 2004.

25. Henri J. M. Nouwen, *The Road to Daybreak: A Spiritual Journey* (New York: Image/Doubleday, 1988), 3.

26. Thomas Merton, *New Seeds of Contemplation* (New York: New Directions, 1961), 34, 35, 32, 47.

27. Thomas Merton, "The Last of the Fathers," in *Honey and Salt: Selected Writings of Saint Bernard of Clairvaux*, ed. John F. Thornton and Susan B. Varenne (New York: Vintage Spiritual Classics, 2007), xlvii.

28. Nouwen, introduction in Gutiérrez, *We Drink from Our Own Wells*, iii.

29. Nouwen, introduction in Gutiérrez, *We Drink from Our Own Wells*, iii.

30. All subsequent Robert Ellsberg quotations are from his *GBA* Interview.

31. *Harvard Gazette*, January 28, 1983, 3, quoted in Deirdre Lanoue, *The Spiritual Legacy of Henri Nouwen* (New York: Continuum, 2001), 32.

32. Nouwen, introduction in Gutiérrez, *We Drink from Our Own Wells*, iv.

33. Henri J. M. Nouwen, *Clowning in Rome*, 20.

34. Jean Vanier, *GBA* Interview.

35. *GBA* Interview.

36. Nouwen, *The Road to Daybreak*, 4.

37. *Instruction on Certain Aspects of the 'Theology of Liberation,'* Congregation for the Doctrine of the Faith, August 6, 1984, accessed September 16, 2017, http://www.vatican.va/roman _curia/congregations/cfaith/documents/rc_con_cfaith_doc _19840806_theology-liberation_en.html.

38. *Instruction on Certain Aspects of the 'Theology of Liberation,'* VII 12.

39. See http://w2.vatican.va/content/john-xxiii/en/encyclicals/documents/hf_j-xxiii_enc_28111959_princeps.html.

40. Gerald Costello, *Mission to Latin America: The Success and Failures of a Twentieth-Century Crusade* (Maryknoll, NY: Orbis, 1979), 273–82.

41. Details provided by the Archdiocese of Oklahoma City at http://stanleyrother.org/ (accessed November 13, 2018).

42. Henri Nouwen, *Love in a Fearful Land: A Guatemalan Story* (Notre Dame: Ave Maris Press, 1985), revised and expanded edition (Maryknoll, NY: Orbis, 2006), 26.

43. With Nouwen on this visit was his executive assistant from Harvard, Peter Weiskel, who also took the photographs included in *Love in a Fearful Land*.

44. Letter XXXVIII to Francis Mancias, November 1544, Henry James Coleridge, *The Life and Letters of St. Francis Xavier* (London: Burns & Oates, 1872), 252.

45. Letter XXXVIII to Francis Mancias in Coleridge, *The Life and Letters of St. Francis Xavier*, 252.

46. Nouwen, *Love in a Fearful Land*, 18.

47. Nouwen, *Love in a Fearful Land*, 102.

48. Nouwen, *Love in a Fearful Land*, 102.

49. Nouwen, *Love in a Fearful Land*, 100.

50. Nouwen, *Love in a Fearful Land*, 84.

51. Nouwen, *Love in a Fearful Land*, 85.

52. Nouwen, *Love in a Fearful Land*, 99.

53. Nouwen, *Love in a Fearful Land*, 99.

54. Nouwen, *Love in a Fearful Land*, 122.

55. António Antunes, *The Return of the Caravels*, trans. Gregory Rabassa (New York: Grove Atlantic, 1988), 167.

CHAPTER 8

1. Thomas Wolfe, *Look Homeward Angel: A Story of the Buried Life* (New York: Scribner, 1929/1957), 504.

2. Henri J. M. Nouwen, *The Road to Daybreak* (New York: Image/Doubleday, 1988), 3.

3. Henri J. M. Nouwen, *Love Henri: Letters on the Spiritual Life*, ed. Gabrielle Earnshaw (New York: Convergent/Penguin Random House, 2016), 85.

4. Thomas Wolfe, *Of Time and the River* (New York: Charles Scriber's Sons, 1935/1999), 260.

5. *GBA* Interview.

6. *GBA* Interview.

7. *GBA* Interview.

8. See his 2001 introduction to *Henri Nouwen: Writings Selected with an Introduction by Robert Jonas* in the Orbis Modern Spiritual Masters Series.

9. *GBA* Interview.

10. *GBA* Interview.

11. Peter K. Weiskel took part in a 2006 presentation at Harvard Divinity School, one of six former graduate students who shared anecdotes about Nouwen's Harvard years. Their remembrances are included in "A Spiritual Mentor's Lasting Influence: Henri Nouwen," March 20, 2006, posted on the News & Events page of Harvard Divinity School's website, https://hds.harvard.edu/news/2011/02/07/a-spiritual-mentors-lasting-influence-henri-nouwen# (accessed September 22, 2017). His contribution is entitled "Possibility and Chaos."

12. Weiskel, "Possibility and Chaos."

13. Michael O'Laughlin, "Henri the Teacher," in *Remembering Henri: The Life and Legacy of Henri Nouwen*, ed. Gerald S. Twomey and Claude Pomerleau (Toronto: Novalis/Maryknoll, NY: Orbis, 2006), 2.

14. O'Laughlin, "Henri the Teacher," 5.

15. O'Laughlin, "Henri the Teacher," 5.

16. Wolfe, *Of Time and the River*, 429.

17. *GBA* Interview.

18. James D. Smith III, "Beyond Tolerance," in "A Spiritual Mentor's Lasting Influence: Henri Nouwen."

19. Michael O'Laughlin, "Lived Religion," in A Spiritual Mentor's Lasting Influence: Henri Nouwen."

20. *GBA* Interview.

21. Henri J. M. Nouwen, *In the Name of Jesus: Reflections of Christian Leadership* (New York: Crossroad, 1989), 10.

22. Nouwen, *In the Name of Jesus*, 10.

23. Robert Ellsberg, from his introduction to Henri Nouwen, *The Selfless Way of Christ: Downward Mobility and the Spiritual Life* (Maryknoll, NY: Orbis, 2007), 10.

24. Søren Kierkegaard, *Fear and Trembling* and *This Sickness unto Death*, trans. Walter Lowrie (Princeton: Princeton University Press, 1941), 341.

25. *GBA* Interview.

26. *GBA* Interview.

27. *GBA* Interview.

28. *GBA* Interview.

29. *GBA* Interview.

30. See http://www.vatican.va/roman_curia/congregations/cfaith/documents/rc_con_cfaith_doc_19751229_persona-humana_en.html.

31. Carl Jung, "The Spiritual Problem of Modern Man" (1928), in *Collected Works*, vol. 10 (Princeton University Press, 1970), para. 148–96, included in *The Portable Carl Jung*, ed. Joseph Campbell (New York: Viking Penguin, 1971), 479 (emphasis added).

32. Nouwen, *In the Name of Jesus*, 10.

33. *GBA* Interview.

34. *GBA* Interview.

35. *GBA* Interview.

36. *GBA* Interview.

37. See http://w2.vatican.va/content/pius-xii/la/apost_exhortations/documents/hf_p-xii_exh_19500923_menti-nostrae.html.

38. See http://www.vatican.va/archive/hist_councils/ii_vatican_council/documents/vat-ii_decree_19651207_presbyterorum-ordinis_en.html.

39. See http://w2.vatican.va/content/paul-vi/en/apost_exhortations/documents/hf_p-vi_exh_19751208_evangelii-nuntiandi.html.

40. See the Community of Sant'Egidio website, "The Community," accessed September 26, 2017, http://www.santegidio.org/pageID/2/langID/en/the-Community.html.

41. Michael A. Hayes, ed., *New Religious Movements in the Catholic Church* (London: Burns and Oates/Continuum, 2005), 8.

42. John Paul II, Address to the Members of the Community of Sant'Egidio, February 8, 2002, accessed September 2017, http://m2.vatican.va/content/john-paul-ii/en/speeches/2002/february/documents/hf_jp-ii_spe_20020208_sant-egidio.html.

43. Brother Alois, *Choose to Love* (Taizé: Presses de Taizé, 2006).

44. *The Rule of Taizé* (London: Society for Promoting Christian Knowledge, 2012).

45. Pope Francis, Homily, Patriarchal Church of St. George, Istanbul, Sunday, November 30, 2014, accessed September 27, 2017, http://w2.vatican.va/content/francesco/en/homilies/2014/documents/papa-francesco_20141130_divina-liturgia-turchia.html.

46. Stephen Pavy, "Blessed Brokenness," in "A Spiritual Mentor's Lasting Influence: Henri Nouwen," https://hds.harvard.edu/news/2011/02/07/a-spiritual-mentors-lasting-influence-henri-nouwen#.

47. See Paulo Freire, *The Pedagogy of the Oppressed*, which eventually sold over one million copies worldwide from 1970. Gutiérrez outlines Freire's methods in *A Theology of Liberation* (1973), 91–92.

48. Freire Institute, "Paulo Freire Biography," accessed September 30, 2017, http://www.freire.org/paulo-freire/paulo-freire-biography.

49. Spring 1970, Harvard Educational Review, http://hepg.org/her-home/issues/harvard-educational-review-volume-40,-issue-2/herarticle/_1026; Summer 1970, http://hepg.org/her-home/issues/harvard-educational-review-volume-40,-issue-2/herarticle/_1026; Fall 1970, http://hepg.org/her-home/issues/harvard-educational-review-volume-40,-issue-3/herarticle/_1038; Spring 1981, http://hepg.org/her-home/issues/harvard-educational-review-volume-51,-issue-1/herarticle/learning-to-read-and-write-in-sao-tome-and-princip; Spring 1995, http://hepg.org/her-home/issues/harvard-educational-review-volume-65-issue-2/herarticle/_317; Fall 1995, http://hepg.org/her-home/issues/harvard-educational-review-volume-65-issue-3/herarticle/culture,-language,-and-race_305 (all accessed September 30, 2017).

50. Paul Freire, *Pedagogy of the Heart* (London: Bloomsbury Academic, 1998), 105, as quoted in Irwin Leopando, *A Pedagogy of Faith: The Theological Vision of Paulo Freire* (London: Bloomsbury Academic, 2017), 5.

51. Nouwen, *Road to Daybreak*, 3.

52. In 1967, Merton created a handwritten chart of his books with a rating scale: Bad, Poor, Fair, Good, Better, Best. There are no books in the "Best" column. *The New Man* is one of eight books he identifies as "Better." See illustration of James Forest, *Thomas Merton: A Pictorial Biography* (Mahwah, NJ: Paulist Press, 1980), 65.

53. Thomas Merton, *The New Man* (New York: Farrar, Straus & Giroux, 1961), 82.

54. Merton, *The New Man*, 64 (Merton's emphasis).

55. Merton, *The New Man*, para. 3, 6–7.

56. The L'Arche Charter, accessed November 13, 2018, http://larche-gwdc.org/about-us/identity-and mission/charter-of-the-communities-of-larche/.

57. Nouwen, *Road to Daybreak*, 4.

58. Nouwen, *Road to Daybreak*, 4.

59. *GBA* Interview.

60. *GBA* Interview.

61. L'Arche Charter.

62. Gustavo Gutiérrez, *A Theology of Liberation* (Maryknoll, NY: Orbis, 1972), 119.

63. Thomas Wolfe, *Of Time and the River* (New York: Charles Scribner's Sons, 1935/1999), 865.

64. Henri J. M. Nouwen, *The Return of the Prodigal Son: A Story of a Homecoming* (New York: Image/Doubleday, 1992), 5.

65. Henri J. M. Nouwen, *Creative Ministry* (New York: Image Doubleday, 1971), 107.

66. Henri Nouwen, *The Selfless Way of Christ: Downward Mobility and the Spiritual Life* (Maryknoll, NY: Orbis, 2007), 91.

67. Nouwen, *The Selfless Way of Christ*, 91.

CHAPTER 9

1. Andrei Tarkovsky, *Sculpting in Time: The Great Russian Filmmaker Discusses His Art*, trans. Kitty Hunter-Blair (Austin: University of Texas Press, 1989), 43.

2. Geoffrey Hosking, *Russian History: A Very Short Introduction* (Oxford: Oxford University Press, 2012), see chap. 2: "The Formation of the Muscovite State."

3. Nouwen, *Road to Daybreak*, 214.

4. Andrei Tarkovsky, *Sculpting in Time: Reflections on the Cinema*, 193.

5. Henri J. M. Nouwen, *Behold the Beauty of the Lord: Praying with Icons* (Notre Dame: Ave Maria Press, 1987), 33.

6. Nouwen, *Road to Daybreak*, 7–8.

7. Although Nouwen does not use the expression, he is closing in on the concept of *visio divina* that substitutes "looking" for "reading." The 2016 exhibition at the Art Gallery of Ontario,

"Mystical Landscapes: Masterpieces from Monet, van Gogh & More" references the work of Evelyn Underhill: mystical encounters tend "to emphasize the personal and Incarnational rather than the abstract and Trinitarian side of Christianity...an experience of adorable Friendship" (409). *Mysticism: A Study in the Nature and Development of Man's Spiritual Consciousness* (London: Methuen, 1912), 409–10.

8. Charles de Foucauld, quoted by Bonnie Thurston, *Hidden in God: Discovering the Desert Vision of Charles de Foucauld* (Notre Dame: Ave Maria Press, 2016), 63. Here she is citing *Charles de Foucauld*, ed. Robert Ellsberg, Modern Spiritual Masters Series (Maryknoll, NY: Orbis, 1999), 83.

9. Brother Charles de Foucauld, "Prayer of Abandonment," Caritas Communities website, accessed October 4, 2017, http://www.brothercharles.org/wordpress/prayer-of-abandonment/.

10. Nouwen, *Road to Daybreak*, 97.

11. Nouwen, *Road to Daybreak*, 177.

12. Nouwen, *Road to Daybreak*, 209.

13. Nouwen, *Road to Daybreak*, 64–65.

14. Nouwen, *Road to Daybreak*, 99.

15. Nouwen, *Road to Daybreak*, 177, 222–23.

16. Daybreak community leader, Joe Egan, tells this story in the Salt and Light Television documentary, *Way of the Heart: Remembering Henri Nouwen*, in the series "Catholic Focus," aired September 21, 2016.

17. *GBA* Interview.

18. *GBA* Interview.

19. Henri J. M. Nouwen, *Adam: God's Beloved* (Maryknoll, NY: Orbis, 1997), 43.

20. Nouwen, *Adam: God's Beloved*, 48 (Nouwen's emphasis).

21. Henri J. M. Nouwen, *The Inner Voice of Love: A Journey through Anguish to Freedom* (New York: Image/Doubleday, 1996), xiii.

22. Nouwen, *The Inner Voice of Love*, 78.

23. Nouwen, *The Inner Voice of Love*, xv.

24. *GBA* Interview.

25. Sue Mosteller, from her introduction to Henri J. M. Nouwen, *Home Tonight: Further Reflections on the Parable of the Prodigal Son* (New York: Random House, 2009), viii.

26. Nouwen, *The Inner Voice of Love*, xvi.

27. *GBA* Interview.

28. *GBA* Interview.

29. *GBA* Interview.

30. *GBA* Interview.

31. *GBA* Interview.

32. Carl Jung, ed., *The Red Book: Liber Novus*, trans. Sonu Shamdasani (New York: W. W. Norton, 2009), 353.

33. *GBA* Interview.

34. *GBA* Interview.

35. *GBA* Interview.

36. *GBA* Interview.

37. *GBA* Interview.

38. Henri J. M. Nouwen, *Heart Speaks to Heart: Three Prayers to Jesus* (Notre Dame: Ave Maria Press, 1989), 14.

39. Henri J. M. Nouwen, *Jesus & Mary: Finding our Sacred Center* (Cincinnati: St. Anthony Messenger Press, 1993), 23.

40. Henri J. M. Nouwen, preface to *Letters to Marc about Jesus: Living a Spiritual Life in a Material World* (New York: Harper and Row, 1988), viii.

41. Henri J. M. Nouwen, *Beyond the Mirror: Reflections on Death and Life* (New York: Crossroad, 1990), 10.

42. *De Foucauld*, Spiritual Masters Series, 70.

43. *De Foucauld*, Spiritual Masters Series, 55 and 12.

44. *De Foucauld*, Spiritual Masters Series, 58 (emphasis added).

45. *GBA* Interview.

46. *GBA* Interview.

47. Henri J. M. Nouwen, *Home Tonight: Further Reflections on the Return of the Prodigal Son* (New York: Doubleday, 2009), 115.

48. Henri J. M. Nouwen, "Finding Our Sacred Center: An Evening with Henri Nouwen," a L'Arche produced video recording of a presentation at Dauphin Way United Methodist Church, Mobile, Alabama, May 5, 1994; V34, Box 331, Henri J. M. Nouwen Archives. Edited and transcribed by the author. The Circus Barum incident is also found in Nouwen's posthumously published *Our Second Birth*, 2006, adapted from the 1998 *Sabbatical Journey: A Diary of His Final Year.*

49. Robert Lax, *In the Beginning Was Love,* ed. S. T. Georgiou (Springfield, IL: Templegate, 2015), 110.

50. Linda Simon, *The Greatest Shows on Earth: A History of the Circus* (London: Reaktion Books, 2014), 17.

51. Nouwen, "Finding Our Sacred Center: An Evening with Henri J. M. Nouwen."

52. *GBA* Interview.

53. *GBA* Interview. The film is *Angels Over the Net*, Daybreak Productions, 1995.

54. Linda Simon, *The Greatest Shows on Earth: A History of the Circus*, introduction; and Henri J. M. Nouwen, "Circus Diary," part 1, June, and part 2, July–August 1993, *New Oxford Review.*

55. Nouwen, "Finding Our Sacred Center: An Evening with Henri J. M. Nouwen."

56. For a much later and more developed reflection on the Rodleighs, see Nouwen, *Our Second Birth*, 127–29.

57. Nouwen, "Circus Diary," part 1, 8.

58. Nouwen, "Circus Diary," part 2, 8–10.

59. Henri J. M. Nouwen, *The Return of the Prodigal Son: A Story of a Homecoming* (New York: Image/Doubleday, 1992), 14.

60. Nouwen, *The Return of the Prodigal Son*, 17–18.

61. *GBA* Interview.

62. *GBA* Interview.

63. *GBA* Interview.

64. *GBA* Interview.

65. Nouwen, *Return of the Prodigal Son*, 139.

66. *GBA* Interview.

67. *GBA* Interview.

68. *GBA* Interview.

69. *GBA* Interview.

70. See http://w2.vatican.va/content/john-paul-ii/en/apost_exhortations/documents/hf_jp-ii_exh_25031992_pastores-dabo-vobis.html.

71. See the Vatican's biography of Mother Teresa, prepared for her canonization in September 2016, accessed October 4, 2017, http://www.vatican.va/news_services/liturgy/saints/ns_lit_doc_20031019_madre-teresa_en.html.

72. Henri J. M. Nouwen, *Life of the Beloved: Spiritual Living in a Secular World* (New York: Crossroad, 2002), 143.

73. *GBA* Interview.

74. Henri J. M. Nouwen, *Our Greatest Gift: A Meditation in Dying and Caring* (New York: HarperOne, 1994), 4.

75. Nouwen, *Our Greatest Gift*, 26.

76. From the data tables provided by United Nations Aids Organization, accessed October 14, 2017, http://aidsinfo.unaids.org/.

77. Henri J. M. Nouwen, "Our Story—Our Wisdom," in Henry J. M. Nouwen, *The Road to Peace*, ed. John Dear (Maryknoll, NY: Orbis, 1998), 177.

78. Henri J. M. Nouwen, *Our Second Birth: Christian Reflections of Death and New Life* (New York: Crossroad, 1998/2006), 62.

79. Henri J. M. Nouwen, "Befriending Death," Address to the National Catholic AIDS Ministry Conference, Chicago, July 1995, excerpted in Henri J. M. Nouwen, *Finding My Way Home* (New York: Crossroad, 2001) and cited in Michelle O'Rourke,

Befriending Death: Henri Nouwen and a Spirituality of Dying (Maryknoll, NY: Orbis, 2009), 92–96.

80. Henri J. M. Nouwen, *With Burning Hearts: A Meditation on the Eucharistic Life* (Maryknoll, NY: Orbis, 1994), 87.

81. Nouwen, *With Burning Hearts*, 87–88 (emphasis added).

82. Nouwen, *With Burning Hearts*, 89.

83. Nouwen, *With Burning Hearts*, 89.

84. René Bazin, *Charles de Foucauld: Hermit and Explorer*, trans. Peter Keelan (New York: Benziger Brothers, 1923), 283.

85. Nouwen, *With Burning Hearts*, 94.

86. *GBA* Interview.

87. *GBA* Interview.

88. *GBA* Interview.

89. *GBA* Interview.

90. Vincent van Gogh, Letter 784, to Theo van Gogh, Tuesday, July 2, 1889, Vincent Van Gogh Museum, accessed October 14, 2017, http://vangoghletters.org/vg/letters/let784/letter.html.

91. Simon Schama, *Rembrandt's Eyes* (New York: Random House, 1999), 685.

92. Schama, *Rembrandt's Eyes*, 685.

93. Schama, *Rembrandt's Eyes*, 685.

94. Schama, *Rembrandt's Eyes*, 685.

CHAPTER 10

1. William King, *A Lost Tribe* (Dublin: Lilliput Press, 2017), 93–94.

2. Daniel Edward Pilarczyk, "The Changing Image of the Priest," *Origins* 16, no. 7 (July 3, 1986): 140–41.

3. James Bacik, *Toledo Catholic Chronicle*, September 29, 1989.

4. Leo Furey, *The Long Run* (Toronto: Key Porter Books, 2004), 151.

5. For a detailed examination of the ecclesiological, media, legal, and historical dimensions of the clerical sex abuse crisis, see Michael W. Higgins and Peter Kavanagh, *Suffer the Children unto Me: An Open Inquiry into the Clerical Sex Abuse Scandal* (Toronto: Novalis, 2010).

6. Donald Cozzens, *The Changing Face of the Priesthood: A Reflection on the Priest's Crisis of Soul* (Collegeville, MN: Liturgical Press, 2000), 131.

7. Robert A. Jonas, *Rebecca: A Father's Journey from Grief to Gratitude* (New York: Crossroad, 1996), xiii.

8. Garry Wills, *Why Priests? A Failed Tradition* (New York: Viking, 2013), 3.

9. Henri J. M. Nouwen, *The Return of the Prodigal Son: A Story of Homecoming* (New York: Image, 1994), 139.

BIBLIOGRAPHY

Abbott, Walter, ed. *The Documents of Vatican II*. New York: Crossroad, 1989.

Adams, D. C. O. *Saints and Missionaries of the Anglo-Saxon Era*. Oxford: Mowbray Press, 1901.

Alberigo, Giuseppe, and Joseph A. Komonchak, eds. *History of Vatican II, vol. 1. Announcing and Preparing Vatican Council II: Toward a New Era in Catholicism*. Maryknoll, NY: Orbis, 1995.

Alden, Dauril. *The Making of an Enterprise: The Society of Jesus in Portugal, Its Empire, and Beyond, 1540–1750*. Stanford, CA: Stanford University Press, 1996.

Allport, Gordon. *Personality: A Psychological Interpretation*. New York: Henry Holt, 1937.

Brother Alois. *Chose to Love*. Taizé: Les Presses de Taizé, 2006.

Anderson, Jane. *Priests in Love*. London: Continuum, 2005.

Antunes, António. *The Return of the Caravels*. New York: Grove Atlantic, 1988.

Aschenbrenner, George A. *Quickening the Fire in Our Midst: The Challenge of Diocesan Priestly Spirituality*. Chicago: Loyola Press, 2002.

Bakvis, Herman. *Catholic Power in the Netherlands*. Kingston: McGill-Queens Press, 1981.

Bazin, René. *Charles de Foucauld: Hermit and Explorer.* New York: Benziger Brothers, 1923.

Bede. *A History of the English Church and People.* Translated by Leo Sherley Price. Harmondsworth: Penguin, 1955.

Benedict XV. *Maximum Illud: Apostolic Letter on the Propagation of the Faith throughout the World.* Washington, DC: National Catholic Welfare Conference, 1919.

Bengtson, Jonathan, and Gabrielle Earnshaw, eds. *Turning the Wheel: Henri Nouwen and Our Search for God.* Toronto: Novalis, 2007.

Bernanos, George. *Cahiers du Rhone.* Neuchâtel: Editions La Baconnière, 1949.

———. *Diary of a Country Priest.* London: Bodley Head, 1937.

Bernard of Clairvaux. *De Consideratione.* Translated by George Lewis. Oxford: Clarendon Press, 1906.

———. *Honey and Salt: Selected Writings of Saint Bernard of Clairvaux.* Edited by John F. Thornton and Susan B. Varenne. New York: Vintage Spiritual Classics, 2007.

Bernstein, Leonard, and Stephen Sondheim. *West Side Story.* London: Boosey and Hawkes, 2000.

Berry, Carol. *Vincent van Gogh: His Spiritual Visions in Life and Art.* Modern Spiritual Masters Series. Maryknoll, NY: Orbis, 2015.

Beumer, Jurjen. *Henri Nouwen: A Restless Seeking for God.* New York: Crossroad, 1997.

Boisen, Anton T. *The Exploration of the Inner World: A Study of Mental Disorder and Religious Experience.* New York: Willett, Clark and Company, 1936.

————. *Out of the Depths: An Autobiographical Study of Mental Disorder and Religious Experience*. New York: Harper and Brothers, 1960.

Braster, Sjaak, Frank Simon, and Ian Grosvenor. *A History of Popular Education: Educating the People of the World*. Abingdon, Oxford: Routledge Press, 2013.

Burns, Kevin. *Henri Nouwen: His Life and Spirit*. Cincinnati: Franciscan Media, 2016.

Carrière, Jean-Claude. *La Controverse de Valladolid*. Arles: Editions Actes Sud, 1999.

Chapman, Dom John. *Spiritual Letters*. London: Burns & Oates, 2003.

Clarke, Kevin. *Oscar Romero: Love Must Win Out*. Collegeville, MN: Liturgical Press, 2014.

Clayton, Lawrence A. *Bartolomé de las Casas and the Conquest of the Americas*. Chichester: Wiley InterScience, 2011.

Coleman, John A. *The Evolution of Dutch Catholicism 1958–1974*. Berkeley, CA: University of California Press, 1978.

Coleridge, Henry James. *The Life and Letters of St. Francis Xavier*. London: Burns & Oates, 1872.

Confoy, Maryanne. *Religious Life and Priesthood*: Perfectae caritatis, Optatem totius, Presbyterorum ordinis. Mahwah, NJ: Paulist Press, 2008.

Congar, Yves. *My Journal of the Council*. Translated by Mary John Ronayne and Mary Cecily Boulding. Collegeville, MN: Liturgical Press, 2012.

Connelly, John. *From Enemy to Brother: The Revolution in Catholic Teaching on the Jews, 1933–1965*. Cambridge, MA: Harvard University Press, 2012.

Costello, Gerald. *Mission to Latin America: The Success and Failures of a Twentieth-Century Crusade.* Maryknoll, NY: Orbis, 1979.

Cozzens, Donald B. *The Changing Face of the Priesthood: A Reflection on the Priest's Crisis of Soul.* Collegeville, MN: Liturgical Press, 2000.

Daniels, Roger. *American Immigration: A Student Companion.* New York: Oxford University Press, 2001.

De Bono, Christopher. "An Exploration and Adaptation of Anton T. Boisen's Notion of the Psychiatric Chaplain in Responding to Current Issues in Clinical Chaplaincy." PhD diss., University of St. Michael's College and Toronto School of Theology, 2012.

de Chardin, Pierre Teilhard. *The Divine Milieu.* London: William Collins Sons & Co., 1960.

de Foucauld, Charles. *Charles de Foucauld.* Modern Spiritual Masters. Edited by Robert Ellsberg. Maryknoll, NY: Orbis, 1999.

Dear, John, ed. *Henri Nouwen: The Road to Peace—Writings of Peace and Justice.* Maryknoll, NY: Orbis, 2002.

Dewulf, Jeroen. *Spirit of Resistance: Dutch Clandestine Literature during the Nazi Occupation.* Rochester, NY: Boydell & Brewer, 2010.

Duke, A. C., and C. A. Tomse, eds. *Church and State since the Reformation*, vol. 7 of *Britain and the Netherlands.* The Hague: Martinus Nijhoff, 1981.

Dunne, Claire. *Carl Jung: Wounded Healer of the Soul.* London: Watkin Publishing, 2012.

Durback, Richard, ed. *Seeds of Hope: A Henri Nouwen Reader.* New York: Image Books, 1997.

Edwards, Cliff. *Van Gogh and God: A Creative Spiritual Quest.* Chicago: Loyola Press, 1989.

Evans, Richard Isadore. *Gordon Allport: The Man and His Ideas*. New York: E. P. Dutton, 1970.

Ford, Michael. *Wounded Prophet: A Portrait of Henri J. M. Nouwen*. New York: Doubleday, 1999.

Forest, James. *Thomas Merton: A Pictorial Biography*. Mahwah, NJ: Paulist Press, 1980.

Foster, Dom David. *Contemplative Prayer: A New Framework*. London: Bloomsbury, 2015.

Frankel, Viktor E. *Man's Search for Meaning: An Introduction to Logotherapy*. New York: Beacon Books, 1963.

Freire, Paulo. *Cultural Action for Freedom*. Cambridge: Harvard University Press, 2000.

——. *Pedagogy of the Heart*. London: Bloomsbury Academic, 1998.

——. *The Pedagogy of the Oppressed*. New York: Seabury, 1970.

Furey, Leo. *The Long Run*. Toronto: Key Porter Books, 2004.

Georgiou, S. T., ed. *In the Beginning Was Love: Contemplative Words of Robert Lax*, Springfield, IL: Templegate, 2015.

Gerrits, G. H. *People of the Maritimes: Dutch*. Tantallon, Nova Scotia: Four East Publications, 2000.

Goddijn, Walter. *The Deferred Revolution: A Social Experiment in Church Innovation in Holland, 1960–1970*. Amsterdam: Elsevier, 1975.

Gutiérrez, Gustavo. *Essential Writings*, Maryknoll, NY: Orbis, 1996.

——. *The Power of the Poor in History: Selected Writings*. Maryknoll, NY: Orbis, 1983.

——. *A Theology of Liberation: History, Politics, and Salvation*, Maryknoll, NY: Orbis 1973, revised 1988.

——. *We Drink from Our Own Wells*. Maryknoll, NY: Orbis, 1984.

Hayes, Michael. *New Religious Movements in the Catholic Church*. London: Burns & Oates/Continuum, 2005.

Heschel, Abraham. *God in Search of Man: A Philosophy of Judaism*. New York: Farrar Straus and Giroux, 1955.

Higgins, Michael W., and Kevin Burns. *Genius Born of Anguish: The Life and Legacy of Henri Nouwen*. Mahwah, NJ: Paulist Press, 2012.

Higgins, Michael W., and Peter Kavanagh. *Suffer the Children unto Me: An Open Inquiry into the Clerical Abuse Scandal*. Toronto: Novalis, 2010.

Higgins, Michael W., and Douglas Letson. *The Jesuit Mystique*. Toronto: Macmillan Canada, 1996.

———. *Power and Peril: The Catholic Church at the Crossroads*. Toronto: HarperCollins, 2002.

Hiltner, Seward. *Preface to Pastoral Theology*. New York: Abingdon Press, 1954.

Himes, Kenneth R., and Lisa Sowle Cahill. *Modern Catholic Social Teaching: Commentaries and Interpretations*. Washington, DC: Georgetown University Press, 2005.

Hosking, Geoffrey. *Russian History: A Very Short Introduction*. Oxford: Oxford University Press, 2012.

Hough, Stephen. *The Final Retreat*. London: Sylph Editions, 2018.

Jonas, Robert A. *Rebecca: A Father's Journey from Grief to Gratitude*. New York: Crossroad, 1996.

Jung, Carl. *The Portable Jung*. New York: Viking Penguin, 1971

———. *The Practice of Psychotherapy*, vol. 16 of *The Collected Works of Carl Jung*. Princeton, NJ: Princeton University Press, 1966.

———. *The Red Book: Liber Novus*. Translated by Sonu Shamdasani. New York: W. W. Norton, 2009.

———. "The Spiritual Problems of Modern Man," in vol. 10 of *The Collected Works of Carl Jung*. Princeton, NJ: Princeton University Press, 1970.

Junkins, Donald. *The Contemporary World Poets*. New York: Harcourt Brace Jovanovich, 1976.

Kandel, Eric R. *In Search of Memory: The Emergence of a New Science of Mind*. New York: W. W. Norton, 2006.

Kasper, Walter. *Leadership in the Church: How Traditional Roles Can Help Serve the Christian Community Today*. New York: Crossroad, 2003.

———. *Mercy: The Essence of the Gospel and the Key to Christian Life*. Mahwah, NJ: Paulist Press, 2014.

Keen, Sam. *Learning to Fly: Reflections on Fear, Trust, and the Joy of Letting Go*. New York: Broadway Books/ Random House, 1999.

Kierkegaard, Søren. *Fear and Trembling* and *Sickness unto Death*. Translated by Walter Lowrie. Princeton, NJ: Princeton University Press, 1941.

King, William. *A Lost Tribe*. Dublin: Lilliput Press, 2017.

Koningsberger, Hans. *Modern Dutch Poetry*. New York: Netherlands Information Office, 1955.

LaNoue, Deirdre. *The Spiritual Legacy of Henri Nouwen*. New York: Continuum, 2000.

Lax, Robert. *Circus Days and Nights*. New York: Overlook Press, 2009.

Leddy, Mary-Jo. *Radical Gratitude*. Maryknoll, NY: Orbis, 2002.

Leeming, David A., ed. *Encyclopedia of Psychology and Religion*. New York: Springer, 2014.

Leopando, Irwin. *A Pedagogy of Faith: The Theological Vision of Paul Freire*. London: Bloomsbury Academic, 2017.

Lochnan, Katharine, Roals Nasgaard, and Bogomila Welsh-Ovcharov, eds. *Mystical Landscapes: From Vincent van Gogh to Emily Carr*. Munich: DelMonico Books, 2016.

McNutt, Francis Augustus. *Bartholomew de las Casas: His Life, Apostolate, and Writing*. Cleveland: Arthur H. Clarke Co., 1909.

Merton, Thomas. *The Asian Journal*. New York: New Directions, 1973.

———. *Learning to Love*, vol. 6, *The Journals of Thomas Merton*. Edited by Christine Bochen. New York: HarperCollins, 1998.

———. *The New Man*. New York: Farrar Straus & Giroux, 1961.

———. *New Seeds of Contemplation*. New York: New Directions, 1961.

———. *Raids on the Unspeakable*. New York: New Directions, 1966.

Moore, Bob. *Victims and Survivors: The Nazi Persecution of the Jews, 1940–1945*. London: Hodder Headline, 1997.

Nava, Alexander. *The Mystical and Prophetic Thought of Simone Weil and Gustavo Gutiérrez: Reflection on the Mystery and Hiddenness of God*. Albany: State University of New York Press, 2001.

Newman, John Henry. *On Consulting the Faithful in Matters of Doctrine* (1859). Lanham, MD: Rowman & Littlefield, 2006.

Nouwen, Henri J. M. *Adam: God's Beloved*. Maryknoll, NY: Orbis, 1997.

———. *Behold the Beauty of the Lord: Praying with Icons*. Notre Dame: Ave Maria Press, 1987.

———. *Beloved: Henri Nouwen in Conversation with Philip Roderick*. Ottawa: Novalis, 2007.

————. *Beyond the Mirror: Reflections on Death and Life.* New York: Crossroad, 1990.

————. *Can You Drink the Cup?* Notre Dame: Ave Maria Press, 1996.

————. *Clowning in Rome: Reflections on Solitude, Celibacy, Prayer, and Contemplation.* New York: Image/Doubleday, 1979.

————. *Creative Ministry.* New York: Image/Doubleday, 1971.

————. *A Cry for Mercy: Prayers from the Genesee.* New York: Image/Doubleday, 1983.

————. *Encounters with Merton: Spiritual Reflections.* New York: Crossroad, 1981.

————. *Finding My Way Home: Pathways to Life and the Spirit.* New York: Crossroad, 2001.

————. *The Genesee Diary: Report from a Trappist Monastery.* New York: Image/Doubleday, 1976.

————. *¡Gracias! A Latin American Journal.* New York: Harper & Row, 1983.

————. *Heart Speaks to Heart: Three Prayers to Jesus.* Notre Dame: Ave Maria Press, 1989.

————. *Henri Nouwen: Writings.* Modern Spiritual Masters. Edited by Robert A. Jonas. Maryknoll, NY: Orbis, 2001.

————. *Here and Now: Living in the Spirit.* New York: Crossroad, 1994.

————. *Home Tonight: Further Reflections on the Parable of the Prodigal Son.* New York: Doubleday, 2009.

————. *In Memoriam,* Notre Dame: Ave Maria Press, 1980.

————. *In the Name of Jesus: Reflections on Christian Leadership.* New York: Crossroad, 1989.

————. *The Inner Voice of Love: A Journey through Anguish to Freedom.* New York: Image/Doubleday, 1996.

————. *Intimacy*. Notre Dame: Fides, 1969.

————. *Jesus and Mary: Finding our Sacred Center*. Cincinnati: St. Anthony Messenger Press, 1993.

————. *Letters to Marc about Jesus: Living a Spiritual Life in a Material World*. New York: Harper & Row, 1988.

————. *The Life of the Beloved: Spiritual Living in a Secular World*. New York: Crossroad, 2002.

————. *Lifesigns: Intimacy, Fecundity, and Ecstasy in Christian Perspective*. New York: Doubleday, 1986.

————. *The Living Reminder: Service and Prayer in Memory of Jesus Christ*. New York: Seabury/Crossroad, 1977.

————. *Love Henri: Letters on the Spiritual Life*. Edited by Gabrielle Earnshaw. New York: Convergent/Penguin Random House, 2016.

————. *Love in a Fearful Land: A Guatemalan Story*. Notre Dame: Ave Maria Press, 1985. Revised edition, Maryknoll, NY: Orbis, 2006.

————. *The Only Necessary Thing: Living a Prayerful Life*. New York: Crossroad, 2008.

————. *Our Greatest Gift: A Meditation on Dying and Caring*. New York: HarperOne, 1994.

————. *Our Second Birth: Christian Reflections on Death and New Life*. New York: Crossroad, 1998/2006.

————. *Out of Solitude: Three Meditations in the Christian Life*. Notre Dame: Ave Maria Press, 1974.

————. *Peacework*. Maryknoll, NY: Orbis, 2005.

————. *Pray to Live: Thomas Merton—Contemplative Critic*. Notre Dame: Fides/Claretian, 1972.

————. *Reaching Out: Three Movements of the Spiritual Life*. New York: Doubleday, 1975.

————. *The Return of the Prodigal Son: A Story of a Homecoming*. New York: Image/Doubleday, 1992.

————. *The Road to Daybreak*. New York: Doubleday, 1988.

————. *The Road to Peace: Writings of Peace and Justice*. Maryknoll, NY: Orbis, 2002.

————. *Seeds of Hope: A Henri Nouwen Reader*. New York: Doubleday, 1989/1997.

————. *The Selfless Way of Christ: Downward Mobility and the Spiritual Life*. Maryknoll, NY: Orbis, 2007.

————. *Spiritual Direction: Wisdom for the Long Walk of Faith*. New York: HarperSanFrancisco, 2006.

————. *With Burning Hearts: A Meditation on the Eucharistic Life*. Maryknoll, NY: Orbis, 1994.

————. *The Wounded Healer: Ministry in Contemporary Society*. New York: Image/Doubleday, 1972.

O'Laughlin, Michael. *God's Beloved: A Spiritual Biography of Henri Nouwen*. Maryknoll, NY: Orbis, 2004.

————. *Henri Nouwen: His Life and Vision*. Maryknoll, NY: Orbis, 2005.

O'Malley, John W. *What Happened at Vatican II*. Cambridge: Harvard University Press, 2008.

O'Malley, John W., Joseph A. Komonchak, Neil Ormerod, and Stephen Schloesser. *Vatican II: Did Anything Happen?* London: Bloomsbury Academic, 2007.

O'Rourke, Michelle. *Befriending Death: Henri Nouwen and a Spirituality of Dying*. Maryknoll, NY: Orbis, 2009.

Porter, Beth, and Philip Coulter, eds. *Befriending Life: Encounters with Henri Nouwen*. New York: Doubleday, 2001.

Pruyser, Paul. *A Dynamic Psychology of Religion*. New York: Harper & Row, 1968.

Radcliffe, Timothy. *What Is the Point of Being a Christian?* London: Burns & Oates/Continuum, 2005.

Rahner, Karl, ed. *Encyclopedia of Theology: The Concise Sacramentum Mundi*. New York: Crossroad, 1989.

Roger, Brother. *The Rule of Taizé*. London: SPCK, 2012.

Rollins, Wayne G. *Soul and Psyche: The Bible in Psychological Perspective*. Minneapolis: Augsburg Fortress, 1999.

Schama, Simon. *Rembrandt's Eyes*. New York: Random House, 1999.

Segundo, Juan-Luis. *Liberation of Theology*. Maryknoll, NY: Orbis, 1976.

Segundo, Juan-Luis, Alfred T. Hennelly, and Robert R. Barr. *Signs of the Times: Theological Reflections*. Maryknoll, NY: Orbis, 1993.

Selderhuis, Herman J. *Handbook of Dutch Church History*. Göttingen: Vandenhoeck & Ruprecht, 2015.

Sheldrake, Philip, ed. *The New Westminster Dictionary of Christian Spirituality*. Louisville: Westminster John Knox, 2005.

Simon, Linda. *The Greatest Shows on Earth: A History of the Circus*. London: Reaktion Books, 2014.

Sipe, W. Richard. *Celibacy: A Way of Loving, Living, and Serving*. Liguori, MO: Triumph Books, 1996.

———. *Living the Celibate Life: A Search for Models and Meaning*. Liguori, MO: Liguori Press, 2004.

———. *A Secret World: Sexuality and the Search for Celibacy*. New York: Brunner/Mazel Press, 1990.

———. *The Serpent and the Dove: Celibacy in Literature and Life*. Santa Barbara: Praeger, 2007.

———. *Sex, Priests, and Power: Anatomy of a Crisis*. New York: Brunner/Mazel, 1995.

Sobrino, Jon. *Archbishop Romero: Memories and Reflections*. Maryknoll, NY: Orbis, 1990.

Sommerfeldt, John R. *The Spiritual Teachings of Bernard of Clairvaux*. Kalamazoo, MI: Cistercian Publications, 1991.

Speaight, Robert. *Georges Bernanos: A Biography*. New York: Liveright/Norton, 1974.

Spink, Kathryn. *Brother Roger, a Universal Heart: The Life and Visions of Brother Roger of Taizé*. London: SPCK, 1986/2005.

Spotlight Investigative Team (Matt Carroll, Kevin Cullen, Thomas Farragher, Stephen Kurkjian, Michale Paulson, Sacha Pfeiffer, Michael Rezendes, and Walter V. Robinson). *Betrayal: The Crisis in the Catholic Church*. New York: Little, Brown & Company, 2002.

Tarkovsky, Andrei. *Collected Screenplays*. New York: Faber and Faber, 1999.

———. *Sculpting in Time: The Great Russian Filmmaker Discusses His Art*. Translated by Kitty Hunter-Blair. Austin: University of Texas Press, 1989.

Thurston, Bonnie. *Hidden in God: Discovering the Desert Vision of Charles de Foucauld*. Notre Dame: Ave Maria Press, 2016.

Twomey, Gerald S., and Claude Pomerleau, eds. *Remembering Henri: The Life and Legacy of Henri Nouwen*. Maryknoll, NY: Orbis, 2006.

Underhill, Evelyn. *Mysticism: A Study in the Nature and Development of Man's Spiritual Consciousness*. London: Methuen, 1912.

van der Post, Laurens. *Jung and the Story of Our Time*. New York: Random House, 1975.

van Gogh, Vincent. *The Letters of Vincent van Gogh*. Edited by Ronald de Leeuw. Translated by Arnold Pomerans. London: Penguin, 1996.

Wall, Duncan. *The Ordinary Acrobat: A Journey into the Wondrous World of the Circus, Past and Present*. New York: Vintage, 2013.

Wills, Garry. *Why Priests? A Failed Tradition*. New York: Viking, 2013.

Wolfe, Thomas. *Look Homeward Angel: A Story of the Buried Life*. New York: Scribner, 1929/1957.

———. *Of Time and the River: A Legend of Man's Hunger in His Youth*. New York: Scribner, 1935/1999.